WITHDRAWN

Instant Art,
Instant Culture:

The Unspoken Policy for American Schools

D0139566

NAHCHAN

Instant Art, Instant Culture:

The Unspoken Policy for American Schools

Laura H. Chapman
Art Education Consultant, Cincinnati, Ohio

TEACHERS COLLEGE, COLUMBIA UNIVERSITY
NEW YORK AND LONDON 1982

821457

Published by Teachers College Press, 1234 Amsterdam Avenue, New York, N.Y. 10027

Copyright © 1982 Laura H. Chapman

All rights reserved. No part of this publication may be reproduced or transmitted in any form or by any means, electronic or mechanical, including photocopy, or any information storage and retrieval system, without permission from the publisher.

Library of Congress Cataloging in Publication Data

Chapman, Laura H.
  Instant art, instant culture.
  Bibliography: p. 191
  Includes index.
  1. Art—Study and teaching—United States. 2. Arts—Study and teaching—United States. I. Title.
N108.C47   707'.1273   82–3318
ISBN 0-8077-2722-9   AACR2

Manufactured in the United States of America
87 86 85 84 83 82   1 2 3 4 5 6

*I dedicate this book to my mother,
Flora Margaret Chapman.*

Contents

Acknowledgments

I WISH TO THANK COLLEAGUES who provided their own critical commentaries on various drafts of the manuscript: David W. Baker, Michael Day, Arthur Efland, Hermine Feinstein, Pearl Greenberg, Vincent Lanier, and Kenneth Marantz. Their assistance should not be interpreted as an endorsement of the ideas I have presented. Carol Strohmaier Hartsock and Judy Timmerman provided typing and editorial assistance, and Jeanette Baus typed the final draft. Patricia A. Renick's contributions are too numerous to inventory, but gratefully acknowledged. In different but most helpful ways Lois Patton, Louise Craft, and Christie Lerch of Teachers College Press facilitated the process of publication.

Introduction

THIS BOOK IS FOR ANYONE who has an interest in the nation's arts and its system of public education, but especially for those who are deeply concerned about the quality of arts education that American youth are receiving in public elementary and secondary schools. *Instant Art, Instant Culture* is a critical commentary on the status of arts education in the nation's schools, with particular emphasis on education in the visual arts. A number of recommendations for improving schools art programs are presented.

Instant art, like many other instant products in our lives, makes few demands on all who participate in it. It requires minimum skill, little or no knowledge, the least possible effort, and practically no investment of time. Instant art is a sham, but it has become the standard fare American schools offer to most of our young people. It is one manifestation of our national ambivalence about the role of art in public education.

On the one hand, most of us want to believe that education is the key to improving the quality of life, and assuring the vitality of American culture. Because we value "culture" and regard "the arts" as part of it, almost everyone will agree that studies in the arts should be included in a proper education for young people. On the other hand, we have inherited a particular view of the arts in this century, a view that makes art seem to be so mysterious, intuitive, and so much a question of native talent or personal preference that teaching art to the young does not really seem to be possible or valuable.

These unreconciled attitudes are reflected in contemporary art education. What many schools offer to children is little more than a token exposure to the visual, performing, and literary arts. Even this exposure is offered grudgingly, as if learning about the visual arts, music, dance, theater, and literature were a bonus or luxury. The instruction offered in some schools is so casual or wasteful of time and resources that many children actually are miseducated in the arts. Many of our young people graduate from high school with the impression that art is undemanding, unless one has talent, and irrelevant to contemporary life, unless one has the wealth and leisure to indulge in it.

These are harsh judgments of arts education today, but I believe they are reasonable conclusions, when we examine

□ the aims, content, and resources that would be appropriate for a basic education in art for youth;

□ the variety of attitudes within our culture and in schools that disparage the study of art and its teaching;

□ the proportion of young people in our schools who are denied access to art instruction with teachers who have adequate preparation;

□ the small amount of time youngsters typically spend in classes taught by qualified teachers;

□ the assumptions that undergird the education of art teachers and severely restrict the content and form of art instruction in school;

□ the preoccupation of theory and research in art education with topics that are narrow in scope or investigated without due regard for their bearing on formal instruction in schools;

□ the major themes in a spate of recommendations for arts education offered by various national organizations, commissions, and blue-ribbon panels.

In this book, I have endeavored not only to provide the reader with facts, cases, and analyses that lend support to these broad judgments, but also to portray how it feels to be a teacher of art in a system of education that places little value on study of the arts. I hope I have captured the aspirations and concerns that many professionals in art education have today.

This book is addressed to two major groups. The first is the new constituency of advocates for the arts in education: legislators, parents, school board members, educators, artists, arts administrators, as well as supporters of the arts representing business, labor, and government. In the last decade, a number of groups within this broad constituency have published resolutions and recommendations on the role of the arts in public life, including their role in education. This new constituency is now functioning as an organized lobby, seeking legislation and funds for the arts at the federal, state, and local levels. In all this activity one can discern an emerging national viewpoint about arts education. Because this book raises fundamental questions about the wisdom of this viewpoint, I hope it will be read and discussed by everyone who is serving as an advocate for the arts and arts education.

The second group to whom this book is addressed is the community of professionals in education: teachers in colleges and universities, leaders of professional associations in education, directors of curriculum in local and state education agencies, and, of course, art educators, most of whom, like myself, wear more than one hat in working to improve school art programs. For college students of arts education, as well as professionals, the book is intended to provoke discussions about fundamental issues, policies, and directions for the future.

I hope my colleagues in arts education will find this commentary informative and generally sympathetic to our field, even though it is critical of some long-cherished beliefs and fails to offer glowing reports on school art programs. Indeed, in our collective efforts to portray the virtues of art in the school curriculum, I believe we have failed to communicate to others the degree to which art instruction is not even offered in schools, or is taught under such poor conditions that our efforts seem to have little constructive effect. Too often, we are falsely accused of shabby practice when in fact we are systematically prevented from teaching effectively.

But those of us in arts education must also put our own house in order. As a professional group we have been all too tolerant of makeshift programs, trivial activities in schools, and the marginal preparation of art teachers. We have contributed to the very problems and attitudes about which we are quick to complain. The perspective on teaching art that I have presented here may not be received favorably by all art educators. But even those who may disagree with particular aspects of this commentary will, I believe, find much that deserves a hearing.

At the end of this book, a number of recommendations for improving art education are presented. These recommendations do not carry the endorsement of any organized group, but it would be wrong to judge that they speak for the author alone. Indeed, I have tried to capture in this one commentary many of the concerns and problems that have been expressed by others in art education. Nevertheless, what I present is one person's viewpoint, and readers who are not persuaded of its merit by the discussion alone will, at least, have acquired information about art education that otherwise might not have been known to them.

Although many of the problems and issues discussed in this book apply to instruction in literature and the performing arts of music, dance, and theater, I have concentrated on the visual arts, for several reasons. First, it is the area in which I have greatest expertise. Second, most of the visual arts are created and encountered in ways that are fundamentally different from the performing and literary arts. As a result, the issues in educational theory and practice are not the same in each of the arts. For example, the preoccupation of schools with the mastery of language has given an importance to the literary arts not enjoyed by the performing and visual arts. Third, in many national recommendations for improving school programs, especially those which have been promoted by the National Endowment for the Arts, the performing arts have been given greatest prominence. In short, the visual arts have not been well represented in discussions of educational reform.

Chapter One presents an overview of the biggest problem we face in art education: the belief held by many Americans that education in art is not really essential for all children. In chapter 2, an agenda for the reform of the curriculum of schools is presented. In this chapter, I urge schools to strive for education of high quality, and suggest that this can be accomplished, in part, through programs of study in which the arts, sciences, and humanities (social studies) are core subjects, all receiving comparable attention. In order to illustrate the kind of attention we should give to the arts, I have presented, in chapters 3 and 4, an outline of some concerns in teaching the visual arts. The concept of art education outlined in these chapters can be found in more developed form in my college text, *Approaches to Art in Education.*

In order to suggest the magnitude of the gap between what our schools should be teaching and what typical instruction is like, chapter 5 examines some common practices in elementary school art instruction. Chapter 6 describes typical patterns of instruction in secondary schools. Chapter 7 suggests how teacher education programs might be improved. Chapter 8 is about theory and research in art education, especially how it reflects and reinforces some practices which are found in schools. Chapter 9 reviews some of the recommendations for arts education which have been shaped by federal programs and forwarded by influential panels of citizens, arts advocates, and educators. Chapter 10 examines some of these recommendations in greater depth, with particular attention to related-arts programs and the model for educational change which has been promoted as a means of reforming arts education. Chapter 11 offers some alternative recommendations for strengthening art education in schools. Chapters 1, 2, 9, 10, and 11 are addressed to problems which are shared in some degree by all of the arts—visual, literary, and performing. The remaining chapters focus on visual arts education.

The reader who is interested in references and more detailed information about some of the data will find these in the appendices, but a word should be said here about the major sources of data I have used in this book.

For much of the information on visual arts instruction, I have relied upon reports from the National Assessment of Educational Progress (NAEP) in art conducted in 1974–75 and 1978–79 by the Education Commission of the States under a subcontract from the National Bureau of Education Statistics.[1] These reports are part of a long-term evaluation program. They offer information on the performance of students at ages nine, thirteen, and seventeen on exercises that measure skills in drawing and in design, as well as knowledge about and attitudes toward art. Some of the questions asked and test results from the National Art Assessment are presented in appendix C, pp. 173–177. The reports allow us to see how student performance varies according to a number of specific factors: age, sex, race; area of residence in the country, and size and type of community; and parents' education. The reports also show how well students perform when art is or is not taught in the school. Information was also collected on children's out-of-school art activities, museum visits, and interest in collecting art.

The National Art Assessment is not above criticism. It does not evaluate the artistic skills and concepts that many art teachers emphasize in schools. It does not capture well the range of values that good art programs do nurture; it does not provide a measurement of the individual improvements of students from year to year; even less does it test students in depth. In spite of these and other possible objections, the information is useful, for it is the only source of nationwide data that suggests how young people are engaged with art, in and out of school.

A second source of information is a national study of secondary school enrollments in selected arts courses conducted in 1978 under the auspices of CEMREL (Central Midwestern Regional Educational Laboratory) by David Rindskopf and his coworkers.[2] This study makes use of existing data on course enrollments in the arts, previously unanalyzed, collected in 1972–73 by the National Bureau of Education Statistics.

A third source of information, not about art in schools but about the adult arts audience, is, like the preceding source, a critical analysis of 265 separate studies of those who attend art museums, concerts, plays, and other cultural events. This 1978 report, published by the Research Division of the National Endowment for the Arts, offers information on the age, race, educational background, occupation, and income of the arts audience.[3] It complements information reported in a fourth major source of data, the surveys conducted by the National Research Center of the Arts, an affiliate of Louis Harris Associates. The Harris surveys of public opinion about the arts are published as *Americans and the Arts*, and data from those conducted in 1975 and 1980 are cited extensively in chapter 1.[4]

The four preceding studies meet most of the customary standards for survey research. The fifth source of information does not meet them. It is an informal survey that I conducted in 1979 through *School Arts Magazine* to which 600 art teachers and art supervisors responded.[5] The questionnaire used in the survey, and the results, are presented in appendix A, pp. 161–170. Those who responded did so voluntarily. Obviously, we cannot know whether these responses are representative of all art teachers and supervisors of art. Nevertheless, I believe the results are worth reporting, for several reasons. First, there is little current information on the character of art instruction in schools. Second, the survey showed a good distribution of responses across grade levels, amount of teaching experience, and geographic regions (as far as could be discerned by postmarks). The art teachers who responded directly influence the education of about 175,000 students. Third, the survey results speak for 600 teachers and supervisors, and the most salient features of their replies are noteworthy precisely because teachers are "where the action is," and yet are heard too rarely.

A note on definitions: For the purpose of this discussion, the *arts* may be broadly classified into three groups—visual, literary, and performing. Normally in this volume, when I refer to the *arts*, or to *art*, the usual intent is to encompass music, dance, theater, literature, and the visual arts within the meaning. Exceptions to this pattern of usage will be apparent in the several chapters which concentrate on the visual arts, where, for brief reference, the term *art* is used to mean the visual arts, specifically. Under the visual arts, we will consider the traditional studio fields of drawing, painting, printmaking, sculpture, and crafts; we will also include photography, film, and television when these are regarded as forms of visual expression. Equally important are the fields of architecture, interior design, and environmental design; graphic and product design; and the visual dimensions of rituals, spectacles, celebrations, and ceremonies.

The reader should understand that I favor a comparable view of music, dance, theater, and literature—a view that would encompass a variety of forms and genres within our own culture, as well as others. Judgments of quality are essential, of course, but in every case, I believe that such judgments are most appropriately made in the light of specific works and the criteria appropriate in a given context. Indeed, through more adequate teaching of the very process of making critical judgments about art, students might be better prepared to recognize varieties of excellence.

I will also refer to *the arts, the sciences,* and *the humanities* as broad fields of study in general education. These distinctions are commonly used in discussions of both college programs and the programs of elementary and secondary schools, but with somewhat different meanings. In most elementary or secondary schools, the general or commonly accepted core curriculum is organized around the study of science, social studies, mathematics, and the practical use of language. Within this scheme, the arts are usually regarded as an enrichment, outside of the regular curriculum. The humanities are reflected in social studies programs which examine human society and thought from the vantage points of a number of disciplines—history, philosophy, cultural anthropology, and political science, among others. In college humanities programs, the study of language and literature are prominent, for both are central in understanding the history of human thought. In precollege education, literature is treated in so-called language arts programs, which have in recent years concentrated on developing "functional literacy"—skill in reading, writing, speaking, and listening—at a level required for everyday life. Indeed, in the pursuit of this aim, schools have given much less attention to the sciences, social studies, and the arts than was typical before the development of functional literacy skills became an issue overshadowing almost all others in public discussions of the curriculum.[6]

In order to draw attention to the problems of achieving some balance in the curriculum of schools, and to address related issues in precollege education, I have cited the arts, sciences, and *humanities* (referring to social studies) as broad fields of study which, in addition to mathematics and the practical use of language, ought to be required in the general education of all students in elementary and secondary school.

A word about levels of education is in order. Most American schools are still organized according to grade levels. For the purpose of our discussion, a high school course or program is offered in grades nine through twelve; a junior high school program includes the seventh and eighth grades; and an elementary school program includes kindergarten through grade six. Many districts have shifted to a "middle school" organization reaching from the fourth or the fifth grade to the eighth grade. Because most teachers are still trained, certified, and employed to serve in the elementary school (kindergarten to sixth grade) or the secondary school (seventh to twelfth grade), chapters 5 and 6 are organized in terms of this division.

Although this book is highly critical of art education in the nation's schools, it is intended to persuade anyone who cares about art education to take constructive action for the improvement of school programs. It is my hope that the majority of readers will find here some of the facts and justifications they may have been seeking in order to harvest greater support for art programs in schools. Art education, as a field of endeavor, suffers from so many forms of neglect that many citizens, arts advocates, and professionals in education seem to assume that conditions cannot be improved. I believe that changes can be made, but not until we dare to question current practices and seek improvements for the right reasons.

1 | Instant Art, Instant Culture: The Unspoken Policy for the Nation's Schools

FEW CITIZENS REALIZE that 80 percent of our nation's youth graduate from high school with little or no instruction in the arts. Most youngsters spend twelve years in school, and during that time receive about twelve thousand hours of instruction, but less than 1 percent of this time is likely to be spent in studying the arts (except literature) with a qualified teacher. The typical high school graduate has a token education in the arts. About ninety hours of instruction in the visual arts is normally required—all of it compressed into a single art course taken in the seventh or the eighth grade. Requirements in music are essentially the same. The study of dance and theater is rare.[1]

Contrary to popular opinion, art instruction is not made available in all of our elementary and secondary schools. Even when something called "art" or "music" is offered, teachers who are well-intentioned but poorly qualified may miseducate children. Many well-prepared teachers of the arts are asked to work under such absurd conditions that they cannot teach effectively. What's more, teachers may be trained in ways that reinforce cultural stereotypes about art. For these and other reasons, many students who graduate from high school know little about the world of art.

1

The Agenda for Discussion

The fact that a typical high school graduate has so little instruction in the arts is one of the best-kept secrets in public education. Many parents, school administrators, principals, and school board members who believe that the arts are taught regularly, as part of the twelve-year curriculum, have never examined *who* teaches art, *what* is taught, *how often*, *when*, and to *whom*. When these facts are examined—as they will be in subsequent chapters, particularly for the visual arts—it becomes clear that most of our schools are not providing even a minimum of education in the arts.

Absent from most of our schools is a climate of genuine approval for children to study the arts, and programs of sufficient duration and quality to enable our high school graduates to learn how art might affect their lives. The message that many of our children get from current practices in schools is this: Art is a "frill" unworthy of being included in the regular curriculum, and hence of marginal importance in adult life. This message is delivered to our children from kindergarten through high school. It is the message we communicate by the limited time and few resources we allocate for instruction, by our failure to monitor the quality of elementary school instruction, by the elective status of the arts in high school, and by the limited expectations we have for student learning in the arts. All of these actions tell our young people that art does not count for much in human affairs.

Even when art is taught in schools, the typical fare we offer to children has little substance. We give children an opportunity to *do* a bit of art now and then—to sing, dance, or act. In the visual arts, they may learn how to use art materials or how to make clever projects that require little mastery and thought. Even in our high schools, art teachers concentrate on skills in performance, often at the expense of cultivating sensitivities and teaching concepts that build an appreciation of the arts. This kind of education reflects an extremely low estimate of the ability of young people to be engaged with the arts. We seem to assume that if children have a chance to do a bit of art in school, our educational responsibility has been met.

The proper study of art, however, involves far more than dabbling with paint, doing craft projects, singing, dancing, and being exposed now and then to the work of creative or performing artists. The arts of visual expression, for example, are evident in almost every visible thing shaped by the human mind—all the artifacts we use, all the images we see, all the constructed spaces we inhabit. Learning about the arts of visual expression (as well as the arts of music, dance, and theater) is just as demanding as, and no less important than, mastering the arts of expression through words and numbers.

Knowledge of the arts, like knowledge in any field, is an instrument of personal power. And because knowledge can be used in social and civic life, one's knowledge of art can be an ingredient determining one's social status as a well-educated person, equipped to participate fully in community and cultural affairs. People who have gained a knowledge of art—beyond the level of amateur performance—are not only more confident in dealing with art in a variety of settings; they are also well poised to influence the kind and amount of artistic activity that a community offers to its citizens. Such persons form the cultural "elite"; they are well educated, and because they are knowledgeable about the arts, they help to determine what does count as art within the larger culture.

Few members of the cultural elite create or perform in the arts, either as professionals or as amateurs; they value art as an ingredient of their social and civic lives, not merely as a hobby. They attend and support the arts institutions in their communities. Most have had the benefit of training in art appreciation, and many grew up in an environment where others approved of their learning about art. In other words, their confidence in art had been cultivated both through formal instruction and through a social climate that encouraged them to study art.

While this kind of interest and confidence in art is influenced by educational opportunity, similar opportunities are not generally available to all children and youths. In fact, few of our schools provide an educational climate in which the study of art is genuinely approved, and even fewer offer programs of sufficient scope, duration, and substance to cultivate an appreciation of art. These opportunities are not now provided to all children, even though they could be and should be a normal part of a child's education. The process of acquiring knowledge about art thus remains a matter of privilege associated with membership in a social class in which such knowledge is valued and provided.

Although a good deal of publicity has been given to the dramatic increase in attendance at art museums, concerts, and plays over the last decade or so, the so-called arts explosion described by Alvin Toffler is not due to the quality and availability of arts education in our elementary and secondary schools.[2] The new arts audience is largely a by-product of the increase in college graduates following the baby boom. Not until college do most young people encounter an environment where the study of art is required and genuinely approved as one aspect of being a well-educated person. More than 80 percent of the arts audience has had some college education, about half have four-year degrees, and many have pursued graduate work. Most are professionals, white-collar workers with an average income well above the national average.[3]

Surely we must ask whether the nation's arts—increasingly supported by public funds—are to be enjoyed by a particular social class, with membership in this class defined almost exclusively by a college education, a white-collar job, and a substantial income. Education, more than any single factor, predicts adult participation in the arts, but because our elementary and secondary schools provide so little art instruction, the majority of high school graduates are not prepared to evelute the arts, least of all those arts which might be cherished for their subtle meanings, complex forms, and precise execution. We seem to assume that the majority of our students will go on to college and can then be introduced to the arts. We forget that the majority of our youth do not attend college.

Is Art Education Really Needed?

The biggest problem in developing art programs in our schools comes from the unexamined beliefs and opinions held by the public, by the arts establishment, and by professionals in education, including arts education. Within each of these groups—and all are potential supporters of art programs in school—there exists a deeply engrained belief that the arts, with few exceptions, can be experienced, comprehended, and created with little or no formal education. Overcoming this fundamental misconception is the first and biggest step we must take. The difficulty in making this first step can be appreciated more fully when we examine how most of us think about art and art education.

Public Opinion

What does the public think about education in the arts? The results from several surveys conducted by Louis Harris Associates offer some insights. Perhaps the most important discovery is that more than 75 percent of the public have the opinion that a person "does not need to study or learn about art in order to understand or enjoy art."[4] This opinion, though widely held, does not take into account the depth of our response to art. In fact, many works of art are so subtle or so complex that it is almost impossible to appreciate them without a background of knowledge. With few exceptions, the more we understand about art, the more likely it is that we will find it enjoyable or profoundly moving. Nevertheless, the idea that art is not a subject that one must study is pervasive within our culture.

Public skepticism about the need for education is also apparent when we shift from the topic of appreciating the arts to the topic of creating art. The 1975 Harris survey suggests that the public believes training is of greater importance in creating certain forms of art, while talent is more crucial in creating other forms. When people are asked to explain why they create art (or not), they report that certain art forms are more demanding of training, as opposed to talent. The approximate order of perceived importance is shown below.[5]

Talent More Important	*Training More Important*
Writing (creatively)	Playing in an orchestra
Singing/drawing, painting, sculpting	Writing/playing a musical instrument
Playing a musical instrument	Dancing (ballet, modern dance)
Dancing (ballet, modern dance)	Drawing, painting, sculpting
Playing in an orchestra	Working in the theater
Working in the theater	Making craft items
Making craft items	Singing

Adults who do not create or perform in the arts say that the most important reasons for not doing so are lack of time, lack of training, and lack of talent (in that order). Among the college educated, a lack of talent is perceived as the greater obstacle in creating art, not a lack of training. It comes as no surprise that among those with a high school education or less, a lack of training is perceived as the greater barrier to creating or performing as artists.[6]

Although most school arts programs emphasize skills for creating or performing art, only approximately 7 percent of the public report "a great deal" of engagement in creating works of art or performing within the arts of music, dance, or theater. Although quite a few adults report some engagement with crafts (about 20 percent), much of this activity appears to be handwork—needlepoint, embroidery, woodworking, and the like.[7] Since there is a vast hobby-craft industry offering how-to-do-it instruction, much of this activity may not require much more than the ability to follow directions, along with sufficient time, and money for supplies.

Why do school programs concentrate on teaching children to make art and perform in the arts when few adults continue with this kind of activity? Educators who favor this kind of school arts program often claim that through the process of making art children will gain a general appreciation of the kind of work artists do and will be stimulated to attend exhibits and other artistic events. The results of the Harris survey, and of several other studies noted in chapters 5 and 6, do not lend uniform support to this claim. For example, over half of the adults who engage in crafts did not attend any cultural institution in their community in the preceding year, and more than a third of those who paint, draw, and make sculpture were classified as "cultural non-attenders." Adults who engage in the performing arts, as musicians or vocalists, as dancers, or as workers in theater, more frequently say they are stimulated by seeing the work of other artists than adults who create visual art or work in the crafts.[8]

Even though the public seems uncertain about the need for arts education, the Harris survey from 1981 shows a high level of public support for arts education in schools, and on a full-credit basis, "just like math or science or English." Over 70 percent of those polled endorsed courses in creative writing; instrumental and vocal music; drawing, painting, or sculpture; and music and art appreciation. Courses receiving less support were photography; acting; ballet or modern dance; and ceramics, needlepoint, weaving, and related crafts. Notice that the crafts, which are not perceived as demanding much talent or training, do attract the greatest numbers of adults into some kind of art activity. Nevertheless, the crafts are least likely to be endorsed as courses for the school to offer for credit.[9]

Overall, public expressions of support for the teaching of art courses increased between 1975 and 1981. This increase in voiced approval for arts education occurred during a period of great emphasis on the "basics" in education and financial distress for the nation and for schools. The public also appears to be willing to finance arts education; however, this willingness has declined slightly. In 1981, a solid 75 percent of the public favored regular financing of arts courses from school funds, a slight drop from the 1975 level of 79 percent.[10]

While it is costly to provide field trips to museums, concerts, and plays, more than 90 percent of Americans say that it is important for young people to attend arts events in the community. The highest endorsement is given to visiting art museums, followed by attendance at concerts, plays, ballet or modern dance performances, and operas. Predictably, the citizens who most clearly favor children's having opportunities of this kind are "frequent" attenders of cultural institutions.[11]

What the Harris surveys show is not that Americans think the arts are a frill in school programs; instead, citizens are not fully persuaded that *education*—formal instruction and training—plays a critical role in one's encounters with art. Americans are willing to have courses in the arts offered for full credit as part of the curriculum, and many see these courses as a regular educational expense. But the general view seems to be that arts education is "nice," not really necessary. As far as the visual arts are concerned, if you believe anyone can enjoy and understand art without knowing much about it, if you believe talent is more important than training in creating fine art, and if you believe anyone can do the crafts, there does not seem to be any compelling need for all young people to study art in school.

The Arts Establishment

Ironically, the Americans who seem to be the least convinced about the need for art education are the cultural elite—the upper 10 percent of the population who support the arts institutions in their communities by frequent attendance, and often through financial support or voluntary work. Within this group of persons who are highly involved in the arts, 85 percent do *not* agree that "You have to study or learn about such things as art or music before you can understand or enjoy them."[12] This same opinion, which implies that education is not really essential in the arts, was held by 78 percent of the general public.

This higher degree of skepticism among the cultural elite is remarkable, especially when we realize that more than 80 percent of the people in this group have some college education. Most have a college degree or have done graduate work. This advanced level of education also explains why many of the elite are professionals and enjoy a median income well above the national average. Patrons of the opera, for example, had an income about $6,500 above the national median in 1976; patrons of the symphony had incomes in the same range. Among those who attend art museums frequently, the income was $3,500 above the national median (see app. B, fig. B. 2); for theater, about $5,000 above; for ballet and modern dance, about $5,500 higher than the national median income.[13]

As a group, the cultural elite also have benefited from education in art to a degree well above the average citizen. For example, nearly two-thirds of those who frequently attend art museums took art appreciation courses in school or college. More than two-thirds attended art museums as children and began making such visits about two years earlier (average age of nine and one-half) than most Americans. More frequently than the general public, regular patrons of art museums report that they had attended museums on field trips arranged through schools, and that they had teachers who stimulated their interest in art and taught them specific things that helped them appreciate art. Seventy-one percent of the cultural elite *disagreed* with the statement "What I was taught in school never really helped me to enjoy or appreciate the arts," compared with 53 percent of the general public.[14]

A number of experiences mediated by formal education in art distinguish the cultural elite from the general public, and taken together these experiences appear to be far more important than the influence of family and friends on later interest in art. We know, of course, that parental education and attitudes have a general impact on children's attitudes about "getting an education." This influence can be traced in art (see chaps. 5 and 6). But there is also no doubt that the art education made available in schools contributes to later interest in the arts, and that the school arts program is especially important for the majority of children whose parents do not have a college educa-tion.

What is striking about the cultural elite is their reluctance to ac-knowledge that formal education in art is really essential for one to enjoy and understand art. Equally striking is their belief that the creation of art hinges on talent more than on training—a belief which assumes that training has been provided. These attitudes would be harmless enough if it were not for the fact that the cultural elite is not just a social class defined by statistics; increasingly, it has become a well-organized lobby seeking to influence national and state policies on the arts and arts education.

In the last fifteen years or so, and largely through the efforts of the cultural elite, a new arts bureaucracy has been formed to promote and to serve the arts within American society.[15] From the growth of this bureaucracy—which was created as a channel for funds from the National Endowment for the Arts—a system of state and local arts councils has evolved, as well as groups of advocates for the arts, whose activities, one might suppose, would enhance school arts programs. In fact, the new arts establishment has offered recommendations which reflect a distrust of formal education in the arts and a skepticism about the value of studying them, which parallels the results from the Harris surveys.

The sympathies of the new arts establishment and its advocates are not directed toward school programs that reach all children and provide for continuous study of the arts. Rather, arts advocates are urging parents, educators, and citizens to endorse ideas that would, if acted upon, *increase* the distance between the "elite" and the public. Among the ideas being promoted by the arts establishment, to be examined more fully in later chapters, are these:

- □ Arts education should focus on the making of art, (which already is the emphasis in school programs). By contrast, the study of art history and the development of art appreciation is not to be given comparable importance in the education of youth.
- □ Arts education should be delegated to artists and community agencies—"deschooled" as much as possible. Arts education is a social service which can not only be provided in a number of settings within the community, but can also be financed and managed in a manner comparable to the operation of United Appeal agencies which coordinate social services.
- □ Arts education need not be considered a regular part of the school curriculum, and need not be financed primarily or exclusively by the regular school budget.
- □ The primary benefits from arts education in schools will come from the use of art to improve children's achievement in other subjects and to make schools attractive places for children. In-school instruction should focus on interrelating the arts and integrating them with other subjects, through activities that involve youngsters as performing artists or as creators who manipulate art materials.
- □ Present and future arts teachers should be trained as "generalists"—as administrative staff who can help to coordinate the arts services offered by the community to school-age youth. The arts generalist can also strengthen the related arts and integrated programs offered in the school.[16]

While much of the rhetoric from the new arts establishment seems to be supportive of more and better instruction for children, the school is not portrayed as the agency primarily responsible for such instruction. One finds no strong arguments on behalf of the principle that all young people should receive a basic education in the arts while they are in elementary and secondary school.

This orientation to the arts in education is particularly unfortunate when it is voiced by groups who seem to represent the "national interest" in the arts. For a comparison, imagine that the national leadership in science or the humanities were to recommend that instruction in these fields be "deschooled," and paid for by some other path than regular school funds. Imagine that such instruction would be delegated to scientists and scholars in a community, most or all of whom would prefer to earn income from their regular line of work. Is it likely that all children would receive a basic education in the sciences, the social studies, and language arts under such a scheme? Who could afford such instruction? The comparison serves as a reminder that our school system, above all else, is designed to offer equality in the opportunity to study science and the humanities and that the same principle should be applied in relation to the arts. In short, the arts leadership has not addressed the issue of equality in the opportunity for children to study art.

The Educational Establishment

Unfortunately, many of the attitudes that cause art to be neglected in our schools are reinforced within the educational establishment—in college departments where teachers are trained, where the leadership is prepared for school administration, curriculum design, research, and teacher education. It is here that the trouble begins for arts education. It begins when knowledge about the role of art in human experience is virtually ignored in the training of school administrators and other educational leaders; neither are classroom teachers and art teachers as well trained as they should be.

In general, faculty in schools of education—the experts in curriculum, in educational psychology, in school administration, in the training of classroom teachers—are not well versed in the arts. Few appear to be familiar with the recent professional literature on education in the arts. Many educators have had little or no instruction in art or in art education beyond a brief course or two that may have been required of all undergraduates or included as part of their initial training as teachers. In almost all debates about educational reform, methods of teaching, evaluation of learning—the educational leadership concentrates its attention on reading, mathematics, writing, science, and social studies. The arts, if mentioned, are not treated as a regular part of the curriculum, but as an extra, an enrichment, or tool for learning subjects other than art.[17]

In addition to this general neglect of the arts in the discussions of the educational leadership, there are special problems with the way that the visual arts are typically introduced into the training of classroom teachers, and, to some extent, the training of teachers in the visual arts. In their initial preparation within the visual arts, many teachers have been encouraged to adopt a philosophy of teaching creative art activities, but without a corresponding emphasis on teaching for appreciation. Teacher education programs also tend to romanticize the role of art in childhood. In much of the literature on teaching art to children, the adult is portrayed as a villain who robs children of their charm, innocence, creativity, imagination, and natural sense of design.[18] While there are genuine risks in all insensitive art instruction, so pervasive is the idea that the children are "naturally" creative in the visual arts that the mission of the teacher may even be defined as that of preventing children from learning about art from informed adults.

Teacher education in the visual arts also has been narrow in scope. Although most art teachers are trained to draw, paint, and create various types of art, they are less likely to have been trained to analyze the practice of making art, especially from an historical perspective. Until recently, few teachers were trained to teach children about art history and issues in judging the visual arts. There is still some resistance to such instruction, both in schools and in teacher education. Because many teachers are urged to see themselves primarily as artists or craftsworkers, relatively few teachers have been called upon to consider the role of the visual arts in public life—to study the economics and sociology of art, for example, or to examine the relationships between the unique objects produced by the artist and all of the mass-produced and mass-marketed goods that young people encounter every day. Indeed, quite a few teachers have been urged to adopt a "personal" philosophy of art education, as if the intensity of one's personal preferences offered a proper and complete justification of educational practice.

Not all of these traditions are unique to the visual arts, but they illustrate some of the weaknesses in educating teachers of the arts which, in turn, compromise the arts education young people receive, if, indeed, they are served by a teacher in the arts.[19] There are pockets of excellence in arts education, but when we examine current practices from a national perspective, we must conclude that the most dominant attitudes held by the public and by professionals in art and education contribute to a pattern of neglect of the arts in education.

Typical practices in our schools prevent the majority of our youth from receiving a basic education in the arts, either by restricting access to instruction so that only the most determined and talented can obtain it, or by so narrowly representing the world of art that youngsters are ill prepared to appreciate it unless or until they go to college.[20] Indeed, if we wanted to design a national educational policy to insure that art would be comprehended and consciously valued only by a privileged social class, we would not need to do much more than translate many current practices into an explicit statement of policy.

A New Attitude Toward the Arts

What is vitally needed today is a radical reconstruction of the way we think about arts education. It is unreasonable to construe art as if it were an enterprise that does not require study or merit status as a major subject within the curriculum, on a par with science and the humanities. It is wrong to treat the arts only as enrichments or electives for talented students, when, in fact, all students should be equipped to deal with the arts knowledgeably, whether they become artists or not, and whether they attend college or not. As a nation, we tolerate art in school, we allow something called art to happen, but we do not really expect much from this instruction. We seem satisfied if children have a chance to dabble in the arts. We permit this level of engagement, and not much more.

This general orientation to arts education in schools does not enhance the public's perception of art as a worthwhile form of human endeavor. And it creates a climate in which the self-fulfilling prophecy operates. Because we do not expect very much from the teaching of art within our schools, we allocate few resources for arts education, and thus make it difficult or impossible for teachers to offer a decent program of instruction. Thus, teachers who enter schools with a strong sense of responsibility for art education may be prevented from teaching effectively, for want of resources to do the job.

What makes these conditions demoralizing for teachers of the arts is not just the inherent difficulty of providing a sound educational program; it is being placed in a position of maintaining the pretense of doing so in the absence of proper support. It must be said, however, that many teachers of the arts have become part of this self-fulfilling cycle. As a professional group, teachers of the arts are not inclined to be militant, even when they feel that they are not treated equitably in relation to allocation of resources, and time. These problems are less acute for teachers in the language arts, but by training and disposition, most arts teachers enjoy creative challenges and are thus more likely to try to "make a silk purse out of a sow's ear" than to complain about teaching conditions which severely handicap their efforts.

I hope this book will help to persuade educators at all levels, the growing community of advocates for the arts, and the general public that the basic education of our children must include basic education in the visual, literary, and performing arts. Arts education is not only a legitimate and terribly neglected mission for the nation's schools; it is, I believe, properly seen as an obligation of our schools. Only through our schools can we provide the nation's youth with an equal opportunity to study art early in life, and hence an equal opportunity to determine how the arts might enrich their lives.

The plight of arts education today, and particularly visual arts education, is not widely appreciated, because: 1) the conditions under which schools offer instruction have not been well documented, 2) the prevailing concepts of "good and sufficient" art education for children are so inadequate that they provide no measure of the gap between the way things are and the way they ought to be. This book then is a critical commentary intended to illuminate and to build an appreciation of the importance of these issues.

2 | Reforming the Curriculum: A New Role for the Arts

THE AMERICAN SYSTEM OF PUBLIC SCHOOLS has always been the target of criticism, but at no time in recent history has the issue of quality in education been more open to reconsideration. I believe we are entering an historic period in which fundamental changes must be made in our expectations for schools.

Consider these factors, among others, which foreshadow a major period of general educational reform: the profound skepticism, both public and professional, about the quality of education children receive in public schools; the lack of overwhelming success for the back-to-basics movement, in spite of a decade of trial and massive expenditures of money; the reexamination of the curriculum that must occur as federal funds are withdrawn from special instructional programs; the growth of interest in evaluating the quality of education, coupled with questions about the influence of the educational testing and publishing industry on the curriculum of schools; the pressure for improvements in public schools caused by discussions of voucher and tax-credit plans.[1]

Excellence in Education

All of these pressures for the reform of public schools offer an unparalleled opportunity for citizens and educators to address the issue of quality in the instructional program of schools. It is clear that minimum competency in the three R's cannot be maintained as the exclusive aim of schools. Changes in the curriculum are needed, and these could be made in a way that would not only address the issue of quality in education, but also assure that the arts have a central position in the curriculum.

Let us begin with the simple but fundamental idea that all children, irrespective of their social class, should be provided with a basic education in the arts, the sciences, and the humanities (social studies). A curriculum built around studies in these three areas is probably the single most well-established standard for quality in the education of youth. It is the kind of education valued by persons who occupy positions of leadership and power in our society.[2] While this standard has not been seriously entertained for public schools in recent history, it might well be revitalized as the issue of quality continues to be linked with the very survival of public schools. A curriculum designed for excellence need not be for the wealthy alone, nor based on the assumption that all students will attend college.

In a curriculum organized around the arts, sciences, and humanities, arts education would become nothing less than a required program of studies. All children would study the performing, literary, and visual arts from kindergarten to at least the tenth grade. If the arts were taught by well-qualified teachers, we should expect coherent and developmental learning about each of the arts. Nothing less is worthy of the nation's young people. And in the long run, nothing less is worthy of the nation's arts and its cultural vitality. If pursued, this goal of required instruction in the arts would not only place the arts on a par with the sciences and the humanities within the curriculum; it would demonstrate that the curriculum *as a whole* has been conceived to provide education of the highest quality.

Educators, together with citizens who care about public education, could cause this direction of reform to occur. Support for this direction of change should not be underestimated, for many classroom teachers, parents, and principals are ready for reform. They know that children are demoralized by drill after drill to develop "test-taking" skills, at the expense (literally) of learning about the larger world—the planet we inhabit, the people with whom it is shared, the vantage points of life provided through studies in the arts. The back-to-basics movement has reduced instruction in the sciences and social studies no less than it has hurt the arts.

The Fractured Curriculum

There are critical flaws in the curriculum many schools now offer, and these flaws affect instruction in all subjects, not only the arts. In many schools, the curriculum is a disaster area, fragmented into all sorts of special channels to such a degree that administrators, parents, and students have little sense of educational priorities beyond the so-called basic skills.

This fragmentation of the curriculum has been caused by a general failure of the educational establishment to reconcile two major demands on schools. The first demand is located in the traditional role of the school as an agency for transmitting organized knowledge to each generation. The second demand is found in our expectation that schools will promote the individual and social growth of children by teaching them to be literate, to have self-esteem, to seek jobs, and so on. The first demand is accommodated by the *content* children learn through instruction based in the major subject fields—science, social studies, and the arts. The second demand is met through the *patterns of behavior and skills* which schools attempt to cultivate—skills in reading, in communicating with others, skills that are essential for securing a job and participating in civic affairs.

When we look at the regular curriculum today, we can see that these two demands are poorly reconciled. What we now see is a curriculum where instructional time for the arts, sciences, and humanities is bartered for time to teach special courses that purport to nurture the individual growth of children—courses that build self-concepts, or teach creativity, skill in critical thinking, perceptual awareness, moral judgment, or other skills. And both of these functions of education—transmitting knowledge and fostering personal development—are placed into competition for time to teach courses intended to make children responsible, self-supporting citizens—courses in career awareness, skills for daily living, consumer education, and so on. In short, the so-called basic skills are taught with little regard for the content children are learning in social studies, the sciences, or the arts.

The curriculum in many schools is a shambles precisely because our concern for the personal development of children and their ability to function as self-supporting citizens has not been matched by equal concern for their mastery of subject matter. Separate instructional tracks and specially funded programs have been created to teach many specific skills and attitudes, and each of these courses preempts time which otherwise might be devoted to studying science, human society, and the arts. As a result, there is said to be no time for instruction in the arts, and very little time actually is given to the sciences and social studies.[3] In the pursuit of all these disconnected aims, schools have not done a good job of teaching children about the arts, sciences, and social studies, nor have they succeeded well in nurturing the personal and social well-being of children. In short, the curriculum in many schools has little coherence in content, developmental sequence, or social emphasis.

Arts education suffers from the same basic problem that we find in the larger educational arena, but with several peculiarities. The heritage of teaching practice and of scholarship in dance, theater, music, and the visual arts has been dominated by claims about the value of arts activities for the individual development of children in such general areas as perceptual awareness, self-expression, and creativity, as if these were unique contributions of the arts to individual development. In addition, the arts have been portrayed as a means for achieving a range of social aims which are not unique to the arts. For example, the arts are said to be means of improving children's interest in school, and thus are described as valuable aids in preventing children from dropping out of school, or the arts may be viewed as therapeutic for the emotionally disturbed child.

This interest in using the arts as "tools" for learning is so prevalent that some educators appear to be uncomfortable with the idea of teaching the arts as an organized yet ever-growing body of knowledge. The prevailing belief is that children should not encounter the arts as subjects for study, since that would make the arts more academic, more intellectual, and less distinctive within the curriculum.[4]

We do not see clearly that knowledge about the arts—intellectual content—can be transmitted, *with* due regard for the personal development of children in art *and* for the purpose of cultivating their awareness of the social dimensions of art.[5] Because we have a habit of placing the developmental, social, and intellectual aims of arts education into a competing, not a complementary relationship, arts education is plagued by the same kind of fragmentation in purpose and effectiveness that we now see in the general field of education.

Faced with the increasingly fragmented curriculum and provided little earmarked time for instruction, arts educators have attempted to latch onto any fragment of the curriculum that seems to be important at the moment. Thus, when truancy is a major concern, arts teachers promise to reduce truancy by making schools more lively. When reading is the most important concern, arts teachers try to boost reading scores through the arts. But this pattern of response—even if partially justified by the importance of such problems—reinforces the impression among administrators that the arts can always be slipped into the curriculum informally. As a consequence of this pattern of smuggling the arts into the curriculum, many administrators feel free to plan the regular curriculum, allowing time and resources for everything except the arts.

Arts educators can and must reverse those habits of thought which have made the arts appear to be unworthy of serious study, and therefore of marginal importance in the curriculum. At the same time, arts educators have every right to challenge an educational establishment that has come to expect no more than "minimum competency" and "functional literacy" as the outcomes of twelve years of schooling. This failure of educational leadership is a classic case of the self-fulfilling prophecy. As expectations have been lowered for students, their actual performance has declined, and public skepticism about the quality of schools has increased.

Indeed, when the arts, sciences, and humanities are proposed as the core content areas for a curriculum, one can see that arts educators have failed to address the basic problem. Arts educators have become so preoccupied with justifying their place in the curriculum that the other side of the justification issue has been missed. Collectively, arts educators should ask the larger educational community *on what grounds* the arts have been excluded from the regular curriculum.

If we look at the most common dimensions of the so-called regular curriculum, a clear pattern of discrimination against formal study of the arts is apparent. There is not daily or required instruction in the arts over a span of nine or ten years, as there is in the sciences and the humanities. On the average, only a half-year of art and a half-year of music is required in twelve years of school.[6] In the elementary school, there is little effort to control the quality of instruction and to assure that art content is appropriate and well presented.[7] What most schools offer to children is a "dose" of the arts for one year, at puberty, as if it were part of an obligatory rite of passage into the world of culture. And that's all. These practices, I submit, cannot be justified on any grounds worthy of consideration for American education.

A Strategy for Change

The root problems of art education cannot be solved without an un-paralleled exercise of leadership aimed at redefining the total curriculum so that the arts are treated as a major domain of study, on a par with the sciences and humanities. The challenge is to modify habits of thought which have discriminated against the arts as a major subject within the curriculum. What we need is not more of the same kind of casual instruction we now see in many schools, but an arts curriculum that would merit status as a required program of study from kindergarten to the tenth grade.

The First Step: Developing an Arts Curriculum

Arts educators should collaborate in the design of a program of study that will encompass all of the arts—visual, literary, and performing. The planning of such a program should begin with the same premises that apply in most subjects. These premises are:

- The school is obliged to provide *a basic education in the arts* to all children and youth. No other institution is so well equipped nor so clearly responsible for assuring that all children have an equal opportunity to become knowledgeable about dance, music, theater, literature, and the visual arts.
- The education children receive in the several arts must be controlled for quality and be continuous, so that learning in the arts, like learning in other subjects, is developmental and cumulative.
- Learning in the arts must be actively promoted and reinforced throughout the rest of the curriculum.
- Learning in the arts must be planned for, supported, and assessed in the same systematic manner one would expect for other subjects.

How can these conditions be met? It is common to assume that in planning an arts curriculum one must begin with a scheme that will not only interrelate the several arts but also integrate the arts into other subjects within the curriculum. As we shall see, these assumptions do not guide the planning process in all subjects; accordingly they should not be regarded as "ground rules" for planning an arts curriculum. Indeed, since the arts are distinct from each other in their modes of creation and encounter, our chief concern is to plan a curriculum that will promote learning about the world of the arts, but in a way that preserves the integrity of learning about each of the arts.

How can one organize a large and complex body of knowledge such as the arts and still maintain the integrity of instruction in each of the arts? Planning principles which have been used in other fields offer clues. Consider, for example, the structure of the typical science curriculum in many elementary schools. First, a clear distinction is made between studies in the life sciences, earth sciences, and physical sciences. Second, within each of the sciences a few major themes are treated again and again at each grade. Third, within each grade, several topics related to each theme serve as the focal point for specific lessons and activities. Fourth, and most noteworthy, neither the themes nor the topics are contrived to impose relationships across the sciences.

The science curriculum is coordinated in two major ways. It is coordinated sequentially, along the lines suggested by cognitive learning theory—from observing particular things and varieties of them, to learning about simple interactions, then simple systems of interactions, then more complex systems and concepts. It is also coordinated along subject-matter lines through the choice of themes and topics appropriate to each of the sciences.

Using similar planning principles, the arts curriculum might well be organized around the visual, performing, and literary arts. This clustering reflects the structure within today's art world. It also recognizes that the performing arts are created, presented, and experienced under conditions which are different from the visual and literary arts. While affinities among the performing arts might be demonstrated to children within this structure, the intent is not to minimize the importance of instruction in each of the arts, nor to suggest that relationships must be demonstrated among them. Within the literary arts, the study and use of language as art should be distinguished from instruction in "basic skills," so that children develop a better sense for the expressive and evocative power of language.

If a coordinating structure similar to that in the science curriculum were adapted to the arts, younger children would learn about the variety of things in the world that may be regarded as dance, music, the visual arts, and so on. In the middle elementary grades, more specific interactions might be studied within each of the arts—in dance, interactions between the shape of the body and its movement through space; in painting, the interaction of color and shape to establish a mood. In the upper elementary grades, more complex problems and abstract concepts could be introduced.

Whatever the coordinating structure—and many models can be

used—the topics or themes selected for the curriculum should be introduced and organized to provide a sound program of study in the respective arts of dance, music, theater, literature, and the visual arts. The coordinating structure should not prevent curriculum designers from planning activities that bridge across the arts, but neither should it require that relationships be found among the arts just for the sake of doing so.

In order to bring the arts into parity with science and social studies, no less than five to five and one-half hours a week should be devoted to arts education in elementary school, excluding the language arts. The language arts already command a disproportionate share of the curriculum and should, of course, include substantial work in creative writing and literature. Hence, this suggested block of time would be reserved for instruction in the visual arts, music, dance, and theater—about eighty minutes per week for each. It should be noted that the professional associations of art and music educators recommend one hundred and ninety minutes per week, respectively, for visual art and music.[8] Additional time for all of the arts can be gained by teaching the basic skills in mathematics, reading, writing—and all other subjects—so that they reinforce or extend arts learning. Before suggesting how this might be accomplished, let me illustrate how the arts might be strengthened in secondary school.

In secondary schools, a program balanced between the visual, literary, and performing arts should be required from grades seven through ten. Various scheduling patterns might be devised. For example, during the seventh and eighth grades, four half-year courses might be required. One of these would be selected from several options in the visual arts, one from several options in the performing arts, one from several options in the literary arts. The fourth course would be selected in any of the arts. A similar pattern of required and open electives might be designed for the ninth and tenth grade.

In the ninth or tenth grade, year-long courses might be designed as an alternative to half-year courses, and some of these year-long courses might be designed to relate the arts. For example, instead of the typical dry comparisons among the arts based upon formalist principles (line, shape, movement, rhythm, and so forth) a course might be designed around the idea of "rites of passage." Students would learn that in almost every generation and culture the arts serve as a means to express important life events. What art forms are associated with birth, with childhood, adolescence? How might the arts enter our lives later—at work, while raising a family, during retirement, even at our death? In such a course, the fine, popular, and applied arts could be treated; cross-generational and cross-cultural comparisons could be made. Other courses might be designed for the academically gifted: world history, for example, but studied through the arts.

If arts programs were designed along these general lines, students entering the ninth and tenth grades would have a background in each of the arts, and thus would be much better prepared to deal with concepts that relate the arts or connect the arts to other topics. Talented students would not be prevented from concentrating their studies in a particular art form. In the eleventh and twelfth grades, art might remain an elective. Students selecting these electives would be more certain of their interest and more thoroughly prepared for advanced study.

The Second Step: Reinforcing the Arts Curriculum

A curriculum effort of the kind I have described is but one facet of a larger plan to secure a decent share of instructional time for the arts. A second step is to build a support system for arts education throughout the rest of the curriculum, and particularly in the elementary school. At the present time, most of a school day at the elementary level is devoted to instruction in the basic skills.[9] Schools spend a fortune on texts, tests, workbooks, and ditto masters for such instruction, to say nothing of materials for teaching science and the social studies.

Here are some questions that all educators must begin to ask. Do the materials employed in teaching the "basic skills" and other so-called tool subjects enhance learning in the *arts?* If not, on what grounds are all those dittos, workbooks, and drills justified as tools for learning? Within social studies texts and activities, is work within the arts portrayed as useful work? Are the artistic achievements of social or cultural groups presented? When a drawing activity is introduced in a science or social studies lesson, does this "art" activity reinforce the visual arts curriculum, and is it consistent with a developmental drawing program that an art educator might design? In physical education, is graceful movement fine for girls, but disapproved for boys? When educators ask questions such as these, it becomes more apparent that thoughtless practice in the rest of the curriculum might undermine or contradict the agenda for arts learning.

This kind of review of the so-called regular curriculum might be accompanied by other actions. Since schools spend so much money on testing and on published materials for teaching basic skills, arts educators (together with their colleagues in science and social studies) should request that all of these materials be reviewed prior to their purchase. Publishers of tests, texts, and related materials should be required to supply school districts with an analysis of these materials, showing what children will be learning about the arts, sciences, and social studies as they are learning to read, write, and compute.

From an inspection of the exercises children encounter in the name of basic skills instruction, one might conclude that the most valuable things in the world for children to think about are dittoed purple outlines of clowns, sailboats, balloons, rubber balls, birds of no particular species, and isolated words like *at, hat,* and *bat.* The indifference to content displayed in such exercises, the amount of time preempted by their use, and their high cost—when they are presented in non-reuseable workbooks or dittos—all help to explain why there is no time, money, or genuine concern for the arts and for other substantive studies in the curriculum.

Larger school districts do have the leverage to withold bids and contracts from suppliers of instructional materials who fail to provide satisfactory evidence that appropriate intellectual content in art, as well as science and social studies, is integrated with all exercises and tests for the three R's. In a fairly short time, one might expect that publishers would develop materials with greater sensitivity to the content children learn. At the level of a single school, staff and teachers might conduct an informal review of the tests and instructional materials they use. Indeed, the more reeducation one can build into the review process, the better.

The Third Step: Evaluating the Aesthetic Environment of the School

Paralleling these efforts, we should examine what children are taught about art on an informal basis through the physical environment of the school. Such a review would concentrate on the aesthetic characteristics of the school. It would examine the images children see and the values that the school communicates to them about art, directly or metaphorically. Children learn about art through the very design of classrooms and through the sensory and behavioral impact of graphic materials and displays. The choreography of movement in and through the school is part of their aesthetic education, as is the kind of sound they encounter during a typical day. There should be artistry in these and related dimensions of schools.

A similar analysis should be made of specific forms of art that children encounter in extracurricular programs. What kinds of painting, sculpture, music, dance, and theater do children encounter outside of the arts curriculum, but under the auspices of the school? Among the images selected for display in halls and classrooms, we should find works of art, or reproductions of them. Special ceremonies, school assemblies, routine announcements at the start of a school day—all might be planned to enhance arts learning, through the inclusion of forms of poetry, music, dance, and drama appropriate to the occasion and the desired response to it. This kind of analysis and planning should result in a greater consciousness of the total school environment as a support system for the arts and aesthetic education.

The Fourth Step: Planning and Staffing

Arts education suffers from neglect in many of the planning and decision-making procedures that shape the curriculum and determine how resources are allocated. Every school and school district should have an annual plan for the improvement of arts education, as well as an extended plan for the next three to five years. The value of planning techniques such as management-by-objectives (MBO) is as much psychological as practical. Such techniques provide a format for placing the arts on the agenda for discussion in budgetary, staff, and other administrative reviews, so that even if arts education is not well supported, everyone has a clear sense of what has been given up, at what price, and on what educational grounds.

Staffing remains a major problem, particularly in dance and theater, where no strong tradition of teacher education and certification has been established. In fact, the main reason why some advocates want schools to employ artists as teachers is to make sure that dance and theater are taught. However, cumulative, developmental learning in the arts cannot be cultivated if artists are employed on a part-time basis or brought in to "do their own thing" without regard for the aims of the curriculum or activities that may precede or follow their temporary involvement.

The most acute staffing problem is in the elementary school, where classroom teachers who have little or no background in the arts are nevertheless called upon to teach them. If specialists cannot be employed to teach the arts, then, at minimum, specialists must be employed to develop the arts curriculum, secure resources, and train classroom teachers on the job through demonstration lessons, workshops, and seminars.

In the long run, dual certification programs in more than one of the arts should be developed. This pattern would give greater flexibility to schools and arts teachers in relation to job assignments. It would be helpful too, if all teacher preparation in the arts were approached with the idea that "making" or "performing" in the arts is not the only path to learning and teaching. Instead, artistic experimentation should be treated as a laboratory component of arts education, in the way science educators use laboratory experience. Learning in art should extend well beyond the child's own ability to sing or dance, to play a musical instrument, to write a poem or paint a picture.

In the short run, the burden of arts curriculum development will have to be assumed by the specialists available within a school or school system, and most likely these specialists will be in the areas of art, music, and reading or literature. In large school districts, arts and classroom teachers might be found with special strengths in the arts and, through temporary reassignment, be brought into the process of curriculum design and teacher education. Strategies for change suitable for local communities can be found, if the commitment to improvement has been made.

A Future for Arts Education

The opportunity exists in the concept of arts curriculum planning and in the pressure upon schools to offer education of high quality to reverse habits of thought and practices which have seriously weakened instruction in the arts, sciences, and humanities, but have encouraged the investment of millions of dollars for instruction devoted to no more than minimum competency. Surely this kind of decision making is the cause of public disenchantment with schools.

The issue in offering arts education is not, as is often said, the lack of time for instruction within the existing curriculum, but the broader question of proper and wise use of available time for all subjects. Rather than slipping the arts into what is mistakenly called the regular curriculum, the total curriculum should be redefined so that the arts are included from the outset, on a par with the sciences and the humanities.

Authentic reform does not lie in the direction proposed by various advocates who favor more emphasis on making art as the essence and end of arts education, or incidental instruction to be offered by artists and community agencies, or more use of the arts as a tool for improving learning in other subjects, or more condensed and abbreviated instruction in the guise of "related art" or "interdisciplinary" arts courses.[10] It is precisely this catch-as-catch-can orientation which has taught school administrators that the arts are not worthy of inclusion in the curriculum on a par with the sciences and the humanities.

Until the arts are treated as a normal, obligatory, and regularly scheduled core subject within the curriculum, there will always be yet another reason for the educational establishment to say, "Sorry, no time and resources for the arts." And if, by our own professional conduct, arts educators provide the fuel for this kind of judgment, shall we then complain about the poor treatment given to the arts in public schools?

There is an alternative path to the reform of schools and the reform of arts education. Let us work toward a concept of education in which the arts, sciences, and humanities are acknowledged as equally important channels of endeavor and equally valuable sources of knowledge about ourselves and the world in which we live. Let that sense of equity in human endeavors be reflected in a revised curriculum that emphasizes all of these areas equally.

If we have the vision, desire, and energy to undertake this agenda for change, the quality and coherence of the whole curriculum will be enhanced, and the arts will be more equitably treated in American schools. We have little to lose, and much to gain, by attempting this kind of reform.

3

Back to Basics: Including Art

WHY BOTHER TO TEACH ART in our schools? In the preceding chapter this question was answered by saying that education of high quality means education in the arts, sciences, and humanities. In this chapter and the next we will examine why art must be taught and suggest the kind of active, planned instruction that children should receive in our schools, taking the visual arts as an example.

If children were able to comprehend the arts without having any formal instruction at all, there would be no good reason to include studies of the arts within the curriculum.[1] In the case of the visual arts, many people seem to believe that children are naturally creative and artistic, or that appreciating is only a matter of exercising one's personal taste, or that learning about art is a special form of self-indulgence for the very rich and the few who are talented. None of these popular beliefs makes the study of the visual arts seem very important in the basic education of young people. These attitudes, among others, may explain why instruction in the visual arts has such a marginal place in our elementary and secondary schools.

What Is Basic Education?

Adults in every society provide a basic education for their children in order to prepare them for their responsibilities as adults. Toward this end, a basic education serves to transmit the cultural heritage to each generation, to develop the skills children will need in order to pursue a rewarding life, and to nurture responsible social conduct. By extension, basic education in the visual arts should illuminate art as part of the cultural heritage and prepare young people to make informed decisions about the role of art in their personal, social, and civic lives. The best way to make sure that all of our children have an equal opportunity to study art is through our schools.

Young people do learn about the visual arts informally, outside of schools, and since they are exposed to visual images of all kinds they develop ideas about the nature of art from many sources—friends and family, other adults in their community, and even from the mass media. What children learn from these sources may, on occasion, be vivid and appropriate, but when these informal channels of education are relied upon to provide valid information about art, many children are likely to be misinformed. For example, from the typical portrayal of artists in fiction and television dramas, one might conclude that most artists are either jealous, impulsive fools or have saintlike genius.

Even if youngsters are not miseducated by their informal exposure to the arts of visual expression, it should be obvious that the most equitable, efficient, and readily available way of accomplishing art education is through our schools, for the school is the only agency that reaches all children. In addition to ensuring that all have an equal opportunity to acquire valid knowledge about art, the school is intended to make the process of learning efficient, coherent, and so intrinsically rewarding that children acquire a love of learning.

In order to grasp the importance of basic education in the visual arts and to appreciate the vital role of the school in providing it, let us examine in greater detail some reasons why the study of art is worthwhile and needed.

Why Bother To Teach Art?

Is art a subject that requires study? Although the obvious answer seems to be yes, we have seen that many people in our society seem to believe that the study of art is unnecessary. A number of these beliefs are embedded in clichés that surface in discussions of art. Consider this sampling of slogans, and notice how deeply engrained is the belief that art does not need to be taught:

□ *Children are naturally imaginative, creative, and artistic.* (Don't teach children art, you'll destroy what nature has given them.)

□ *I don't need to know anything about art to know what I like.* (A knowledge of art doesn't aid judgment.)

□ *Art is a gift, a talent you are born with.* (Train the talented, but don't waste time trying to teach the untalented.)

□ *If you have to explain it, it isn't art.* (Art is self-evident, it can't be illuminated by explanation.)

□ *People who try to explain art are barking up the wrong tree.* (Teachers who try to explain art are misguided.)

□ *Art is a universal language everyone can understand.* (Understanding of art is not influenced by education.)

□ *Art is caught, not taught.* (Exposure to art is infectious.)

□ *I can't draw a straight line with a ruler.* (Art is skill in drawing; the clumsy can't learn about art.)

□ *Art is fun, enjoyable.* (Art is a form of entertainment.)

□ *Art is play.* (Art is never work, doesn't require disciplined study.)

□ *Art is therapy.* (Art is for people who are abnormally troubled.)

□ *Art is anything you can get away with.* (There are no criteria for judging art.)

□ *Art is life, life is art—that's all there is to it.* (Anything can be called art.)

□ *Art speaks for itself.* (Teachers aren't needed.)

The attitudes reflected in clichés such as these must be set aside. Not only do these unexamined beliefs demean the hard work, intelligence, and cultivated skill required to create and appreciate art; they are easy-to-use excuses for not teaching art or for avoiding the effort of developing programs that might result in a more enlightened understanding of art. At minimum, we should expect our schools to produce citizens who are informed about the role of art in everyday life, its historical significance, and the importance of art to those who create it. Let's examine why these expectations are not likely to be met without formal instruction.

Art in Everyday Life

Few children (or adults) really understand how their attitudes and their conduct can be affected by the visual forms they encounter every day.[2] For example, the visual character of my front yard or shop, or the arrangement of my personal space seems to be nobody's business but mine, but my decisions about these spaces will determine the kind of environment you will see the moment you enter my space. If all of us make our decisions with little or no regard for how they affect others, we can create a world unfit for anyone to live in. Consider, for example, how much we have come to depend on disposable convenience items—paper cups and napkins, plastic dishes and dinnerware, throwaway containers for drinks and food. What we gain in immediate convenience, we lose in the presence of a litter-filled world. The study of art should cause us to think about issues such as these.

Studies of the visual arts are important because so much of our basic understanding of the world is built from what we see. Encounters with advertising, television, all kinds of products, and buildings are powerful and unavoidable ingredients of our lives. The characteristics of such forms—their design, style, material, form, symbolism—all influence how we respond to them, shaping in subtle and obvious ways our habits of thought and conduct, our sense of time and place, and our personal identities. Our children are bombarded with messages that tell them the "good life" is tied to material wealth and ownership of things. But few children are being taught to think about the human effort that goes into mass-produced items or how the visual form and function of objects can be planned to affect our response to them.

The visual, spacial, and material world we live in is not simply a given, but a large-scale expression of our individual and collective values. Few children will become artists, designers, or architects, but every child will become a citizen who will have some freedom to select, arrange, or influence the kind of images, products, and spaces he or she will encounter. In the absence of well-developed skills in perceiving visual forms and understanding how visual forms can convey meanings, we are prone to treat many of the things we see and use without sensitivity, grace, or regard for the human effort behind their creation. The ability to see and decipher the meaning of visual forms and ordinary objects is an acquired skill, one that few children will develop to a significant degree without formal instruction.

The Artistic Heritage

A second reason for teaching art is that few children grow up in homes where it is a commonplace thing to talk about the work of artists, designers, architects and craftsworkers, or to study the works created by artists of the past and present.

The accomplishments of artists and others who devote their lives to art certainly are worth knowing about, not only because their efforts are superb models of individual achievement, but also because their work can teach us about our own potentials. From the artistic heritage we can learn much about feelings and concerns that have been grasped by the human mind and given visual form.[3] Even if we are unable to examine masterpieces firsthand, studies of the artistic heritage can teach us that there are more telling, poignant, and powerful examples of human imagination than we may encounter in ordinary life—the sculpture of Michelangelo, the paintings of Giotto, Raphael, Picasso.

Unless we have had some instruction in art, we are not likely to develop a sense for the depth and scope of achievement in art. It is not enough to see original works of art, or slides or reproductions: We must learn the value of thinking about what we see. The depth of our understanding can be improved by reading, discussion, and reflection. Such skills are vital if young people are to gain *intellectual* access to the heritage of art—past and present—and to the insights it can offer.

It may be true that the more subtle aspects of art cannot be grasped by the very young and the mentally handicapped, but education early in life, more than any other single factor, predicts whether as an adult one is likely to have an interest in seeing works of art. As we have noted, the dramatic rise in the size of audiences who attend art museums and arts events parallels the growth in the number of college graduates. It does not come from improvements in school art programs. Of the adults who attend art museums, 83 percent have some college education.[4] But what knowledge of the artistic heritage, and interest in it, do we cultivate in the majority who do not go to college? Very little. Do we really mean to exclude all those students—about 75 percent—from the prospect of appreciating the kind of art that museums and galleries display?

Consider that in the college environment most students do have the opportunity to study art, to attend museums or galleries, and to engage in conversation about art. Even more important than these activities is a general climate within the college that says, in effect, that it is a good thing to learn about art. At this level of education, most students sense that there is social and institutional approval for them to study art.

These several conditions for learning about art rarely are matched in our elementary and secondary schools, even though they should be. The high school graduate who does not attend college is too often left with the impression that the art in museums and galleries is for "other folks." Even at the college level, faculty who teach art appreciation courses, often must begin with concepts that could have been introduced in the fifth, sixth, or seventh grade. College-bound or not, our children deserve better instruction, and with it, the opportunity to respond more fully to works of art.

The Artistic Process

A third theme for basic education in art recognizes that few children grow up in homes where they are actively encouraged to draw and paint, cut and paste, model clay, and participate in other activities that test their skills as makers of images and objects. Educators have long claimed that every child benefits from making art. Indeed, educators have been so extravagant in their claims about the value of art activities in childhood that one would think that making art is all children need to do—a solution to almost every educational problem. For example, art activities have been proposed as a remedy for low achievement scores, emotional distress, lack of creativity, juvenile delinquency, dropping out of school, and lack of a positive self-concept, among many other problems.[5] What we forget is that these and other possible values that may be realized from making art very likely could be achieved by other paths, and perhaps with greater success.

If we are genuinely interested in basic education in art, there are two main reasons for engaging children and youths in the process of making art: 1) to teach them how art can be made, or 2) to use the art-making experience as a stimulus for discussions about the kind of work artists do. In teaching art, studio activities should have essentially the same role that laboratory work has in teaching science. In teaching science, laboratory work is intended to cultivate general skills and attitudes that will be of equal use to the few who will pursue science as a career and to the many who will deal with science as citizens, not as scientists.

Just as there are limits to the technical training our schools can provide in science, so, too, are there limitations in the technical training that our schools can offer to students who may wish to pursue a career in art. The development of specific occupational skills in creating art is beyond the scope of basic education, but occupational awareness is not. Indeed, if art programs are carefully planned, students who are motivated to seek a career in art should be well informed about occupational choices in art, not only in the various studio and design fields, but also in those which require skills in interpreting art—art history, criticism, teaching. Even students who have no desire to pursue art as a vocation can benefit from an awareness of occupations that employ the arts of visual expression, for throughout their lives they will encounter the products of those occupations.

The arts of visual expression, in short, affect the quality of life enjoyed by every citizen, and to a greater degree than we ordinarily assume. For this reason, the most general aim of basic education in art is "enlightened citizenship in the arts."

What Should Be Taught?

Education is a dynamic process that does not end when children leave school. Because it is impossible to teach children everything that might be useful or interesting, it is important to be very selective in what we teach and in how we use the limited amount of time available for art instruction in schools. In this way, we can better equip students to continue their own lifelong learning in art. This requires planning and a clear sense for priorities.

One of the most pervasive problems in art education is the absence of carefully planned programs, particularly in elementary schools. A related problem is that many well-planned programs are so concentrated on making art—teaching children to draw, paint, model clay, and so forth—that one would think this kind of activity is totally sufficient for education in art.

Let me illustrate the gap between the popular conception of art education—engaging children almost exclusively in making art—and what we should teach children. A suggested set of aims for basic education in art is outlined below.[6]

A Curriculum Framework for Basic Education in Art

Functions of General Education	*Major Goals for Art Education*
Encourage personal fulfillment	Encourage personal response and expression in art
Transmit the cultural heritage	Promote awareness of the artistic heritage
Improve the social order	Promote awareness of the role of art in society

Sub-Goals. Encourage Personal Response and Expression—Help students learn different ways to
> generate ideas for expression through art
> use visual qualities for artistic expression
> use media to create expressive qualities

perceive visual qualities as sources of feeling
interpret the meaning of visual qualities
judge the significance of their art experience

Sub-Goals. Promote Awareness of Artistic Heritage—Help students learn
how members of the artistic community
generate ideas for their work
use visual qualities for artistic expression
use media to express their ideas
perceive and describe art
interpret works of art
judge and explain works of art

Sub-Goals. Promote Awareness of the Role of Art in Society—Help students
understand how people in a given society or culture
express various beliefs in visual forms
use visual qualities for artistic expression
use media to create expressive forms
perceive visual qualities
interpret visual forms
judge visual forms in the environment

The premises are simple: We want children to study art from the
vantage points of both the creator and the perceiver. Whether children
are studying the art of adults or extending their own abilities, their
activities should be purposeful, directed toward "big ideas" and questions that keep turning up in art. Some of these ideas and questions are
suggested by the aims listed in this outline of curriculum goals: What
are some of the wellsprings of art? Where do artists get ideas for their
work? How are images given form? How can media be used express-
ively? What is involved in perceiving visual forms? How have people
interpreted art and judged it?

As you can see, if teachers were to pursue these suggested aims
and themes, children would still make art, but teachers would have to
provide substantially more time for youngsters to study the historical
and social dimensions of art than most programs today provide. The
suggested aims are charted in three broad groups in order to highlight
these neglected aspects of art education. In the "live" classroom setting, of course, good teachers organize activities so that there is a
natural flow and fusion of ideas.

Beyond the question of aims is the question of priorities in teaching.
Among teachers of art at all levels of instruction in our schools, priority
has been given to making art—that is, for studio-based art programs.
In most schools, children are introduced to picture-making through
drawing, painting, and printmaking, as well as sculpture and crafts.

These art forms are certainly worth teaching. But children should also learn about architecture, design for advertising, products, and publications, or about photography and other forms of art. However, relatively few teachers appear to be dealing with these art forms, primarily because they have only been trained to work in the studio arts and crafts. In other words, a studio-based program may actually restrict learning in art to whatever children can make by hand.

Almost all art teachers are strongly committed to studio-based programs, and many seem to believe that what children learn through making art will "transfer" to other art forms, and perhaps to children's behavior beyond art. For example, during the 1960s, when schools were criticized for not producing more creative scientists for the space race, art teachers were quick to suggest that creativity in art could contribute to this goal of enhancing scientific creativity. In the research literature on artistic creativity, however, there is very little to suggest that any transfer of learning is likely to happen unless teachers illustrate the connections between ideas and directly teach for transfer.[7] Many teachers also seem to assume that making art enhances children's perceptual skills and appreciation of art. This is not likely to occur, however, unless the teacher explicitly demonstrates the connections between making art, perceiving it, and appreciating it.[8]

What about teaching children to look at works of art and introducing them to the artistic heritage? Teachers do not usually give this area as much attention as it deserves. Particularly at the elementary level, many teachers still seem to think that children may be inhibited in doing their own art if they are asked to see, discuss, or think about the art of adults. But active and skillful looking can be nurtured, and in a way that does not intimidate or inhibit their creativity. Indeed, with good training, teachers discover that this kind of instruction can be as lively, non-threatening, and creative as studio instruction.

Even in secondary schools, many teachers are still reluctant to teach art history or develop skills in critically analyzing art. This lack of enthusiasm can be traced, in part, to the fear that students will want to copy the styles of other artists, rather than to be inventive. Some teachers, again, have had little training in critically analyzing art, or they may have had such dull art history courses in college that they shy away from this area.

Perhaps the greatest need in art education is for instruction that illustrates the role of art in foreign cultures, as well as in contemporary life in America. When art teachers do introduce children to visual forms in a social or cultural context, a typical approach is to study the arts of a particular culture—the Eskimos, the Japanese, the Africans, the Northwest Indians, or a similar group. But teachers must also be well prepared to deal with the contemporary visual environment as an expression of people today—our aspirations and our conduct.

The studio training of art teachers and their education in a fine arts tradition may well explain the general neglect in school programs of the public, collaborative, and technological arts, to say nothing of the popular arts that arise from mass-merchandising. In relatively few schools or teacher preparation programs will you find solid teaching about the aesthetic, metaphoric, or functional aspects of architecture; of urban, industrial, or graphic design; of photography, television, and film; or of the ceremonial arts in which visual forms are used to commemorate important life events. It is as if much our own visual culture were alien territory to art teachers—one they were unable to understand through the concepts about art that they have acquired.

Obviously, there are many exceptions to these broad descriptions of art education practice today, but for the purpose of understanding the most dominant patterns of instruction, I think it fair to say that studio instruction remains the single most pervasive emphasis in art education and that most children are short-changed in understanding the artistic heritage and the functions of art in social life.

Toward Basic Education in Art

Basic education in art must center on the *subject* of art. This seems to be an obvious point, but, as we have seen, there is a long tradition in education of insisting that art should contribute to a wide range of values other than learning about art—as if art were only a means to education, never the content to be taught. Such general aims as "developing a positive self-concept," "nurturing creativity," "improving eye-hand coordination," and "fostering cognitive growth" are little more than empty slogans. They offer little guidance for teaching art, unless we take time to examine what they mean in the specific context of the subject of art.[9]

For example, it is sometimes claimed that art contributes to the development of a child's positive self-concept. We should ask how the study of art makes that contribution, and what aspects of a child's "self" might be affected by the study of art. Unless we can identify specific connections of this kind, we have no basis for saying that art is a means of developing a positive self-concept. In fact, other subjects and experiences might be more important to building one.

If we want to work with the notion of self-concept in art, we might begin by asking questions such as these: What images in the history of art deal with the self of the creator (self-portraits)? What can anyone learn about the self of a person by studying the physical appearance of persons, their visual presence? To what extent is our sense of self defined by the reactions of others to our visual presence? Should it be? Can the ability or inability to create art, or to talk about it knowledgeably, affect how we feel about ourselves or about others? Questions such as these do make a specific link between studying art and developing children's understanding of the self. An outcome of this kind of knowledge may be self-understanding, but it will be uniquely tied to the study of art.

We should also ask whether the things we say we want to teach can, in fact, be influenced by instruction. The improvement of eye-hand coordination, for example, is sometimes cited as an objective for art activity. But eye-hand coordination initially depends on physiological development, and teachers have little direct control of that. Many perceptual and manipulative skills are also specific to individual tasks. I may be masterful at the keyboard of a piano or typewriter, but not skilled in using clay or watercolor. The purpose of teaching art is not to improve some vague notion of eye-hand coordination, but to improve specific skills relevant to art.

Empty claims about art education, when thoughtlessly repeated, may prevent us from thinking about what we really can teach children about art. For example, it is easy for us to say that children are naturally artistic, but if that is really true, why teach art? Art would be like recess—little more than a supervised opportunity for children to do what comes "naturally." Unfortunately, art is treated in just this way—like recess—in many elementary schools.

Perhaps the most neglected aspect of planning is determining the relative importance of what we teach, and when it should be taught. For example, many teachers do seem to assume that most of their students will go on to college and will learn about the artistic heritage—past and present—as part of their general education program there. But the assumption is wrong: The majority of students do not go to college. Should they be denied the opportunity to become familiar with art history? Similarly, within the everyday life of most citizens and in the history of art, what is the relative importance of being able to make a macrame belt or plant hanger? Should schools devote time to activities that one can learn to do easily from a how-to-do-it book? We might well agree that children should study the fiber arts, but this does not mean children can be expected to *do* all of the fiber arts.

More generally, we must begin to adopt a viewpoint about teaching art that concentrates on the job of imparting knowledge about the subject of art. We have a long history of introducing the arts in schools as a form of physical activity or as a manipulative tool to achieve a variety of ends. In the past, we have been so eager to treat art as a technique for achieving other educational purposes that we have not fully considered whether children are learning anything about the world of art, or, if so, what they are learning. It is time to correct this imbalance and to recognize that art is a form of human endeavor worthy of study. Even with all the apparent "openness" and variety in art, there is, nevertheless, a significant body of knowledge about art that should be transmitted to youngsters.

In summary, basic education in art is a general, not a technical or vocational, education. It is education for enlightened citizenship in a democratic society. In preparing youth for their role as citizens, the major functions of basic education are: to cultivate those abilities which hold some promise of making one's life satisfying, to transmit the cultural heritage to each generation, and to nurture responsible social conduct.

Art must be considered a fundamental concern in basic education because art is undeniably a significant part of the cultural heritage, because the experience of art holds some promise of making one's life more satisfying, and because art enters into the civic and social aspects of our lives. The talented career-bound student is not penalized by a basic education in art. Indeed, there is greater assurance that varieties of talent will surface under programs designed to offer basic education.

4

Basic Education in Art: Guidelines for Programs

How can basic education in art be provided in our schools? Curriculum time and resources for art education are limited. These are hard facts, but they apply to all subjects. The more central questions are these: Do educators have a commitment to teaching art? If so, how strong is that commitment? What steps may be taken to secure adequate resources? Are existing time and available resources being used to maximum advantage?

The Question of Commitment

The first requirement for building an art program is to make a public announcement of one's commitment to this important mission. Ideally, school boards, parents, administrators, classroom teachers and arts specialists, as well as members of the local community of artists—all should join to issue a statement of commitment to the concept of basic education in art for every student. The language in any written statements should make it clear that art is a required subject, not merely an "enrichment," or "bonus" that might be eliminated in hard times.

Second, physical and human resources must be allocated for art
education. Money is not the chief obstacle in securing adequate resources for art instruction; the major barrier, again, can be traced to an
attitude that art is "nice" but does not deserve equal treatment in our
schools—especially in allocation of resources. Most teachers work
under less than ideal conditions, and they are willing to improvise, if
they work in an environment where all teachers are treated fairly and
given tangible support. Rarely do we consider whether art receives the
same consideration in resource allocations that we give to other subjects.

Outright prejudice against the teaching of art becomes apparent
when we ask questions that challenge current practices. For example,
in elementary schools the scheduling of art classes almost always is a
by-product of allocating time for other subjects. The classroom teacher
often reserves afternoons and Fridays for art, because children, like
adults, are less attentive and energetic at these times. But why do we
assume that art is not a subject that requires concentration, effort, and
study? Why is fatigue thought to be less important in studying art than
other subjects?

In secondary schools, bands and athletic teams are provided with
nearly professional equipment and uniforms, and adequate time and
space, while art teachers have little or no access to slides, films, books,
or supplies. Why is the teaching of art not given equitable treatment in
budgeting and facilities?

Or suppose that the funds devoted to the purchase of reading texts,
workbooks, and testing services in elementary schools were taken as a
standard for proper support of an educational program, and one were
to claim that a comparable amount should be allocated to art. In 1979, a
midwestern city spent over sixty-two dollars per student per year for
reading materials, and many of these were workbooks and dittoed
worksheets. In this same district, a junior high school visual arts
teacher received *eighty cents* per student per year for expendable
supplies.[1] Reading is surely important, but the emphasis placed upon
teaching and testing reading—at the expense of the rest of the curriculum—may have contributed to children's disenchantment with
schools. In some districts, resource allocations for reading have made a
shambles of the rest of the curriculum, which, among other functions,
should introduce the content that can make reading seem worthwhile
to children.[2]

When we examine the grounds on which schedules and resource
allocations are determined, we can see that art too often is given
leftovers and a marginal existence, thereby reducing the likelihood

that effective teaching can be accomplished. It is from unexamined actions such as these, and their consequences, that citizens and educators reveal their lack of commitment to art education. It is from this marginal treatment of programs that children are taught that art does not count for very much, either in school or in life. An authentic commitment to art education will be evident when there are equitable resource allocations for art.

Who Should Teach Art?

The teacher is the most important ingredient in education. Teachers of art, like all good teachers, must have a broad understanding of their field, be sensitive to individual differences in students, have excellent skills in communication, and be committed to teaching. These skills and attributes are not the inevitable result of the teacher's own ability to make art. In other words, artists are not necessarily good teachers. Similarly, the skills that students need in order to make informed judgments about art are not automatically cultivated when their education emphasizes making art. The importance of a well-informed teacher of art is not fully appreciated by many school administrators or parents.

In most fields, teachers and students work from textbooks and employ a variety of instructional materials developed by nationally recognized experts in that field. When approved for use in schools, these texts and curriculum materials offer some assurance to everyone that the subject matter—science, mathematics, social studies—will be represented to children accurately, efficiently, and fairly. This traditional way of assuring fairness and accuracy in the presentation of a subject does not operate in art. Why not? It is easy to forget that the teaching of art rarely occurs through the use of a textbook or by following a curriculum that has been prepared by a team of experts.

In most subjects, teachers do have a choice of student texts, teacher manuals, and other curriculum materials, which have been designed by experts in the subject field. Although a few textbooks and instructional materials for teaching art have been published, there is no established tradition in art education of introducing teachers to their actual use with children or of evaluating the content of published teaching aids.[3] Art teachers who have been taught in a studio orientation may, in fact, resist the use of bookish or academic teaching aids, preferring to draw upon their own knowledge of art.

In art, each teacher is not only placed in the position of having a ready command of the content, but also of designing the art curriculum singlehandedly, while teaching full-time. These conditions make it imperative for school districts to employ teachers of art who have a broad knowledge of art, are highly skilled in curriculum planning, and thoroughly familiar with resources for teaching art.

Figure 4.1 outlines some of the most fundamental questions that art teachers face in planning an art program.[4] It is worth repeating that when teachers do use textbooks and other detailed resources for instruction, they have, in effect, relied upon experts to help them answer such basic pedagogical questions as: What shall I teach? Why? When? How? and so on. In the absence of comparable resources which can be used by art teachers in the classroom, it is essential for school districts to employ not only art teachers, but also art supervisors or art curriculum specialists who can work with art teachers to improve the quality of their planning. Far too many "programs" in art are little more than a series of short-term activities and projects lacking educational coherence.

Designing an Art Program

The problems of selecting and organizing content for instruction in the visual arts are far more complex than they are in subjects which have always been taught through texts or in an analytical way. Planning an art program may be especially difficult for teachers who have been encouraged to approach art so intuitively and personally that their own conceptual grasp of the subject may be weak. Individual enthusiasms, fads, and easy-to-teach projects are too often taken as the basis of instruction. There is no single magic formula for an effective program, but there are basic concepts, relationships, and principles that should be considered in planning.

Concepts One Can Teach

CONCEPTS ABOUT WORKS OF ART: Art is not nearly as mysterious and intuitive as it is often said to be. Art can and should be taught within a framework of concepts—general concerns which guide our thought about particular works of art. The quality of almost every discussion about art, or activity in art, does depend on an understanding of certain key concepts and the phenomena to which they refer. For ex-

Figure 4.1. Major Components in Planning.

WHY	WHAT	HOW	TO WHAT EXTENT

Goal	Approach to Study	Content Possibilities	Teaching Materials and Activities	Student Materials and Activities	Desirable Outcomes
To help children learn to generate their own ideas for personal expression.	Observing nature and the constructed environment.	Children's direct perception of land, sea, sky, the seasons, the weather, or structural forms in nature, and of buildings, roads, signs, walkways.	Techniques to heighten children's perception—discrimination of lines, colors, shapes; multisensory awareness; perception of symbolic aspects and contexts or purposes.	Means of recording and interpreting perceptions, cameras, sketches, diary, or tape recorder; direct work in a medium.	Children generate ideas for personal expression from their observations of nature and the constructed environment.

Note: From *Approaches to Art in Education* by Laura H. Chapman, copyright © 1978 by Harcourt Brace Jovanovich, Inc., and reprinted with their permission.

ample, within the visual arts, concepts bearing directly on works of art encompass a number of specifics—examples, types or subtypes of phenomena—some of which are briefly noted below.

Art forms: architecture, painting, sculpture . . .
Types of products: residential architecture, mural painting, mobiles . . .
Media: paint, clay, wood, steel . . .
Forming processes: casting, carving, constructing . . .
Aspects of design: linearity, color quality, action of shapes . . .
Perceptual qualities: light to dark, narrow to wide . . .
Inferred qualities: bold, delicate, active . . .
Subject or themes: still life, landscape, love, hate . . .
Symbolism: conventional or explicit (heart=love), implied (steel=
   coldness) . . .
Interpretive stance: objective, subjective, imaginative . . .
Stylistic features: organic, geometric, open form, closed form . . .
Function or purpose: to inspire, contain liquids, provide warmth . . .

Children are not born with a prior knowledge of these concepts, nor do they automatically learn to perceive the phenomena to which these concepts refer. The recognition of "color qualities," for example, is learned, and it varies from one culture to another. Neither do children grasp the value of knowing about color qualities (or any other aspect of art) without sensitive and memorable opportunities to apply what they have learned.

Concepts such as these, though essential to understanding works of art, cannot be grasped through a rote learning of terms, definitions, and examples. Concepts must be given life and meaning by connecting them to the actions of people and to the settings where the action is. Knowledge is dead unless we can use it in a particular context.

CONCEPTS ABOUT THE CREATION AND USE OF ART: It is easily forgotten that almost every art activity or discussion of art involves three elements: a *person* interacting in a *setting* with a *work of art* or some aspect of a work of art. If we are not sensitive to the dynamic nature of these interactions, we are likely to fall into the trap of teaching skills and concepts in a dry, sterile way. The concepts which bear on works of art must be connected to events or people in the world of art, to the child's life, or vividly illustrated in relation to the life of a people in a social or cultural group. If we fail to connect what children are learning in school with the larger world outside of school—or with the work of people who devote their lives to the creation and study of art—children do not see much point in what they have been taught. They have no way to judge whether their in-school activities have authenticity and utility beyond the school environment.

Let me illustrate. It is a safe bet that every year thousands of youngsters across the nation make Halloween masks in school as an "art" project. Many sixth graders have had six encounters with Halloween art, if not with masks. We must ask ourselves how many of our sixth graders have learned that masks are, in fact, an art form—a product found in actual use by many cultural groups, as well as in museums? How many youngsters understand that artists and historians have studied masks and have thus extended our grasp of the functions of masks in other cultures? Have students examined the conditions under which they may have put on a masklike expression without wearing a real mask? Are they acquainted with the way contemporary artists have probed the idea of masks in sculptural form or in painting. Have they inquired into the relationships between the plastic mass-produced masks available in stores, those made by their own hands, and those found in other cultures? Exploring concepts about the creation and use of art gives active meaning to concepts about works of art. When we make connections of this kind, we are also teaching concepts so that they forward the aims of the art program.[5]

The Balancing Act

One of the most persistent problems in teaching art is that of achieving adequate balance in what we teach. If we prematurely restrict children to a particular approach to working in art or thinking about it, we may well develop habits that prevent them from appreciating other approaches. For example, if the art program emphasizes representational art, but does not provide much opportunity for the exercise of imagination or the exploration and analysis of design, we are limiting children's horizons. Individual appreciations and skills certainly can be honored and cultivated, but children should be challenged to work with more than one orientation to art in the interest of their long-term growth and understanding.

BIASES IN ART TEACHING: This need for balance and contrast in viewpoints can be appreciated more fully when we consider some of the peculiar biases that may lead to a subtle form of indoctrination. For example, if children are only introduced to art as something *they* can make, how are they to learn about the art of other cultures or about art created from technologies that children cannot personally use? Or consider a teacher's desire to have students create original art. The most influential aesthetic theories of the twentieth century do place a premium on originality. Thus, when children use conventional symbols or forms in their art work, a teacher may see this as undesirable. It is equated with a loss of individuality and lack of innovation in art. But children should also learn that conventional symbols have a place in art. Symbols with well-established meaning play an important role in the arts of the church, for example; and they are important today in art forms that are designed to communicate with the public—billboards, television advertisements, and traffic signs.

In the same way that art instruction may be dominated by unexamined doctrines about "excellence" in works of art, so too may teaching be biased through unexamined doctrines about the persons who create art and doctrines about the creative process. For example, many teachers do not really think designers and architects are artists, because architects and designers are not totally free to express themselves in their work. But all artists work within limitations, particularly those imposed by their choice of a medium. So too, must designers and architects deal with economic issues, the needs of the client, and other limitations imposed by the technologies of mass production and engineering. When we identify content for instruction, we must do so responsibly—in the light of the history of art, including the historical development of the way we ourselves have come to think about art.[6] Clearly, we cannot teach everything to children. In this sense, any decision about content will reflect some bias in judgment. But there are criteria that we can employ in making decisions. Let us examine some of them.

FAIR PLAY: THE DIVERSITY OF ART: The concepts of art we present to youngsters not only must be representative of different value systems within Western thought and artistic practice, but also must reflect selected sociocultural groups outside of the European mainstream. This imperative recognizes that our society is culturally pluralistic.

Experience in all walks of life amply demonstrates that we can approach cultural differences with either a superficial or a genuine concern for fair treatment. Too rarely do we apply this principle of fair treatment to the task of teaching art. In virtually every subject that touches on human values and beliefs, we insist that young people be taught to respect cultural differences and to base their own judgments on adequate information and thoughtful comparison. These principles are equally applicable to the teaching of art.[7]

In a democratic society built from a nation of immigrants, there is not one cultural heritage, but many. The diversity of cultural traditions in American society is so great that any attempt to represent all of them in a curriculum is clearly impossible. However, each of us in some measure is like all other people, like some other people, and like no other person. Basic education in art must seek to develop in all youth an appreciation and understanding of art within the culture that is the heritage of the majority of Americans—that is, European or Western culture. But we should also illuminate for all children the achievements and traditions of particular ethnic and minority groups, thereby nurturing a fundamental understanding of different cultures, as well as esteem for the contributions individuals make within a culture.

For the purpose of general or basic education, art programs that concentrate exclusively on the restoration of pride in an ethnic or minority cultural group are just as inappropriate as programs that fail to reflect anything except the majority culture. The sensitivities needed for appreciation of any culture are built from contrasts and comparisons with one's own cultural identity.

FAIR PLAY: CONTINUITY AND CHANGE IN ART: A detailed study of the history and varieties of world art is beyond the scope of basic education, but appreciation of diversity, change, and continuity in art can be developed to a threshold that makes it possible for students to understand historical-cultural differences in art. Several principles should be followed in selecting examples of works of art for historical-cultural studies.

The examples of art that we present to students should be selected to: 1) encompass historically significant and contemporary art forms; 2) illustrate the impact of changing values and technologies on the character of art; 3) demonstrate similarities and differences in the treatment of selected media, themes, structures, styles, and functions of products in different cultures; 4) invite comparisons with images, artifacts, and environments that we experience every day; 5) offset stereotypes about those who create art. To the extent possible, of course, children should also study original works of art.

From Plans to Practice

For readers who are interested in curriculum design, figure 4.2 shows one of many workable plans for instruction during a year. It is a unit, or "modular," plan which provides for a concentrated study of art forms which are selected to achieve a balance between two- and three-dimen-

Figure 4.2.   Example of a Modular Plan for a Year.

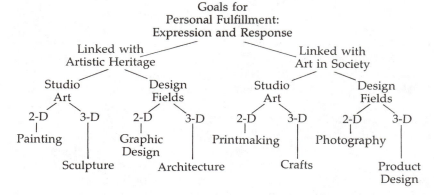

Note: From *Approaches to Art in Education* by Laura H. Chapman, copyright © 1978 by Harcourt Brace Jovanovich, Inc., and reprinted with their permission.

   If units of instruction are planned around art forms, as suggested here, eight units might be the core of the program for a year. While these art forms meet the criteria for adequate scope, they by no means illustrate every possibility.

sional art. The general plan is useful in a wide range of schools, including those with a high rate of student mobility or absenteeism. The modular or unit approach to planning the art curriculum has the obvious advantage of allowing students to pursue a topic in some depth, but with clear points of transition to sustain interest throughout the year. The absence of a tight linear sequence makes it possible for students who are not able to attend school for the whole year to benefit from coherent instruction during part of a year. Variations in emphasis and in the art forms selected for study can be made in order to build understanding from year to year. In the high school, one or two units might be extended into a full course. A wide range of topical units of study, based on key concepts, can be developed by teachers to suit their unique schedules and levels of instruction.

   A planned program of basic education in art does allow for individualized instruction, even though it imposes a structure on teaching. It should be noted, moreover, that many teaching techniques and curriculum materials are advertised as means of individualizing instruction, but actually may require all students to complete the same standard assignments, with the rate of completion being the single point of individual difference. This limited notion of individualizing instruction is quite common in teaching reading and mathematics, especially when a mastery of standard assignments is closely tied to performance on highly publicized tests. In some instructional "packages," dialogue with the teacher is hardly required at all.

Relatively few aspects of art instruction, as here presented, would lend themselves to such a packaged and mechanistic approach to "individualized" teaching. Dialogue remains the single most humane way to assure that students know they exist as individuals and that someone cares about what they see, feel, think, and imagine. Little of the content in art that is worth knowing about can be fully programmed, or reduced to simple yes and no answers. Neither will students learn much about art through projects that involve little more than the mindless manipulation of media. There is, in short, no substitute for a knowledgeable teacher of art who is sensitive to students and skilled in cultivating creative and critical thinking.

Making It Happen

Our schools must employ well-qualified, full-time teachers of art whose chief interest is teaching children and youth. Beyond this, it should be obvious that art teachers must have access to the supervisory help of experts in art curriculum development, in-service education, and resource development. Toward this end, a full-time curriculum specialist in art, employed in a supervisory post, ought to be available for every twenty-five to thirty art teachers employed in a school district. Part-time assignments could be arranged in smaller school districts, if there is an art teacher who has had advanced training in curriculum and resource development.

The employment of a full-time, certified elementary school art specialist, for every twenty to twenty-five classrooms of kindergarten through grade six, is the best assurance that students will have access to qualified instruction. No less than sixty minutes weekly should be allocated for visual arts instruction with a specialist, with twenty to forty minutes weekly of additional time allocated for follow-up activities conducted by the regular classroom teacher, and these activities should be planned in consultation with the art specialist. At least one-half hour of consultation time must be provided to both teachers— the classroom teacher and the art specialist—every month.

In the junior and senior high school, the study of art should be required, and instruction with certified art teachers should be made available in every year from the seventh to at least the tenth grade (as suggested in chap. 2). The absence of such requirements in junior and senior high school leaves about 80 percent of our young people with no art instruction beyond the typical half-year junior high courses in art and music. As students are enrolled in the required secondary school art courses, staff needs will be comparable to those in English and in all other required subjects. If this seems to be an extraordinary suggestion, it is only because we have beome so accustomed to thinking that effective education in the arts can be accomplished in a half-year in junior high school. It can't be.

Some Tools of the Trade

Elsewhere I have described the kind of rooms, spaces, and schedules necessary for effective teaching and have suggested plans for using community resources to strengthen the instructional program.[8] Physical resources for an effective art program extend well beyond the conventional studio supplies, small tools, and equipment. Access to original works of art and cultural artifacts is essential. District and school art collections, field trips, and circulating exhibitions—all are means of assuring that students are able to study original works of art. Additional resources and brief descriptions of their use are outlined in the following list.

NONSTUDIO ART RESOURCES

Original Works of Art
Audiovisual Media
> *Tape recordings* for interviews, narratives by historians, critics, artists. May be used alone or with slides.
> *Telephone* for live interviews with artists.
> *Records or tapes* with filmstrips or slides (such resources are becoming more numerous); excellent for independent study, review.
> *Films, slides, filmstrips* provide excellent materials on a wide range of art forms.
> *Overhead transparencies* of maps, diagrams of studio processes difficult to demonstrate.
> *Television,* for in-school series on art.

Printed Media
> *Books, magazines,* for examples of superior book illustration; books and magazines about art for students to read.
> *Reproductions* of postcard size for matching and sorting, large sizes for display and study.
> *Charts and flashcards* for review of art vocabulary, art processes and concepts.
> *Photographs* (black and white, or color), as examples of art and as means for study of environmental and architectural phenomena.

Other Tangible Aids
> *Models and replicas* for visual study, made of wood, paper, plastic—for example, human skull, skeleton, architecture.
> *Samplers* of media, processes; for example, Navajo weaving on small frame.
> *Real objects* from nature and everyday world, organized to illustrate phenomena or concepts.
> *Commercial games, toys* such as Montessori-type materials, puzzles, magnetic boards, magnifying glasses, prisms.

In seeking resources, the teacher's ability to think about art education in a comprehensive manner is of critical importance. Not only does a general command of the subject of art permit flexibility in the actual process of teaching, but it produces an awareness of the gap between resources presently available and those which are needed. As a professional group, art teachers are probably too proud of their ability to make ingenious use of limited resources. This pride is misplaced when it accustoms people to thinking that art can be at the bottom-of-the-barrel and still be well taught. Finally, to the degree that teaching is based on short-term plans, art teachers are further handicapped in anticipating needs, projecting budgets, and outlining timetables for the acquisition of resources.

In summary, the major obstacles to effective art education are not financial, but attitudinal. Any school district that has a uniformed marching band, an extracurricular or curricular athletic program providing uniforms, equipment, space, and a specialized coaching staff could, if seriously committed to basic education in art, muster the resources to provide an art program of high quality.

Unacknowledged prejudices within the culture and in the educational community systematically exclude youth from the opportunity to study art. These prejudices must be brought to the attention of parents, teachers, administrators, and the arts constituency itself. Clearly, if resources are not provided, if qualified staff are not employed, and if basic education in art is not seen as an obligation in schools, instruction will be trivialized. At minimum, we should insist that judgments about school art programs be based on a thorough examination of the conditions under which art is taught. In the next several chapters, we will review some of these conditions, first at the elementary level, then at the secondary level. From this review, the magnitude of the task of changing attitudes and school practices should become apparent.

5 | *The Most Crucial Years: Art in the Elementary School*

EARLY AND CONTINUOUS EDUCATION during the elementary years is just as vital in art as in any other subject. However, it is during these years that many youngsters receive poor art instruction which impairs the growth of their interest, knowledge, and skill in art.

Who Teaches Art?

All school districts should employ certified teachers of art to work with children in the elementary school. However, in over half of our elementary schools, either the classroom teacher is responsible for teaching art or no art is taught.[1] In most schools, the classroom teacher is responsible for all subjects—reading, writing, arithmetic, science, social studies, music, art, and so on. But few classroom teachers are well prepared to teach art. In spite of the fact that the classroom teacher is responsible for teaching art, many states do not require *any* college courses in art for an elementary school teaching certificate (twenty-six states in 1979).[2] Even when some college preparation is required, the college courses offered to classroom teachers may be weak. Many classroom teachers receive no more than a brief introduction to the so-called principles of art and a survey of theories of children's growth in picture-making. Most courses also show teachers how simple art media and projects can be introduced to children; for example, tempera paint, crayon, cut paper or collage, clay, and papier-mâché.

Because many elementary school principals have the same meager preparation in art as the classroom teacher, principals may believe that art is being taught if children's drawings are displayed here and there in school, or if holiday decorations are made. Often the elementary program consists of little more than allowing children to color with crayons, to cut and paste paper, or to make simple craft projects. Nevertheless, if elementary principals are asked, "Is art taught in your school?" 90 percent reply, "Yes." Surely the quality of instruction must be questioned, for in two-thirds of our elementary schools, art is taught for less than an hour per week, and in about 40 percent of the schools the principal will admit that no objectives or curriculum for art instruction have been identified (see fig. 5.1).[3]

In the past, many school districts provided the classroom teacher with on-the-job help in teaching art by employing art resource teachers, art consultants, or art supervisors. Through special workshops, short courses, and some demonstration teaching, the art consultant was able to improve the quality of the art instruction offered by the regular teacher. In 1973, about one school in four had programs based on this kind of working relationship. But this support system is often the first to be cut under financial pressure. For example, there were 435 art consultants in California in 1970; by 1978 only 50 were employed.[4] In the absence of these services, the quality of art instruction cannot be monitored or improved.

Specialist art teachers are employed in about 18 percent of our elementary schools, but few have been given a teaching schedule that permits anything more than "instant" art instruction for large numbers of children. Art teachers may be assigned to teach 500 to 1,500 youngsters.[5] A typical class schedule only permits children to have about one art lesson every other week, or about fifteen lessons per year. More often than not, teachers of art do not have an adequate classroom, nor do they have supplies, equipment, or storage space; books, slides, reproductions, and original art are also lacking. This kind of teaching environment makes it impossible for art teachers to do justice to many of the philosophical concepts that may have been emphasized in their college programs. Monitoring "individual growth and development," for example, is exceedingly difficult if you meet with 500 to 1,500 individuals once every two weeks.

These scheduling patterns place teachers of art in the position of

Figure 5.1. Access to Art Instruction: Elementary Schools.

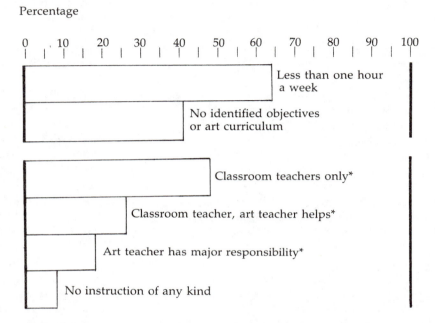

Percentage

Note: Data from A. Harnischfeger and D. Miller, "Resources for Art Education in the Nation's Elementary Schools: Opportunity, Time and Instructional Staff Qualifications" Technical Report no. AH-78. St. Louis: Central Midwestern Regional Educational Laboratory, 1979, p. 11.
    Asterisk indicates inference from data reported (survey did not ask whether both the art teacher and classroom teacher shared responsibility for instruction, but inferences about this role and who had primary responsibility for teaching art could be made from data reported in several other categories).

having to shortcut instruction in order to retain a semblance of order and sanity in their work. Children may thus be introduced to whatever the teacher finds easy to teach, easy to manage, and reasonably attractive or appealing to youngsters. The result, in far more cases than any of us may wish to admit, is *mis*education in art. A steady diet of gimmicks, short projects and other instant-art lessons teaches children—and not very subtly—that art is undemanding, fun, and without content that requires much thought.

The amount of art instruction that most children receive in elementary school is meager and of dubious quality. In most schools classroom teachers—many of whom have little or no formal education in art—are given the primary responsibility for teaching art. In fact, most youngsters are denied access to instruction with qualified art teachers. Even when art teachers are employed, their programs may be undermined by absurd scheduling practices and totally inadequate resources. In no other field would we expect teachers to be effective without reasonable working conditions.

The Biggest Handicap: Myths

Poor teaching conditions impair the effectiveness of the few elementary art teachers who are employed in schools, and inadequate preparation restricts the effectiveness of the regular classroom teacher. But the underlying cause of these conditions is certain fundamental attitudes, thoughtlessly perpetuated in education, which make the teaching of art to children seem unnecessary. Indeed, the concepts that we have acquired about the role of art in childhood are the true reasons why we continue to allow teachers who have little or no knowledge of art to teach art, and why we think that art education is somehow taken care of if children do a bit of art now and then. Let us examine some of these beliefs.

The Child as Artist

In much of the professional literature on education in art, writers have expressed great admiration for the child's "natural" artistic and creative ability.[6] The roots of this admiration can be traced to a romantic view of the role of art in childhood. Adults tend to see childhood as a period of innocence, joyful discovery, and imaginative play that should be cherished and protected while it lasts. In addition, adults who have been trained in twentieth-century art have been sensitized to value "child art," especially the odd compositional devices, striking color qualities, imagery, and abstract symbol systems that children often employ when they are left on their own to make pictures. Many adults who claim that the child is an artist seem to cherish the naiveté and charm of childhood and to admire childrens' untutored art work. These values support a philosophy that calls for very little or no adult intervention in the art-making process of young children.

Art Should Not Be Taught

The belief that teaching art to the young is unnecessary and potentially damaging is widespread. If we believe that children are naturally artistic and creative—equipped by nature to function as artists—then normal instruction in art does not seem to be necessary, and, if the child's naiveté is lost, may actually be considered harmful. All that seems to be required for the proper art education of children is to provide them some opportunity to use art materials. It follows that art activities for children can be supervised by any sympathetic adult who appreciates what children create. Under this view, almost anyone who enjoys children can teach art; no specialized knowledge of the subject is needed. If you hold this view, you do not have to employ specialist teachers of art. You do not have to require classroom teachers to study art in order to receive an elementary school teaching certificate. You do not have to plan a curriculum, and you do not have to provide resources beyond the most simple and easily managed art supplies. Current practices in schools mirror these beliefs.

Artistic Ability Is Inborn

In this romanticized view of child art, it is assumed that artistic ability—creativity, imagination—is something every child possesses in some degree. Artistic ability is thus regarded as a natural endowment that will be displayed by all children who are permitted to exercise it. However, what we treat as a natural endowment in the very young child we usually interpret as a "special gift" in the older child. This imperceptible shift in our thinking occurs when we try to explain the decline in children's self-confidence in making art that develops around the fourth grade.

Around the fourth grade, children do become more critical of their work, and many find that making art is less appealing than it used to be. At this age children are sensitive to peer and adult judgments of their performance, and many children have acquired definite notions about "good" art. If instruction in the early grades has been meager, children have probably acquired the idea that talent in art shows in your ability to draw or paint things realistically, and that if you cannot produce art of this kind, you have no talent.

If children in the upper elementary grades do not continue to make art with the spirit of joy, curiosity, and self-confidence typical of early childhood, teachers, too, are inclined to say that those children are not talented in art. We shift our teaching from the premise that every child is an artist to the premise that some children are talented while others are not. By "talent," we usually mean that confidence and interest in art is paralleled by a growth in artistic skills.

In the upper elementary grades then, we find two major attitudes about the role of art in education. The first is that schools should offer opportunities for children to make art in order to nurture the gifted and talented; the second is that art activities should be included in order to "prop up" the confidence of the child who is losing interest in making art.

However, instead of working on skills that produce competence and authentically bolster the child's self-confidence, we typically offer children in the upper elementary grades a steady flow of art projects that guarantee artlike effects with a minimum of skill and effort. Examples? Place chips of wax crayon between pieces of wax paper, iron the paper flat, and display the result in a window as a "stained glass design." Pour plaster into a plastic sandwich bag, hold it with two hands until it hardens, remove the bag, and paint "a design" on the abstract form. These and other manipulative activities may be justified by saying that they encourage experimentation and develop open-mindedness toward art. But what we are really teaching children through such activities is that art is easy, fun, undemanding, and instantly possible if you call it an "experiment" or a "design." This fundamental miseducation of children is not simply permitted in schools; it is often taken as good and sufficient art education.

Through such activities, schools actually *teach* children that art is frivolous. If, in the early years of school, we avoid teaching skills for making and appreciating art, shall we then wonder why a crisis of confidence and drop in creativity occurs around the fourth grade? Confidence is built upon the growth of skills and an authentic feeling of accomplishment. In our desire to preserve the naiveté of children, we provide in the early elementary grades little more than an opportunity for children to make art. The skills many children acquire from this occasional and casual experience are not sufficient to carry them beyond the fourth grade—the level at which most become critical of their work. Indeed, art educators who teach introductory college courses can safely assume that most college students who are not majoring in art, including classroom teachers, will approach studio activities at a level comparable to that of the fourth grade.

Making Art Equals Art Education

This self-defeating cycle of thought and practice can be attributed, in large measure, to the belief that art education occurs when children make art, and that nurturing children's ability to make art is the major, if not exclusive, aim of art education. This network of beliefs indoctrinates children to an extremely narrow view of art, and it reduces art to whatever one can learn through direct participation.

One of the values claimed for allowing children to make art is that the activities nurture creativity. But we seem to have a definite idea about the character of "creative art," especially when it is produced by the young child. The art of the young child must appear to be spontaneous, free, and uninhibited in imagery. This kind of art has aptly been called "the school art style."[7] So much are these qualities valued that children who like to draw with fine details or display a concern for accuracy are sometimes judged to be inhibited, uncreative, and unimaginative. And so much are these spontaneous qualities of child art held in high regard that art activities which might call for planning, discipline, control, and systematic exploration—such as architectural projects, or those involving graphic and industrial design—are rarely made available to children.

We rationalize our preference for direct and relatively undisciplined child art by saying that children do not yet have the necessary motor skills or have not yet developed a cognitive structure that would warrant more demanding art activities. At the same time, however, we do require the young to learn to read and write. When children make letters into words, and words into sentences, they are learning to encode and decode the meaning of complex visual symbols. Exceedingly fine judgments and motor skills are called into play for these subjects, but not for art.

The school art style is a unique by-product of the values held by adults under whose auspices it is created. These values support a limited definition of creative child art and of art forms that are suitable for youngsters to encounter. A young Andrew Wyeth would likely be judged uncreative, and a young Walter Gropius might be excluded from pursuing studies in architecture. It is proper to regard teaching of this kind as a form of indoctrination, precisely because it so often occurs under the guise of freedom of expression and because the assumptions undergirding it are taken as matters of faith—rarely examined critically. We do not, in any other subject dealing with human values, treat so lightly the possibility of indoctrinating youth.

The second reason cited in order to justify studio activities is that personal experience is the best teacher. The corollary is that people who do not make art cannot possibly know much about art that is worthwhile. Nevertheless, if a basic education in art is defined by what children can learn through personal experience in making art, much that is worth knowing about art may be omitted from the curriculum, and much that is trivial may be included, simply because children can do it. No child can make a Gothic cathedral, build a skyscraper, or engage in *making* all of the objects and images that might be worthy of study in art. And many children in our schools are engaged in projects of marginal value simply because children enjoy them and can do them easily.

The doctrine of learning by doing (and its variants—learning by trial and error, learning by discovery) does not attach high value to knowledge that might be acquired from others. In order to dramatize the underlying weakness in this view, we might consider whether, in order to teach youngsters about drug abuse, crime, and sex, we would encourage them to abuse drugs, to commit crimes, or engage in sex. These examples may seem extreme, but they are intended to illustrate that our enthusiasm for the doctrine of learning to *do* art should be tempered with reason. There are limitations to what children can learn if we insist that making art is the only valid way to learn about the subject.

Art as Panacea

Art is frequently regarded in our schools as a tool for learning about everything except art. The aims of basic education in art are not served well by the common practice of diluting art instruction by trying to integrate or correlate art with other subjects. Some activities typical of this approach are: making a mural about the travels of Marco Polo, building a model of the solar system, and illustrating lessons on health or safety. Activities such as these can result in learning some few things about art, but there are several problems with integrated or correlated activities.

First, one justification for teaching art in connection with other subjects is that art activities help to make the process of learning academic subjects more interesting, concrete, and active than standard textbook teaching. Art activities are thus seen as nonacademic—without significant content to be taught and learned—little more than a means of teaching something other than art. In such cases, art activities have the same status as any audiovisual technique or any other activity format (e.g., games, guest speakers) in facilitating learning; art is simply one of many means for presenting ideas, and not necessarily the most effective one. When art is seen exclusively in this fashion, what the student is learning about art does not matter as much as what the student is learning about the other subject. Nevertheless, many educators seem to equate art education with almost any use of materials associated with art—crayons, paint, clay.

Second, when there is an effort to integrate the study of art with other subjects, children may be miseducated. For example, in connection with their studies of Northwestern American Indians, fourth grade children may be permitted to make "totem poles" from cereal boxes, decorating the boxes with cut paper shapes that echo the motifs of the Northwest Indians. A teacher may justify this kind of activity by saying that it integrates art into social studies and teaches children about the art of the Northwest Indians. Surely one must ask how this process of making a model totem pole from empty cereal boxes bears on Northwest Indian art and culture. It is, of course, a kitsch or "school folk art" project of the kind educators usually justify on the grounds that children enjoy making art.

But this kind of encounter with the art of the Northwest Indians hardly does justice to their culture, to the meanings embedded in the totem pole as an art form, or to the artistry in many other artifacts within the culture of native Americans. What children often learn through easy-to-make decorative projects of this kind is so superficial or misleading that the school is really engaged in a form of educational malpractice. When we use art activities to entice children into learning, irrespective of what we are teaching them about the world of art, the activity is no better than a bribe.

Third, while the desire of teachers to make learning an active, vivid process for the student is understandable, the act of planning correlated or integrated activities almost always begins with a subject other than art. The result is a search for projects or activities that link art to science, art to reading, or art to the study of mathematics. While effective teaching of art can occur along these lines, rarely are teachers inclined to reverse the thought process and to ask, for example, how children's knowledge of mathematics can enhance their learning in architecture or sculpture, or whether, through reading, children might improve their skills in deciphering the symbolism in works of art. This failure to see other so-called basic subjects as tools for learning about art demonstrates, again, that art is not really treated as part of the regular curriculum. Instead, art is treated as an open-ended experience easily modified, eliminated, or added after all other subjects are planned.

The improvement of elementary school art instruction cannot occur in a climate of uninformed opinion that treats art as little more than a tool for learning other subjects. Instead, priority should be given to the development of regular and continuous instructional programs which focus on basic education in art. The planning of such programs must proceed from the premise that art is a subject for study in its own right and that the content to be treated in art should determine whether and how other subjects will be brought to bear on art content.

The Art Teacher Speaks: Practices and Problems in the Elementary School

What children are being taught about art in elementary school is worth noting, especially when one considers the scope of the visual arts. It is instructive to examine the results of a survey that I conducted in 1979 through *School Arts Magazine* in which 187 art teachers voluntarily responded to questions about their art programs (see appendix A). About half of these teachers had less than five years of experience, the remainder had more than five years. Collectively, these teachers served over one hundred thousand students.[8]

The core elementary school art program is reflected in the art forms that more than 75 percent of the teachers said that they would teach during the year: drawing, painting, printmaking, basic design, collage, weaving or stitching, mixed media for pictorial work, sculpture, and ceramics. Among the art forms cited by 25 percent or less of the teachers were photography, moviemaking or television, architecture, and special fields of design—industrial, environmental, interior, and fashion.[9] The small interest displayed in design in everyday life can be attributed, in large measure, to the studio and craft orientation of most teachers of art. This orientation, in turn, dominates most teacher education programs.

In a brief survey, it is impossible to ascertain a teacher's philosophy, but several questions were asked about aims and emphasis in teaching art. Most teachers saw themselves as "developing openness to new ideas, originality, imagination," "making art relevant to students' natural interests and experience," and "building perceptual skills and the ability to use media." These themes dominate much of the professional literature of art education. The statements least characteristic of their programs (and the teachers were forced to choose among statements) were: teaching children that "art results from trial and error, patience, and dedication"; setting "high standards, letting students know I expect the best from them"; and "nurturing an awareness of the uses of art in everyday life." The latter of these statements, endorsed by only 3 percent of the teachers, parallels the infrequent mention of the design fields and architecture as art forms that would be introduced.[10]

Art teachers were also asked to respond to a series of questions about interrelating the arts, correlating art with other subjects, and art history instruction. About half of these art teachers reported that they frequently or regularly correlate or integrate art activities with academic subjects. Another third reported that they do so occasionally, "when the art doesn't get lost." When teachers do plan such activities, social studies and the language arts are the major points of connection with art.[11]

In general, elementary school art teachers are more inclined to relate art to academic subjects than to interrelate the several arts. Only 15 percent reported that they interrelated the arts "frequently," and most teachers say that the primary focus for such instruction is to develop awareness of all the senses—sound, touch, motion, and so on.[12]

Only one-fourth of these teachers provide instruction in art history on a regular planned basis; most (61 percent) treat it informally. The most common approach is to emphasize historical designs and techniques in relation to a studio activity. The second most common approach is to treat the visual arts of a selected culture or period, not chronologically. Seven percent believe that art history instruction is not essential in the elementary grades, and 4 percent claimed they were not knowledgeable enough to teach it.[13]

I also invited teachers to respond to questions about practices that bring visibility to the art program or make use of community resources. Of those responding,

73 percent hold a major art exhibit or art festival during the year;
45 percent lead field trips to museums or galleries;
35 percent have local artists visit or exhibit work at school;
23 percent offer workshops or classes for administrators or teachers; and
23 percent have parents serve as art-program volunteers.[14]

If we invert some of these proportions, we can see that the children taught by over half of these art teachers will not visit a museum or gallery, and two-thirds will not see the work of local artists in their school during the year. Lack of time and resources are the biggest problems teachers face in arranging opportunities for children to see original works of art.

It is instructive to examine other problems faced by these teachers. When I asked them to indicate the two problems of greatest concern in relation to teaching schedules, budgets, and space, I obtained these results:

51 percent   inadequate space, equipment, storage
32 percent   not enough preparation, planning time
32 percent   class periods too short
32 percent   classes too large
28 percent   too many classes to teach
25 percent   inadequate budget, supplies, resources[15]

Keeping in mind that only two problems were to be chosen from a list of six, space and scheduling problems appear to be more pressing concerns for these elementary school art teachers than budgets for supplies. In many elementary schools, no art room is provided. It is not uncommon for an elementary teacher to be asked to teach art from a small cart wheeled from room to room, and to present from this "art cart" totally different art lessons in a first grade, a fifth grade, then second grade, back to a sixth grade, and so on. Class schedules can be equally absurd. As an elementary school art teacher, for example, I taught in fifty-five different classrooms, one lesson per classroom every two weeks, with the length of a lesson ranging from thirty minutes to forty-five minutes. Conditions such as these are not unusual. A student-teacher ratio of 1:570 makes a mockery of the concept of individualizing instruction, yet this is the average ratio obtained in our survey.

The idea that many art teachers are frustrated as artists gains some support from this survey. Several questions probed the artist-teacher role. Over half of these teachers cited as a major job-related problem "not having enough time for my own studio work." Although 88 percent thought it was valuable or essential for the art teacher to be a practicing artist or craftsworker, only half had exhibited their work within the last three years and few (about 10 percent) were highly active exhibitors. The expectation that one can teach and pursue one's own artistic career is set up in most teacher education programs, but many teachers evidently find that both pursuits cannot be fully realized while teaching full-time.

How Well Are We Teaching? Student Achievement

As we have seen, art teachers are employed in relatively few of our elementary schools, and many work under conditions that prevent them from teaching students continuously. When we look at measures of student achievement in art, we should keep in mind that classroom teachers have the major responsibility for instruction. For a national picture of students' performance in art and whether it has improved or declined over a period of time, the only source of data is the National Assessment of Educational Progress, which in 1974–75 and 1978–79, tested students' achievement in art.[16] Scores from the 1978–79 assessment allow us to compare the performance of students at ages nine, thirteen, and seventeen with students of the same ages in the mid-1970s. The art exercises that students completed for the assessments measured their knowledge of art, attitude toward art, and skill in drawing and design (for some sample questions and results, see appendix C, pp. 174-175). Scores on the National Art Assessments reflect the percentage of students within each age group who perform satisfactorily. For all nine-year-olds, the questions and instructions were presented orally.

The First National Art Assessment, 1974–75.

Several exercises from the assessment conducted in 1974–75 can be cited to illustrate that learning between the fourth and the eighth grade is not very great. Consider, for example, drawing skills. One exercise calls for children to draw a picture of four people sitting at a square table (see appendix C, p. 174). The drawing is made up by the child, not copied. About 20 percent of the nine-year-olds attempted fore-shortening (tilting the plane of the table to show it in space). This kind of skill is not the only one that art educators might like children to develop, nor is it necessarily the most important. But the skills for representing objects in space can be taught. Nevertheless, thirteen-year-olds scored at nearly the same level as the nine-year-olds on this skill. Likewise, children can be taught to draw a person in a manner to suggest the figure is running, in motion. But on an exercise calling for children to draw a picture of a running person, the fourth and the eighth graders again scored at about the same level on such points as showing the arms bent and the body leaning forward in the direction of the motion.[17]

From the 1974–75 assessment we learn that in schools where the principal says that art is taught (irrespective of who teaches it), the instruction is not uniformly associated with a statistically higher score (see fig. 6.2, p. 82). On the drawing and design exercises, for example, the nine- and thirteen-year-olds who attend a school where art is taught do not score significantly higher than the national average. However, nine-year-olds who attend a school where art is not taught score significantly lower on drawing.[18] Hence, the presence of instruction, regardless of its quality, appears to have some bearing on drawing skills.

Scores on knowledge about art also appear to vary with opportunities for study in school. At ages nine and thirteen, students who attend a school where art is taught score signficantly higher than the national average, and those who attend a school where art is not taught score significantly lower. Since children who attend schools where art is taught may be advantaged in other ways, we cannot conclude that their knowledge about art comes only from the school art program. We can say that in the absence of such programs children are less likely to acquire knowledge about art.[19]

In order to determine whether students value art as an important realm of human experience, students were assessed in a number of ways—one exercise gave them the opportunity to respond to reproductions of art in a way that showed how open they were to different styles of art and to experimentation in art. The results show that nine-year-olds have a fairly well-developed concept of art that leads them to react negatively to works of art based on experimental uses of media and works which portray mystery, sadness, or fear. Although thirteen-year-olds display somewhat more positive attitudes toward various types of art, the scores for both age groups are not statistically significant in relation to attending a school where art is taught.[20]

Among other facts of educational significance, the 1974–75 National Art Assessment tells us that among our nine-year-olds,

27 percent do not think it is important for them to express themselves through art;
34 percent do not create art outside of school;
38 percent have never been to an art museum;
46 percent can offer no answer when asked, "Why is art important?"[21]

Overall, the nine-year-olds who score above the national average on the assessment are white, live in big cities, and have parents who have some college education. Children from this background attend museums often and create several kinds of art outside of school.[22]

It stands to reason that in-school art instruction is the best way to equalize opportunities for children who do not come from these advantaged circumstances. However, art teachers are least likely to be employed in schools with a high proportion (80 percent or more) of minority students. In 1974–75, nearly half of the elementary schools with predominantly white students were served by an art teacher or art consultant. Only one school in five was likely to have these services if the school had a high minority enrollment.[23] On the question of equality of opportunity, these facts speak for themselves.

The Second National Art Assessment, 1978–79

On all of the major art objectives which are included in the National Art Assessment, there are no significant differences between the scores of nine-year-olds tested in 1974–75 and in 1978–79 (see table 5.1).[24]

Table 5.1. Mean Performance Levels, National Art Assessments, Nine- and Thirteen-Year-Olds

	Exercises in Mean	Average (%)		
		1974–75	1978–79	Change
Overall Score				
Age 9	34	36.9	37.6	0.7
Age 13	48	49.9	47.7	−2.2*
Perceive and Respond to Aspects of Art				
Age 9	Too few exercises for meaningful average			
Age 13	6	55.1	55.3	0.2
Value Art				
Age 9	22	40.2	41.1	0.9
Age 13	27	54.9	51.6	−3.3*
Produce Works of Art				
Both ages	Too few exercises for meaningful average			
Know About Art				
Age 9	Too few exercises for meaningful average			
Age 13	7	37.0	34.4	−2.7*
Judge Quality of Works of Art				
Both ages	Too few exercises for meaningful average			

*Change is significant at the 0.05 level.
Note: Adapted from National Assessment of Educational Progress, *Art and Young Americans, 1974–1979: Results from the Second National Art Assessment,* Report no. 10-A-01 (Denver: Education Commission of the States, 1981), p. 5.

For several of the objectives, not enough exercises were administered to nine-year-olds to report a meaningful average, but significant changes occurred on specific items. For example, nine-year-olds showed improvement between the two assessments on items testing their skill in perceiving differences in technique in works of art, and in offering acceptable reasons for their art judgments (design unity, mood or feeling).[25] They were also more successful in a drawing exercise calling for fluency—producing sketches of ideas for paintings. However, skills in creating art were not uniformly improved. For example, fewer nine-year-olds in the late 1970s were successful in producing a coherent or unusual design (for a necklace).[26] Even though museum visits by nine-year-olds increased (up by 7 percent), few nine-year-olds were able to correctly answer four exercises calling for knowledge or familiarity with art history.[27]

Although we see no major trends in the achievement of nine-year-olds between the two assessments, there are marked declines in the scores earned by thirteen-year-olds (see table 5.1). The sharpest declines were in valuing art as an important realm of human experience, particularly in openness to different styles of art and experimentation in art. In the late 1970s, thirteen-year-olds also were less positive about the value of studying art unless they might want to make it a career.[28] Since this negative trend in valuing art is significant, even for students from advantaged backgrounds, we may infer that it mirrors the increasingly conservative mood of the nation, and, of course, its impact on the elementary schools these thirteen-year-olds would have attended from about 1972 to 1978.[29]

In addition to this disturbing trend among early adolescents, not unrelated to their experience in earlier years, we see a signficant decline in thirteen-year-olds' scores on knowledge about art. Most of the questions on knowledge about art asked students to identify from several possibilities the correct name of the artist or the national origin of a well-known work of art pictured in the exercise booklet. Although few questions of this type were asked, even these "academic" aspects of art appear to have been neglected in the last decade.[30]

On both the first and second assessments, the scores of students do, of course, increase with age, but since art instruction in schools is meager, at least some of this gain in scores may be attributed to the general experience that students acquire with age. In the light of the emphasis placed on basic skills in reading and mathematics during the last decade, I believe we may say that the decline in scores for thirteen-year-olds reflects a decrease in their opportunity to study art in school. On both assessments, it has been found that childrens' participation in and understanding of art is a matter of privilege, associated with their parents' education and social class, which, in turn, affects the likelihood that students will attend a school where art is taught by a teacher trained in art. The decline in scores on valuing art, even among advantaged thirteen-year-olds, is not encouraging—to say the least.

Although something that school principals call art is taught in the majority of our elementary schools, the achievement of students does not indicate that this instruction is adequate or that it has improved in the last decade. Nor is the achievement of children in art likely to improve as long as classroom teachers continue to be given primary responsibility for almost all of this instruction, and yet, in many states, continue to be certified without any college courses in art. In few fields other than art would we expect persons who are untrained in the subject to be competent to teach it to others. Nevertheless, this assumption functions as an unstated policy in many of our elementary schools.

The kind of on-the-job assistance that classroom teachers need in order to be effective can be provided by art supervisors or art consultants, but these services are often the first to be eliminated in a financial crunch. The absence of art consultants or supervisors is particularly damaging to the quality of instruction precisely because teachers of art are not widely employed and because there is no established tradition in art instruction of using texts and other carefully researched instructional materials to supplement the classroom teacher's own knowledge. In the absence of extensive training and support services in art, classroom teachers are inclined to believe (erroneously) that almost any activity that requires the use of crayons, paint, and other art materials can be equated with art education.

In the relatively few schools where art teachers are employed, their effectiveness may be impaired by unreasonable class schedules, and lack of space and resources. As a result of these conditions, many teachers who are well qualified and certified to teach art are unable to give their best to students. What most parents, principals, and members of school boards typically hear about are the exemplary schools in their districts, or programs of excellence that are well publicized in national journals. The impression is often formed from these stunning successes that arts education is in very fine shape.

Unfortunately, what the majority of our students in elementary school receive in the name of art education is meager, and likely to be presented in a way that inadvertently teaches them art is a frill, instantly produced with minimum effort, and fundamentally useless in life, unless one plans to become an artist. The magnitude of our disservice to children does not seem to have been grasped by the larger community of educators and arts advocates. In order to comprehend the importance of art education in the elementary school and the consequences of its neglect, we must understand that most children have little opportunity to study art beyond elementary school. Our next chapter, accordingly, will focus on art in secondary schools.

6 Rites of Passage: Art in the Secondary School

We HAVE LOOKED at the situation in elementary schools, where almost all instruction in art is offered not by art teachers but by classroom teachers, many of whom are not well trained in art. It is even more sobering to realize that by the time they leave school, about 80 percent of our nation's youth have had no instruction in art from a reasonably well-qualified teacher beyond *one* required course during junior high school, usually in the seventh or eighth grade. What expectations do we have for this brief course in art?

Art in the Junior High School

Instant Art, Instant Culture:
The Junior High School Program

Consider the dilemma of the junior high school art teacher who is faced with seventh- or eighth-grade youngsters, most of whom probably have not had continuous art instruction in elementary school, and all of whom are undergoing the storms and stresses of puberty. This teacher is now expected to work an aesthetic miracle in one course, or ninety hours flat—assuming that no class time is lost to fire drills, pep rallies, school assemblies, illness, or what have you.

The ninety hours of instructional time allotted for this one required art course may be scheduled on consecutive school days for half a year (the other half reserved for music, home economics, industrial arts), or the teacher may see the youngsters for ninety hours on an every-other-day schedule, five classes every two weeks throughout a full year.

In any case, time is of the essence; the art teacher knows quite well that this one required art course is both the first and the last opportunity for the majority of students to study art with a specialist teacher. The art teacher at this level plans a program carefully. Selections of content are usually made in advance; the agenda, the pacing, and the flow of activity have been anticipated. Instruction commences.

But if the art teacher is working in one of the many schools participating in a variety of social service programs or programs which take advantage of state and federal funds for special courses, one thing can be counted on. Many students will be grouped and regrouped into these special programs by manipulating their art schedule. What does this mean? Let me draw on my own experience as an art teacher in an inner-city junior high school.

Because of the scheduling arrangments for an individualized remedial reading program available to certain students three days a week in a junior high school where I taught, I was expected to accomodate all of the students in a single art class on the remaining two days of the week. As the year progressed, and the reading schedules changed, my official roster for this third-period art class listed 58 students, of whom 20 might be in class on any given day, but never the same students for two consecutive days.

This example may seem to be trivial, but in this school, several other special programs also were in operation, and in each case the programs were closely monitored because they were financed with funds earmarked for specific purposes. The constant reshuffling of students into and out of these "individualized" programs (and for all manner of other tests of performance and counselling) also affected instruction in science, social studies, English, music, and so on. Whatever educational coherence may have been gained for these special programs was purchased at the cost of making an educational disaster area for the rest of the curriculum. Art classes were treated as a temporary "holding pen" for one-third of the seventh- and eighth-grade students whom I taught.

The point is not to condemn special programs or to minimize the importance of counselling and testing, but to illustrate again how the fracturing of the curriculum by the scheduling of special programs, especially those supported under federal or state funds, can so dominate a school curriculum that all semblance of coherent instruction is lost. Even in schools where such programs are not disruptive, the art period tends to be seen as an open hour, easily expendable for student counselling, testing, and any other activity which may require students to be withdrawn from class.

If the junior high school art teacher does have access to students for ninety hours of instruction, there remains the problem of making art intelligible and memorable. The teacher must decide whether to try for depth or for breadth in representing the world of art to young people. Not everything can be taught; that is known.

In relation to making art, instruction in elementary school is so conceptually weak and meager that when children enter the seventh grade, art teachers often find that they must begin with concepts and exercises that could have been introduced in the second or third grade. For example, if the art teacher has a studio-based program, the rudiments of painting and color mixing will be taught again in the seventh grade, even though a good command of these skills can be cultivated *with instruction* in the elementary grades.

Unfortunately, the absence of early and continuous instruction in art cannot be overcome in a short time. In the case of painting, for example, one cannot create expressive art without some ability to control the color, the amount of paint, the direction of the brush stroke, and so forth. The ability to control paint requires practice well beyond that of an occasional opportunity to paint in elementary school.

Because so few students enter junior high school with these and related art-making skills, many do not have the self-confidence to create art. The art teacher is therefore caught in a double bind. Skill cannot be developed overnight, but neither is it wise to insist that youngsters create art without feeling some achievement in doing so. Early adolescents, moreover, have developed notions about "good" art, and they are embarrassed if their work is not up to these standards. The fourth-grade syndrome—loss of confidence in the ability to make art—persists, but now it is exaggerated. Standards are the issue for teacher and student alike. Moreover, the results of my *School Arts* survey suggest that junior high school art teachers, to a greater degree than either the elementary or senior high school art teacher, will "set high standards and let students know the best is expected from them."[1]

This one required art course in the seventh or eighth grade is the last opportunity for the study of art that we make available to the nation's youth. It is a token art education in duration and often in content. It is, I believe, properly viewed as a social ritual through which we endeavor, on a national scale, to impart "culture" to the adolescent. This one required course in art—this quick dose of art—is ritually administered to youngsters at puberty as if it were part of a rite of passage. What we seem to ask from this single course is that it serve as a long-lasting magic potion, permanently infusing the student with a sense for art, and hence for "culture." For many early adolescents, the effect is closer to that of a fast-acting purge, a decisive removal of further interest in art, especially for the majority who do not see themselves as talented in making art.

The Art Teacher Speaks: Practices and Problems in the Junior High School

The survey conducted through *School Arts* suggests that a typical junior high school art program does engage students with many of the same art forms they encountered in an elementary school program taught by an art specialist. More than 75 percent of the junior high school art teachers in the survey planned to teach drawing, painting, basic design, printmaking, sculpture, and ceramics. This was the "core" program which most students would receive from these 168 art teachers.

The average number of different art forms cited by the junior high/middle school teacher was eleven. We do not know how the teaching of these art forms may be distributed across classes, but it is my impression, based on program plans developed by college students and many observations in schools, and also on curriculum work with experienced teachers—that at the middle school/junior high level, teachers often do plan for breadth across ten or more art forms.[2] By simple arithmetic, we can estimate that any given art form is likely to be taught for a very short block of time. Instant art again, but with more pressure on students for disciplined and skillful performance.

In many other respects, the junior high school art program is similar to the elementary school program (see appendix A, pp. 163-70). For example, given twelve statements of aims for art education, most junior high school teachers say, like the elementary school teachers, that they emphasize "building perceptual skills and the ability to use media." "Nurturing awareness of the uses of art in everyday life" was (again) least often endorsed as an aim. Over two-thirds of the junior high school art teachers reported that they do not formally introduce studies of art history. Overall, junior high school art teachers are less inclined than elementary school teachers to integrate art with other subjects and with other arts.

About half of the junior high school art teachers listed as major problems large classes, inadequate facilities and equipment, unruly or apathetic students, and not having time for doing their own studio work.[3]

Student Achievement: Does One Course Make a Difference?

One quick dose of art in early adolescence does not make a substantial difference in students' knowledge about art, skill in art, or attitudes toward art (not, at least, as these kinds of learning are measured by the National Art Assessments). In the preceding chapter, we noted that scores of thirteen-year-olds declined on measures of valuing art and knowledge of art in the 1978–79 assessment. One can see from table 6.1 that this negative trend also is found in the scores of the seventeen-year-olds tested in 1978–79, who would have been enrolled in junior high art classes in the mid-1970s. The art instruction that both groups of teenagers received, some of it in junior high school, does not appear to have had a positive influence on their knowledge about art or their ability to find value in it.[4]

Other results from both assessments also suggest that the brief exposure to art that most children have in junior high school courses has little bearing on their performance as high school students. On a number of measures of skill in representational and expressive drawing, as well as of knowledge about art and skill in perceiving and judging it, the seventeen-year-olds who had only taken one art course since the seventh grade scored at a level close to that of seventeen-year-olds who had taken *no* art courses since the sixth grade.[5] In order to score higher than the national average on all major parts of the assessment, it appears that students must take from four to six art courses beyond the sixth grade or be from an advantaged home which provides many out-of-school art activities. One art course in the seventh or eighth grade is simply not enough.[6]

Even if one wishes to question whether the National Assessments in Art are appropriate measures of student learning, it should be obvious that basic education in art is exceedingly difficult, if not impossible to accomplish in ninety hours flat. The kind of instruction children receive in elementary and junior high school is no less a problem than the amount of time made available for it, for the studio-

Table 6.1. Mean Performance Levels, National Art Assessments, Thirteen- and Seventeen-Year-Olds

	Exercises in Mean	Average (%)		Change
		1974–75	1978–79	
Overall Score				
Age 13	48	49.9	47.7	−2.2*
Age 17	54	56.3	54.4	−1.9*
Perceive and Respond to Aspects of Art				
Age 13	6	55.1	55.3	0.2
Age 17	6	65.5	65.8	0.3
Value Art				
Age 13	27	54.9	51.6	−3.3*
Age 17	27	61.2	57.2	−4.0*
Produce Works of Art				
Both ages	Too few exercises for meaningful average			
Know About Art				
Age 13	7	37.0	34.4	−2.7*
Age 17	14	50.3	50.2	−0.1
Judge Quality of Works of Art				
Both ages	Too few exercises for meaningful average			

*Change is significant at the 0.05 level.

Note: Adapted from National Assessment of Educational Progress, *Art and Young Americans, 1974–1979: Results from the Second National Art Assessment*, Report no. 10-A-01 (Denver: Education Commission of the States, 1981), p. 5.

based programs offered in most schools do not, as is commonly assumed, contribute in a significant way to students' knowledge about art and general appreciation of it. Even some of the skills one might expect to see in drawing are not well developed through such programs.[7]

Art in the High School

The Neglected Majority: The High School Program

Beyond the seventh or eighth grade, students do not study art unless they elect to do so. Few American high schools require study in any of the arts as a condition for graduation.

100 percent   require no study of dance or theater;
 98 percent   require no music;

97 percent   require no visual arts;
95 percent   require no English literature;
94 percent   require no American literature.

Subjects not required in high school programs are not really basic; they are optional, if they are offered at all.

The impression many people seem to have is that high school art programs are strong, and therefore not in need of improvement. In fact, opportunities for the study of art are severely restricted in high schools, and elective courses in art are not as available as we assume. Only three electives in the arts are offered in the majority of the nation's secondary schools: band (84 percent), chorus (68 percent), and a visual art studio course, Art I (64 percent). In nearly one-fourth of the nation's high schools, *courses in the visual arts are not offered in any form, and in 43 percent advanced courses are not offered.* Art I is usually considered a prerequisite for advanced high school courses in art, but in nearly half (46 percent) of our secondary schools, even this general studio course is not offered.[8]

When Art I is offered in a high school that includes grades nine through twelve, the art classes will serve students who have attended different elementary and junior high schools. Consequently, the teacher cannot assume that all students have had an equivalent background of instruction. For these reasons, Art I is frequently a more disciplined version of seventh- or eighth-grade art. Seventy-five percent of the high school teachers in the *School Arts* survey teach drawing, basic design, painting, printmaking, sculpture, and ceramics— essentially the same core program that we found in the elementary and junior high school.[9]

Damaging Attitudes

ART IS AN "EASY" SUBJECT: Art I, as well as specialized studio classes that may be available, such as crafts or ceramics, are commonly regarded as "soft," nonacademic electives by school counselors and administrators, and by many students. Counselors often recommend art as a suitable elective for unruly students or for those who are not enthusiastic about academic work. Counselors make these recommendations believing either that art is therapeutic, or that if students cannot do academic work, they can at least "use their hands." Hence, teachers of art frequently complain that their classes are treated as a dumping ground for problem students.

High school art teachers react to these attitudes in several ways.

Some establish a highly structured program with specific assignments, deadlines, and strict criteria for judging performance, in order to prove to students (and counselors) that art is demanding. Some teachers establish prerequisites for advanced art courses and make admission to courses beyond Art I a privilege for students to earn by superior performance. In some cases the art teacher interviews each student to establish that the student really wants to work hard in class.

In contrast to this pattern of tightening up requirements in order to discourage all but those seriously interested in art, other art teachers enjoy the challenge of working with students who are perceived by nearly everyone else as "problems." Such teachers may strive to make the art-studio environment a refuge for those students who otherwise dislike school. Troubled students may well be aided by the individual attention offered in this kind of environment. But if there is a positive effect for some students, it is not always linked to achievement in making art. More likely it is due to the caring attitude of the teacher and the exploration of the human values and personal feelings that a good art program also emphasizes.

Regardless of the teacher's attitudes toward students whom others have found "difficult," there are two predictable features of high school programs. First, the student who is college-bound will not be encouraged to take art electives. Art has so little intellectual respectability that many colleges and universities will not count high school art electives toward admission. The student who is academically oriented may prefer to avoid art classes, especially if those are perceived as easy or if the classes attract students who have a reputation for unruliness. In either instance, counselors in high schools feel justified in steering the academically gifted student away from art classes. Art history, of course, is a different matter, but art history is offered only in 6 percent to 7 percent of the nation's high schools[10]

ART IS "MOSTLY" FOR THE TALENTED: A second predictable feature of high school programs is that they are designed to serve students who may want to pursue art as a career or those who want to develop their skills as amateurs. Neglected are the vast majority of students whose knowledge about art will come into play as they select and arrange ready-made products, as they create and use the spaces within their homes and places of work, or as they visit galleries and museums. While amateur participation in making art can be rewarding in adult life, teaching art as a hobby cannot be regarded as a major responsibility of the high school. In any case, the making of studio art and crafts tends to be dominant in high school art programs, and because of the specialized equipment and classrooms needed for such activities, the art courses available in high schools typically can accomodate less than 20 percent of the total enrollment in a given school.[11]

Programs developed for talented students certainly are important, but these must be evaluated in relation to occupational opportunities and requirements. A high school art major—a student who has taken all or almost all of the fine arts and crafts available—is not likely to be well prepared to find employment in art immediately following high school. Most vocations in art require advanced study in a professional art school or university art program, or technical training program. Moreover, the student who aspires to become a painter, sculptor, or printmaker, or who hopes to earn a living by making hand-crafted objects will find that even advanced training does not provide a reasonable guarantee of earning an income from producing art.[12]

Although high school art teachers take pride in their best students and naturally want to encourage those students to pursue careers in art, teachers too rarely inform students about the realities of occupational choices in art. For example, young artists who attempt to exhibit their work in commercial sales galleries often are shocked to learn that the gallery commission is 40 percent to 60 percent of the sale price. The young artist who has been taught to press for innovative imagery, form, concept, or technique also will find few galleries willing to exhibit unconventional work, because it is hard to sell.

Moreover, the prevailing work ethic in the fine arts is not to compromise one's artistic vision for the sake of earning money. The young artist who is faithful to this ethical principle and whose work is not marketable is thus forced to earn an income from another source. Even if a job is found in one of the commercial arts, the young artist may feel that "it's only a job," and does not give scope to his or her talent.

The fine arts and crafts are high-risk occupations. This fact should not be used to discourage talented students from pursuing art, but neither should the aspiring artist be kept ignorant of the conditions that operate in the marketing of art and the development of careers in art.

High school art teachers who have been trained in the studio arts and crafts may not be well informed about the "survival skills" needed to pursue art as a full-time career. Only recently have universities and art schools developed courses that address the working conditions, economic status, and legal rights of the artist and craftsworker. The high school art teacher who has not kept abreast of the emerging issues, programs, and service operations for artists is ill-prepared to offer wise counsel to the student who is considering a career in art.

Furthermore, the high school teacher trained in the studio arts and crafts may unwittingly demean many of the occupations in art from which talented students might earn a livelihood. Few art teachers have sufficient training in the commercial fields of art to appreciate them as art forms or to value the skills required of those who work in them. It is not uncommon for those who have been trained in the fine arts and crafts to regard artists who engage in the so-called commercial arts as people who have prostituted their talent for economic gain or popular appeal.

The commercial fields of art—graphic design, product or industrial design, interior design, fashion design, and architecture, photography, film and television—are rarely offered in high school art programs. Students who might succeed in these fields are not given sufficient prevocational experience or counselling to permit them to judge whether they have the interest or ability to pursue these fields. Similarly, students who might have both the interest and ability to pursue careers in art criticism, art history, and museum work have little in-school experience to cultivate or assess those abilities.

The Art Teacher Speaks: Practices and Problems in the High School

The 189 high school art teachers who responded to the *School Arts* survey offer the same core program as the junior high school teachers, but added attention is given to selected crafts. The design fields are not emphasized. For example, 57 percent teach batik, but only 22 percent teach architecture; 38 percent teach enamelling, but only 12 percent teach interior design; 42 percent teach jewelry, but only 4 percent teach industrial design; 69 percent teach weaving or stitching, but only 15 percent teach fashion design; 74 percent teach lettering, yet only 6 percent teach urban or environmental design.[13]

These art teachers most frequently endorsed, as statements that characterize their programs, the following: "[I] make sure students know I'm aware of their effort, progress, achievement" and "[My program] builds perceptual skills and the ability to use media." Least frequently endorsed as characterizing the art program were the statements "[I] make art exciting, special, different from anything else" and "[My program] nurtures awareness of the uses of art in everyday life." Most of these teachers introduce art history informally in connection with studio activities (52 percent), and in doing so, they emphasize the study of historical designs and techniques. Courses devoted exclusively to art history were provided by 7 percent of these high school teachers.

About one-third of the high school teachers reported that they regularly or frequently integrate art into academic subjects, usually with English or language arts. Courses that show inter-relationships among the arts are much less frequently reported. More than a third of the teachers believed that they were not knowledgeable enough in the other arts to interrelate them in a program.

High school teachers enrich their programs in a number of ways. The majority have a major art exhibit or art festival each year (78 percent), and many arrange field trips to museums or galleries (60 percent). Nearly half sponsor an art club and arrange in-school exhibits or visits by local artists. Forty percent have students enter the Scholastic Art Exhibits, a national program of competitive exhibits.

The situational problems of greatest concern to the high school art teacher are inadequate classroom space and budgets. The reader will recall that scheduling problems and class size were cited more frequently by teachers at the lower levels. At all levels of instruction, about half of the art teachers said that they were concerned about not having time to do their own studio work. Most of these teachers also believed that they had gained greater parental and community support for their efforts than support from school administrators.

In this chapter, and in chapter 5, I have identified patterns of instruction in elementary and secondary schools which I believe to be typical, rather than exemplary. The bearing of these and other widespread practices on achievement in art can be further discerned by examining, again, selected results from the National Assessment in Art.

The Net Effect of Art Instruction

Opportunity and Achievement

The opportunity to study art obviously has some bearing on achievement. One can see from figure 6.1 that enrollments in art classes decline from the seventh grade, when about 77 percent take art, to the eleventh grade when about 16 percent do. The fact that art is not a required course beyond the seventh or eighth grade probably accounts for the dramatic decrease in high school art enrollments compared to

Figure 6.1. Estimated Percentage of Students Enrolled in Art for 1974–75, by Grade Level.

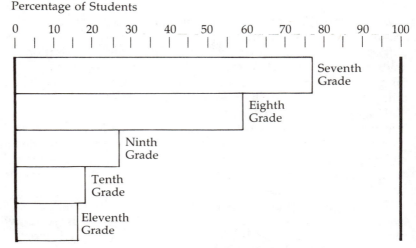

Note: Data from National Assessment of Educational Progress, *Art and Young Americans, 1974–79: Results from the Second National Art Assessment,* Report 10-A-01 (Denver: Education Commission of the States, 1981), p. 18.

No significant change was reported for 1978–79.

junior high school enrollments. Since these enrollment patterns did not change significantly between the 1974–75 and 1978–79 art assessments, secondary school programs do not appear to have been eliminated or cut back in a way that affects national enrollment patterns.[14]

What About Out-of-School Experiences?

Opportunities to learn about art can come from visits to art museums. According to the National Assessment in Art, a majority of students at all three ages (nine, thirteen, and seventeen) have never visited a museum or gallery, or have visited only once. Students in schools where art is not taught are less likely to have visited museums and galleries than students who attend schools where art is taught. Especially for minority students and students whose parents do not have a college education, the school serves as a vital connecting link to the museum experience.[15] The proportion of students who had attended museums at least once increased between 1974 and 1979, by 7 percent for nine-year-olds and 5 percent for thirteen-year-olds, but not for older students. These trends for younger students might be explained by the higher proportion of adults who are college educated, attend museums, and, as parents, provide such opportunities for their children.[16]

Almost all children create at least one kind of art outside of school. The most common activity at each age is drawing. Interest in making some kind of art outside of school appears to increase from age nine to thirteen and drops by age seventeen. At each age, more children create two-dimensional art—pictures in various media—than three-dimensional art such as sculpture, pottery, or jewelry. Participation in such activities remained unchanged for nine-year-olds between 1974 and 1979, but declined significantly for teenagers, especially seventeen-year-olds.[17] Although we know little about the quality of this engagement, the achievement scores of students who create from four to six kinds of art outside of school are, at all ages, higher than the national average.[18] Unfortunately, children's judgment about the importance of making art and confidence in their art ability decreases at each age.[19]

Children's museum visits and their involvement in making art outside of school are well above the national average if their parents have some college education and above-average income, but are below the national average if their parents do not have these socioeconomic advantages.[20]

Does Art Instruction Make A Difference?

As we have seen, student achievement, as measured by the National Assessment in Art, varies considerably in relation to opportunities for participating in art as well as to a number of background factors, the most important of which are socioeconomic. Even so, it is instructive to consider the gains students make between the ages of nine and seventeen and to examine their relationship to art instruction. Some of these relationships are shown in figure 6.2, based on data from the 1974–75 assessment, when student performance was relatively high, and hence when instruction might be assumed to be stronger than in the late 1970s.[21] Significant differences in achievement are associated both with the presence and with the absence of art instruction in schools. In

Figure 6.2. Students' Achievement in Art Related to Whether Art Is Taught in the School.

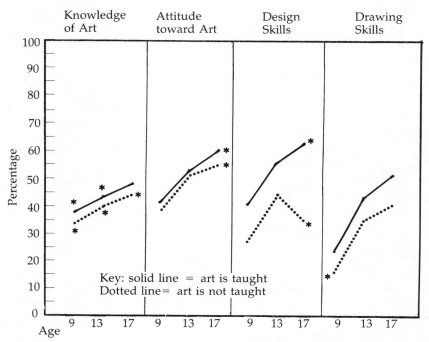

Note: Data from National Assessment of Educational Progress, *Art Technical Report: Exercise Volume* 06-A-20 (Denver: Education Commission of the States, 1978), pp. 146, 155; *Art Technical Report: Summary Volume,* Report no. 06-A-21 (Denver: Education Commission of the States, 1978), pp. 14, 22.

*Asterisks denote statistically significant values.

the absence of instruction, students at all ages score significantly lower on knowledge about art, nine-year-olds have less skill in drawing, and seventeen-year-olds score lower on design and positive attitude toward art. Regrettably, the presence of art instruction does not have a uniformly significant impact on achievement. Art instruction bears on knowledge about art for students at ages nine and thirteen, but not at age seventeen. For seventeen-year-olds, art instruction is associated with greater design skill and more positive attitudes toward art; for younger students it is not.[22] Since seventeen-year-olds *elect* art, and may be assumed to have a special interest in the subject, the bearing of instruction on these scores requires a closer look.

The relationship of achievement to the amount of art instruction that a student has received is suggested in figure 6.3. Seventeen-year-olds who have taken only one art course since grade six score below the national average on all major parts of the assessment. While the addition of two or three classes is associated with a slight increase in achievement, scores are not significantly above the national average unless students have taken four to six classes in art.[23]

Whether art is or is not taught, the achievement scores of students tend to increase with age, and thus reflect, in some degree, what is generally regarded as a natural developmental pattern. However, there are several noteworthy exceptions. First, on both assessments, art instruction seems to have a clear effect on the design skills of students at all ages. Moreover, only in the area of design is instruction sufficiently strong to suggest that instruction outweighs other socioeconomic factors as causes of student achievement. Second, and contrary to what we might expect as a normal pattern of growth, the improvement in scores among younger students from age nine to thirteen—on perceiving art, valuing it, and critically judging it—is

Figure 6.3. Average Scores of Seventeen-Year-Olds on National Art Assessment Tests Related to Number of Art Classes Taken Since Grade Six, and National Average.

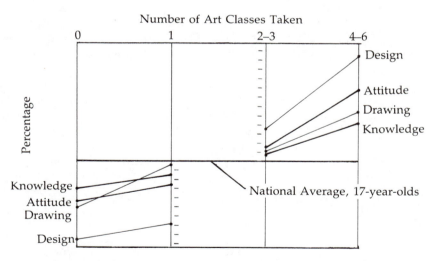

Note: Data from National Assessment of Educational Progress, *Art Technical Report: Summary Volume,* Report no. 06-A-21 (Denver: Education Commission of the States, 1978), pp. 14, 22; *Design and Drawing Skills: Selected Results from the First National Assessment of Art,* Report no. 06-A-01 (Denver: Education Commission of the States, 1977), pp. 86–89, 102.

All results are statistically significant except for drawing with one class, two to three classes, and four to six classes. Each unit reflects a score that is one percentage point higher or lower than the national percentage of students who satisfactorily completed each subtest.

more than double the improvement seen from age thirteen to age seventeen. Between age thirteen and seventeen, the most distinct gains in art learning are in knowledge about art, especially as it is conditioned by a general grasp of history and chronological time. However, this developmental trend is not unusual.[24] Even so, scores on knowledge of art are unnecessarily low, even for older students who have taken a number of art courses.

For example, only 15 percent of the seventeen-year-old students who had taken four to six courses in art could identify Picasso's *Three Musicians* as an example of Cubism (a third of the nation's youth guessed it was Pop Art).[25] Perceptual skills which are vital to examining works of art do not appear to be well cultivated. For example, when presented with a reproduction of a self-portrait by Van Gogh and four other works (one a drawing of cypress trees by Van Gogh), only 10 percent of the students who had taken four to six art courses could visually determine that both the cypress drawing and self-portrait were done by Van Gogh.[26] These and other responses suggest that the additional art classes taken by these students do not result in a general familiarity with the work of well-known artists, or with broad stylistic distinctions, or with major developments in the history of Western art.

In summary, the results of the National Assessment are informative, but not altogether encouraging. They demonstrate that the majority of youngsters on the verge of graduating from high school have not had a continuous and basic education in the visual arts. Most have not had the opportunity to attend museums and galleries with any degree of regularity. Although most students make some kind of art out of school, and in-school programs emphasize making art, there is little reason to believe that this participation is sufficiently informed, or focused, or continuous to support even a modest appreciation of what the creative process in art requires or what art can contribute to one's life. The decline in scores for thirteen and seventeen-year-olds shown in table 6.1, and particularly the declines in "valuing art as an important realm of human experience," suggest that the quality of students' engagement with art has deteriorated in the last decade.

Secondary school art electives are not as available to students as most people seem to assume. And when art programs are offered, few are designed to teach art to students who will not go on to college or to the college-bound student who will be majoring in a subject other than art. Programs are geared to the talented or to amateur participation in making art, and skills and concepts that promote an appreciation of art and its use in everyday life are generally neglected. What the majority of students know about art and can do in art has been defined by the meager studio/crafts instruction they have received before high school or what they have learned on their own outside of school. Can these limited patterns of opportunity to study art be changed? The answer, of course, is yes. One place to begin is teacher education, the subject of the next chapter.

7 The Most Important Ingredient: The Reform of Art Teacher Education

MANY OF THE CHARACTERISTICS of elementary and secondary school art instruction today are by-products of the kind of education teachers of art have had in college. The reform of teacher education is urgently needed, but this cannot be accomplished without a guiding image of the role of the teacher and the kind of curriculum to be taught.[1]

The Teacher as a Person

The art teacher shares with all teachers a general responsibility for being an adult whom students can respect as a person. In earlier decades, respect came to teachers simply because they were called teachers. Parents, for the most part, required their children to show respect for teachers, and the preparation of teachers emphasized the importance of being a model for students. Teachers were asked to see the process of education as a matter of nurturing individual growth and a spirit of cooperation among students. In the last several decades, this "growth and nurture" metaphor for education has been replaced by other guiding images and metaphors for the process of teaching young people.[2] Some of these are noted below.

Metaphors in Education

Central Metaphor	*Terms Reflecting Central Metaphor*	
Growth	Child	GROWTH
		NURTURING growth
		ATMOSPHERE for learning
	Classroom	CLIMATE
	Child	DEVELOPMENT
		WHOLE Child
		UNFOLDING of art activity
Business		BUSINESS of teaching
	School	WORK
	School	PLANT
	Pupil	PERFORMANCE
		FUNCTIONAL literacy
	Performance	CONTRACT
	Learning	TASKS
		INVENTORY of objectives
		COST accounting
Computers		COMPUTER-assisted instruction
	Instructional	INPUT
	Pupil	OUTPUT
	Teacher-Pupil	FEEDBACK
	Instructional	SYSTEMS
	Task	ANALYSIS
		FORMATS for teaching
	Information	RETRIEVAL
Military	National	DEFENSE Education Act
	President's	TASK FORCE on Education
		OPERATION Head Start
	Teacher	CORPS
	Teaching	STRATEGIES
		TACTICS OF TEACHING
		LOGISTICS of scheduling
	Pupil	DEPLOYMENT strategies
		IMPACT of Title IV
		TARGET POPULATIONS for Title III
Reason		DOMAINS of knowledge
		MASTERY of content
	Structure of	DISCIPLINES
		STRUCTURE of knowledge
		FUNDAMENTAL ideas
	Pursuit of	EXCELLENCE
	Methods of	INQUIRY
		HIGHER-LEVEL mental abilities
		HIERARCHY of abilities

Because metaphors such as these can guide our thinking about education, their acceptance can profoundly influence how we treat students and teachers. For example, when educators speak of teaching and learning as if it were a military mission; is the enemy, perhaps—the student? And who are the "targets" of educational strategies and teaching tactics, if not pupils? What do we say about our sensitivity to education when we rely upon images from computer technology, speaking of teacher "inputs," or pupil "outputs" and "feedback"? Even if we grant that certain aspects of education require the application of business and accounting principles, and that education should prepare one for useful work, the language borrowed from business and cost-accounting has contributed much to the dehumanization of educational thought.

These and other impersonal images of teaching do not give proper weight to the role of the teacher as a person and as a professional whose potential influence on the life of students is multifaceted. The ideal teacher, I believe, displays personal and professional maturity. Within the classroom we should witness a dynamic interplay of the teacher's empathy with students, but with a psychological distance from students that allows the teacher to control interactions and to exercise professional judgment.

As a person, the teacher must have enough experience in the world to appreciate human nature and the forces that motivate conduct. There must be some consciousness of one's role as an authority in the classroom, but this authority should be displayed in one's expertise in the subject matter and in interactions with students. Self-respect, an understanding of human problems, and caring about others' viewpoints are essentials. To these sensitivities, we add reason. We must ask that the teacher be able to analyze his or her own values and behavior, to see what is really at stake in the process of teaching, and to decide wisely—ethically—what should be done. The restoration of public confidence in teachers can be forwarded by giving more attention to the principles which ought to govern the conduct of teachers.

Traditionally, college programs have relied on course work in educational psychology and human development to nurture these and other sensitivities in teachers. These courses should not sidestep the issues our teachers are eager to talk about—racism, sexism, drug abuse, economics, pollution, the generation gap, the system. Young teachers want to face these problems for themselves, knowing very well that they will face them in the schools.

On these and other major social issues, the future teacher must learn to distinguish between personal judgments and professional responsibilities, for whether we wish to acknowledge it or not, a public school teacher is employed to transmit a host of social values. Teachers are not free to "do their own thing" in classrooms. Unfortunately, if their college coursework fails to deal with the social and ethical dimensions of education, teachers may be left with the impression that their classroom obligations are limited to those which are written into an employment contract.

I have emphasized the need for teachers who are sensitive to human nature and to the ethical dimensions of teaching because the teaching of art—insofar as it deals with the expression and discernment of human values—is a moral enterprise. It is not, fundamentally, a job in which teachers are free to impart their own beliefs, artistic preferences, and personal enthusiasms to young people without much regard for the responsibilities that go with teaching in schools. While most teachers of art are encouraged to identify with the role of the artist and to function as free spirits within the institutional setting of the school, there are a number of problems related to this orientation. Let us examine a few.

Should the Teacher Be an Artist?

Students who enter the field of art education may do so primarily because they are interested in working with young people, or because they really wish to pursue their studio art but also want a regular salary and job security. There is a spectrum of motivations between these two extremes. But in the eyes of the many college students who really want to be full-time artists, and even in the eyes of some university studio instructors, the decision to teach art is often regarded as proof that the artist is not good enough to make a living from his or her art.

The idea that the teacher of art must be a practicing artist is widely held: Over 80 percent of the 600 art teachers who answered the *School Arts* survey thought it was "essential" or "valuable."[3] This overwhelming endorsement is not surprising, since college and university programs attempt to develop the prospective teacher's identity as an artist. In fact, the completion of studio courses still weighs heavily in state certification standards for art teachers.

The collegiate emphasis on the teacher's ability to perform as an artist is troublesome for a number of reasons. First, it is based on the assumption that the primary mission of the teacher is to engage children and youth in the process of creating art and handcrafted objects to the virtual exclusion of teaching youngsters about forms of art that cannot be made "by hand." As we have seen, courses in architecture, interior design, and industrial and advertising design are not often included in the education of art teachers.

Second, in programs that prepare teachers, studio courses in art may not be balanced with in-depth studies in the history of art or art theory. Indeed, because of the high value placed on spontaneity and novelty of expression in twentieth-century art, the study of art history and theory may be downplayed by faculty, because it is seen as handicapping the art teacher's growth as an innovative artist. In the absence of a broad perspective on the world of art, teachers of art are prone to elevate their own preferences in studio work to a level of artistic and educational significance that is totally unwarranted.

The kind of art history instruction that the prospective teacher receives in college may also contribute to the neglect of art history in schools. Introductory art history courses may be taken in large, impersonal lecture halls and require little beyond learning the names of artists, titles of works, dates, stylistic labels, and one or two distinguishing characteristics of a work. In the absence of lively discussions about works of art, artists, or the cultural milieu in which works are created, young teachers are likely to find art history uninformative, dull, and therefore of little personal or educational importance.

Third, teachers need to realize that youngsters are socially conditioned to attend to a wide range of conventional symbols and artifacts—from numbered-painting sets to outdoor signs—with some awareness that these are examples of art and design. The teacher who expects innovation from children is likely to be greeted, instead, with children who want to draw "Snoopy" or other borrowed images. The focus on experimentation and individuality in much studio instruction may leave art teachers unprepared to comprehend the aesthetic, social, and educational significance of the visual environment, especially mass-produced forms, mass-circulated images, and design motifs that have mass appeal.

Fourth, the emphasis on studio instruction may fail to cultivate in the young teacher an appreciation of language as a means of teaching about art. Verbal studio instruction in painting, sculpture, and other art forms may consist of little more than brief descriptions of class assignments, casual observations about works in progress, and a final criticism of the studio assignments during which students are exposed to peer and teacher judgments of their work. In a studio critique, it is not unusual for personal preferences and outright biases to pass as adequate justification for one's judgment. Some college instructors dismiss the value of a more searching analysis of the student's work by appealing to the idea that "if you have to explain what you've tried to do, it isn't art." The college art student may not be exposed to many teachers who, through the skilled use of language, illuminate the visual and expressive dimensions of studio art.

Fifth, the inefficiency or inappropriateness of studio instruction in teaching the young may not be critically examined. There are many differences between the studio activities one can provide to a large group of children in a school and the studio activities offered in a college program. In college studio courses, the young teacher—as a future artist—may be admonished to avoid creating imitative art, but in art-education methods courses he or she may be urged to do the opposite. For example, the teacher may learn to help children make simulated "mosaics" in paper, but without thinking through what children do and do not learn about mosaics if they are engaged in this process. Similarly, teachers may not be asked to consider in depth the educational significance of, say, engaging children in a four-week macrame project as compared to a four-week examination of architecture.

In addition to strengthening teacher education along these lines, the quality, scope, and use of the studio preparation offered to art teachers needs to be reviewed by faculty in art and art education.

One of the most common complaints of the art-education major is that studio teachers react more favorably to the work of students majoring in fine arts than to that of students majoring in art education. The complaint is not without foundation, and several explanations may be offered for this real tendency to downgrade the art work of the student who plans to teach art.

Although fine arts faculty are, by definition, art educators, most prefer to be identified as artists, not as teachers of art. Given this orientation, fine arts faculty may assume that the prospective teacher of art is not very serious about becoming an artist. Studio faculty may perceive the job of teaching art to children as relatively undemanding (except for stamina, patience, and skill in organization) and, as a consequence, set lower expectations for the artistic performance of the art-education major than for the fine arts major. If children are seen as amateurs in art, their teachers need not be much better than amateurs—or so it seems.

Within a single department of art, the proportion of studio instructors who make the prejudgment that art education majors are "less able" or "less interested" in art is probably small, but the effect of even one studio teacher's having that attitude is felt acutely by almost every art-education major. Most prospective teachers of art resent any suggestion that they are second-rate students. Even when students do not feel this kind of prejudice, a number of other more subtle attitudes may cause the art-education major to be treated as something less than a serious student of art.

First, more women than men are enrolled in college art and art-education programs. As a profession, teaching the young has long been regarded as women's work. Until recently, young women seeking a vocation felt that they had few options beyond the so-called helping professions, chiefly nursing and teaching. Young men who chose teaching as a career often were burdened with having to defend their lack of aspiration for another, more competitive profession.

Second, women who enter art teaching, in particular, also are burdened with a cultural stereotype that art is a subject of "natural" interest to women—an extension of some biological urge to decorate the nest or adorn the body. By the same stereotypic reasoning process, men who show an interest in art have sometimes been prejudged as effeminate. Coexisting with these attitudes is the fact that professional recognition in the world of art is still largely reserved for male artists.[4] In 1976, according to one survey, over one-third of Americans (including the college-educated) agreed with the statement, "Most great artists will always be men rather than women."[5]

Third, the studio art faculty in most colleges and universities is still predominantly male. Some of the faculty, in addition to holding a patronizing attitude toward the work of women art students, engage in sexist games and chauvinistic criticism to such an extent that the female art student is intimidated. Although sexist games may be played both ways, it is rare that the studio guidance and criticism received by women is free of a sexist bias. Women who are told by a male studio instructor that they "paint like a man" are usually expected to take the remark as a compliment. One need not be a radical feminist to understand that for many women students of art and of art education, the task of learning about art is complicated by the prerequisite of having to learn how to take an art class with a male instructor.[6] The woman student is also faced with the task of developing an identity as an artist without the benefit of continuous exposure to the numerous models of artistic excellence that are available to male students. Although such models exist, the history of women's achievements in art is not yet well documented, and the dominance of males on art faculties does not provide women with a strong basis for self-identification with the role of the artist.

The effect of these two cultural loadings—that teaching is a maternal activity and that art, for women, is a decorative urge—is not fully appreciated. It is, however, reflected in the coursework typically required of art-education majors. Courses in jewelry and the fiber arts—weaving, batik, fabric design—are frequently taught in departments of art education, rather than in departments of fine arts, because such courses may be required for state teacher certification, but not for a fine arts degree.

The history of this separation of fine art from the crafts, especially of fibers and jewelry, is too complex to trace fully here. Suffice it to say that in the first several decades of this century, art teachers (mostly women) were not trained in fine arts departments but in departments of home economics or in teachers' colleges where the "home" arts of design, decoration, and manual training in the crafts were emphasized, along with drawing, painting, printmaking, sculpture, and the study of ornamental design in history. In 1917, federal legislation supporting industrial arts and home economics education increased the demand for teachers in those two subjects and caused a realignment of teacher education course requirements.[7] In the new industrial arts programs, greater emphasis was placed on technical processes in working with wood, metal, and other materials than on aesthetic design and handcrafting objects. In home economics programs, greater emphasis was placed on the analysis and choice of ready-made attire and household goods than on handwork.

In changing the departmental structures of universities to accommodate these and other trends, the handcrafts survived primarily as course requirements for art teachers. Since the decorative arts and crafts were considered appropriate studio activities for women to pursue without having to compete in the male-dominated fine arts, they were offered in the female-dominated teacher education program.

Consider also, that in the early decades of this century, the art teacher often was faced with children of first- or second-generation immigrants whose families still depended on craft work and "cottage" industries. In spite of the "melting pot," many of these families maintained a strong tradition of creating handcrafts for ethnic and religious holidays. Teachers of art were trained to respond to these facts. This legacy is apparent not only in course requirements in the crafts but in the folk art orientation of many school activities.

These and other historical factors have resulted in a greater emphasis on the crafts and decorative arts in the education of the art teacher than in that of the fine arts major.[8] This legacy may explain, in part, the high regard art educators have for art made from inexpensive materials or available resources, art that stems from the decorative surface design in folk art, and, more generally, their preoccupation with techniques for using a medium, rather than using a medium to make an artistic statement.

The young teacher of art is, I believe, encouraged to think about art in terms of experimentation with a broad array of media and techniques, and with design as surface decoration. Irrespective of the level at which art is taught or supervised, art teachers seem reluctant to deal with the idea that art is socially useful, and unprepared to deal with art history as much more than a source of designs and techniques for craft work and studio art.

The student majoring in fine arts, by contrast, is more likely to be urged to deal with interactions between form, content, and means of expression. Imagery, concepts, symbolism, and themes are more central concerns, including themes established through the "pure" or abstract use of color, line, and so on. In contrast to the art-education major, the fine arts major is more likely to be urged to make an artistic statement through a series of works, choosing media and techniques appropriate to the statement. Design, too, is more likely to be approached as a dynamic, multilevel structure through which one's expressive intent may be fully realized.

It could be argued that such differences in studio preparation are less important than sustained in-depth work in creating art—whether pursued in many media or more selectively. Sustained effort should lead one to a sense for the nuances and breadth of possibilities in art. There can be no doubt that studio courses for teachers should be directed toward this end. But it is also true that the greater one's commitment to creating one's own art, the more likely it is that one may resent other intrusions on one's time and thought processes. This conflict of interest between making art and teaching art is evident even among faculty who work in university art departments.

The energy consumed in creating art and the energy required for effective teaching are comparable, and prospective teachers should be forewarned that few teachers are able to sustain both activities at the same level of intensity for very long. "Depth" in studio preparation at the undergraduate level, while certainly desirable, may succeed in bringing the prospective teacher to the threshold of wanting to pursue the making of art as a career, and thus set the stage for frustration at having to teach art to the young. The issue, as I see it, is not whether the teacher of art should be trained under the artist-teacher model. The key questions are: 1) What kind of education in art should we provide in schools? and 2) How can teachers best be prepared to offer education of that kind? These questions cannot be answered without some reference to the kind of instruction children and youth should receive in schools.

The Teacher as Interpreter of Art

The skills required to teach the lay public and youth about art are not the inevitable result of deep engagement with studio activities. The role of the teacher is not that of a creator of art, but that of a translator, interpreter, and lifelong student of art. The kind of understanding and experience one needs in order to teach art is defined, not by the teacher's personal imperatives as a creator of art, but by the imperatives of preparing young people for their role as informed citizens, able to participate in a wide range of matters that bear on art.

Suppose we could agree that art education in public schools has three major functions: creating in youths an awareness of the artistic heritage; encouraging personal response and expression; and developing an awareness of the role of art in society. Where does this leave us in teacher education? It leaves us with a set of topics and problems that need to be accounted for in the preparation of teachers. It leaves us with a general framework for examining what teachers need to know in order to become informed professionals within the world of art and persons skilled in teaching others about that world.

As we reflect on the preparation of teachers relative to the artistic heritage, we can see that present course requirements in art history are minimal surveys, inventories of artifacts with names, dates, and places. Advanced courses should be required, for they are more likely to treat more complex and challenging ideas; to teach how artists are influenced by their personal histories and cultural milieus, the effect of existing technologies on the character of work, and the influence of prevailing standards of "good" art on the style and idiom of particular artists. Studies that develop skills in analyzing and interpreting art—art criticism—are equally important. Ideally, the prospective teacher should be able to encounter any work of art, describe it, and offer reasonable explanations for the expressiveness found in the work. There is much room for improvement in this whole area of historical and critical preparation.

The teacher's personal skill as an artist is less important than the teacher's ability to communicate to students what the experience of creating art means and to engage students in this process. An analogy for this dimension of teaching may be found in coaching athletic performance. We expect the coach to be a connoisseur of sport and to know how to elicit skilled performance from others. A good coach may not have been a superb player on the field. Indeed, many were of average ability. But every effective coach is a superb student of sport and understands how the performance of players can be improved.

If teachers are to help children and young people toward the goal of personal response and expression, they obviously need to know about children, their modes of learning, and their milieu. But teachers also need better preparation in classroom methods of helping children to generate ideas, refine them, use media, and perceive, interpret, and judge art. Foundation studies in art history, studio, and art criticism are of little direct use in the classroom unless teachers can translate that content into appropriate activities for children and youth.

Teachers also need to learn ways to bridge the gap between art activities in school and art forms that children encounter out of school. More attention should be given in teacher education to the conceptions of art that young people acquire from the mass media, from the environment of discount stores, and from the youth culture itself. These social dimensions of art can be illuminated through courses which draw upon cultural anthropology and the sociology of art. We need teachers who are much more aware of the way in which social movements influence art, the bearing of art on the lives of people in our own and other cultures, and the way media and forms can shape styles of life. This kind of background is rarely acquired through art history courses.

Finally, as we prepare teachers in the subject of art, we should be keenly aware of contemporary aesthetic doctrines and the changing character of art. I learned the importance of this kind of awareness through my own experience. As an undergraduate I studied design with a teacher who had studied in the Bauhaus, an influential school of art in Germany prior to World War II. One of the doctrines my teacher proposed (and I accepted as rule) was this: "Respect the nature of the material." Wood is wood, you let the grain show; clay is clay, you let the mark of the forming process show on the surface and use earth-colored glazes. So uncritically did I accept these rules for "good" art that for many years I was unable to look at painted sculpture made of wood without prejuding it as bad, or to appreciate highly decorated clay objects with smooth, glossy surfaces. "Form follows function" was another doctrine, but it did not explain that form can be invented without reflecting particular functions. Consider Buckminster Fuller's geodesic dome, and the many functions it might serve. Surely the same risk of teaching narrow standards and principles exists today. This risk can be minimized by knowing the origin of aesthetic ideas and the value systems from which they stem.

The Teacher as a Professional

Another responsibility of the art teacher is to be informed about the profession of education and take part in the improvement of it. The prospective art teacher usually takes courses in the history and philosophy of education, educational psychology, curriculum, and methods of teaching—all as orientation to the profession. The problem is to achieve some integration of all these studies at both a theoretical and practical level.

Curriculum development—planning an art program—is an area of study that can help teachers to integrate their knowledge about art, about students, and other information derived from their course work in education. Skills in planning are usually developed through designing individual lessons. Curriculum planning from kindergarten to twelfth grade should also be addressed. Intermediate levels of planning—for a year or several years—as well as the familiar lesson plan, also require attention. In teacher education, we have, I believe, concentrated on planning lessons as isolated events, as if each lesson had no bearing on anything else. This practice may actually encourage the prospective teacher to think of an art program as little more than a series of short-term, unrelated activities.

As an agenda for professional studies, an emphasis on curriculum would require that a prospective teacher be able to articulate why it is important to teach art and to formulate goals for an art program in such a way that art instruction would be clearly related to the functions of general education in American schools. Further, it would require the teacher to identify the patterns of behavior involved in meeting these goals on the basis of what the prospective teacher knows about art and about the teaching-learning process in art.

The selection of content for art instruction deserves more attention than it gets. The prospective teacher should be able to identify what students should be asked to perceive, judge, and create, and be able to offer good reasons for the amount and kind of attention given to various aims and content. What to leave out of an art program is just as problematic as what to include.

With this broad view of what is possible and desirable, the prospective teacher should be able to determine the sequence and pacing of instruction, how individual differences can be met, and what teaching materials—studio supplies, books, films, and so forth—should (ideally) be available in the school. The prospective teacher should draw upon studies of children's development and educational psychology to answer these questions, but the teacher should also recognize that not every answer to important questions will be found in this research literature. Some guideposts are available, however, and they are useful in determining what we ask of youngsters in the various grades.

Finally we get to the how. Here we come to grips with the real classroom situation, considering teaching methods appropriate for the students and the goal being sought, and all the details of arranging materials and using time and space wisely. We are also back to the qualities of the teacher as a person, his or her ability to relate to students, to analyze what is being taught, and to learn from the experience.

Teaching methods must be given attention, but not in the usual sense of presenting a single method as if it were a solution to all problems. Indeed, we want to assure that teachers are not locked into a single way of preparing for an activity, motivating students, presenting problems, and guiding their efforts. Teachers must have the skill to move freely from open-ended situations to detailed explanations of procedures, from organizing large groups for cooperative action to dialogue with individual students, from prepared lectures to spontaneous, yet reflective discussions. Some of these skills can be developed by practice teaching and other rehearsal techniques, but in the classroom, the teacher's general maturity, based on experience with people from all walks of life, is the most natural ground for truly responsive teaching.

Evaluating student progress in art is a matter of learning to identify aims, to monitor student performance, and to determine whether day-to-day assignments are building toward the larger patterns of behavior decided upon as program goals. The prospective teacher who can make decisions of this kind—and all of them are tied to curriculum questions—is not as likely to take warmed-over college problems into second-grade classrooms or resort to one-time activities that have little more value than being fun and consuming time.

In the future, it will not be enough for the teacher to be able to plan, implement, and evaluate classroom activities. An art program is not limited to the classroom. We must prepare teachers to create a general awareness of art in the school and community, not merely responding to the status quo but insisting that decisions about the art program be made as carefully and be as well publicized as they are in other subjects.

The art teacher should be made aware of the possibilities for community involvement, bringing in guest panels, taking advantage of loan exhibitions, art fairs, local talent, and similar resources. The art teacher who is satisfied with remaining in his or her classroom is likely to gain little support for the art program and secure little cooperation from the guidance staff and school.

Art teachers should also be aware of the forces—social, political, and economic—which are shaping education at the federal, state, and local level. Collectively, teachers form a powerful lobby and can, through their participation in the political process, help to ensure that their professional concerns are reflected within policies that affect schools. If we have learned anything from the last several decades, it is that federal and state legislation, as well as local policies for schools, can have a clear curriculum bias for or against the arts. The emphasis on measurement and cost accounting in school programs, the urgent demands of citizens for job-relevant skills and for education of high quality, a growing awareness of legal issues—all are examples of trends that can influence the character of teaching in general, and also art education.

Finally, and most vital to the health of the profession of art education and its practice, we must address the ethical dimensions of teaching art, especially in schools that are tax-supported. Among these dimensions are the responsibilities of schools for basic education and the meaning of basic education in relation to art education; the relationship of knowledge about art to the quality of life enjoyed by all citizens, both children and adults; and, of course, the conduct appropriate for teachers who work in schools.

College faculty in charge of teacher education programs must dare to imagine a future for art education better than the status quo, venture beyond the current realities, and more fully prepare teachers to deal with art as it may affect the lives of children and adults. We must expect art teachers to be well grounded in the subject of art and have well-developed skills in enabling students to interpret art. The teacher's basic competency in art must be matched by the ability to help students experience art as a unique way of making sense out of the world. Of paramount importance is the teacher's ability to work within the institutional demands of the public school and to plan and carry out an art program that not only is effective with students, but also reaches into the rest of the school and community. We must expect teachers not only to keep informed of broad developments in the profession, but to influence the direction of change through their individual and collective voices. In teacher education programs that focus almost exclusively on the teacher as an artist, this larger perspective may be lost, and with it, the opportunity to understand our past and to shape our future.

8

The Research We Have; The Research We Need

IN THIS CHAPTER, we will look at the kind of theory and research that art educators have pursued, some of the unmapped territory for which research is needed, and how research affects teaching practice.* At the outset, it should be noted that many of the same ideologies which have shaped teacher education and school practices have influenced the character of theory and research in art education. A ripple effect can be traced from the typical background that most of us have in art education to our sense of mission, the character of our research, and our judgments about the importance of research.

Misplaced Skepticism: Attitudes Again

Most of us who work in art education have been trained in programs that placed a premium on our development as artists. In such programs, many of us were taught to value art as a form of individual

---

*Chapter 8 is adapted from my article "Research Means 'Searching Again,' " in *Art Education* 32 (1979): 6–10, with the permission of the publisher, the National Art Education Association, Reston, Va.

expression and to trust the kind of personal knowledge gained through studio experience. Through much of our professional litera- ture, a good many of us have been urged to see the child as someone to be protected from the adult world of reason, fact, and tradition.[1]

We are quick to polarize *objectivity* and *subjectivity* as if these orienta- tions are never fused, interdependent, or complementary. Many of us have acquired an outlook that splits reason from feeling and places each in a separate domain, one labelled *cognitive*, the other *affective*. This tendency to separate reason and feeling is deeply embedded in Western thought. It is evident in much of the general literature on education. Often the arts are regarded as matters of feeling or intui- tion, and opposed to intellectual pursuits. This split is exaggerated in art education, and it has inhibited the development of art education as an intellectual discipline. As a professional group, art educators are probably less receptive to theory and research than most educators, and this skepticism about the worth of organized knowledge contri- butes to the public impression that art, and the teaching of art, are not intellectually demanding.[2]

What is research? Research means "searching again"—inquiring carefully into some matter of special concern.[3] Although each of us may search for authentic knowledge through the private exercise of conscience, research is a more elaborate and public process. It is carried out and reported in a controlled manner so that others can verify that we have not misled ourselves. Because errors in thought, misperceptions, unquestioned values, and unexplained events can cause a good deal of human misfortune, we have, as a species, evolved some fairly elaborate systems of inquiry to produce reliable, coherent, and useful knowledge about the world in which we live.

Research does not thrive in a climate of yea-saying, or in contexts where knowledge from research is rejected out of hand. Research activity thrives on curiosity and doubt. It invites us to question whether our beliefs and practices are really as well founded as we usually assume they are. We are not likely to value research or the disciplines of scholarship required to produce it if, for example, we believe that knowledge comes primarily from personal experience, or if we are certain that the best way to learn is by trial and error, or if we distrust systems of thought in which words and concepts serve as records of ideas and events.

In art education, our lack of comfort with traditions of academic inquiry and research can be seen in the way we typically envision our teaching role. The autonomy we have learned to enjoy in the studio seems to make it legitimate for us to exercise a comparable degree of freedom when we step into the role of teacher. Within the classroom, as in the studio, we want to feel free to express our personal commitments to art, to follow our intuitions, try out new ideas, and learn by trial and error. We seem to equate "academic" teaching with mastering textbook knowledge, drill, and always having to do things one way. We do not want to acknowledge that creative teaching and learning can occur within science, history, or other subjects. And we are reluctant to contaminate art teaching with anything that seems too factual, conceptual, or bookish.

This conception of our teaching role is congruent with the orientation we have brought to research. We are inclined to be skeptical of research because it is "academic" and does not seem to provide an opportunity for us to express our thoughts and feelings creatively. And we are inclined to justify this anti-research position by asserting that art is too mysterious, too complex, or so inherently different from other human experience that research, even if undertaken, is a pointless exercise. These attitudes, which have impeded the growth of scholarship in art education, have also left their mark on the kind of theory and research that we have generated.

The Big Picture: The Character of Our Research

What we art teachers tend to value as a basis for effective practice—identifying with the role of artist and understanding child art—has influenced the overall shape of the research literature in art education. Certain types of research have been of particular interest to art educators, and thus are more abundant. So, too, have the content and general scope of research in our field been determined by our traditional interests.

Types of Research

Research is usually considered under three basic categories: historical, philosophical, and observational (empirical) research. Basic research differs from applied research. Applied research attempts to provide information of potential use to teachers, while basic research is undertaken with no purpose except that of seeking knowledge. Even basic research, which seems to be remote from classroom activities, can influence how we think about teaching and have a greater effect on our work than we may realize.

In spite of the fact that some form of art has been taught in American schools for over a century, historical research into the theory and practice of art education is not abundant.[4] Why? If we truly valued historical perspectives on art and on education, more scholarly effort would surely be devoted to historical research, and more of us would benefit from it. Among other benefits, those of us in art education might find it less necessary to "reinvent the wheel," map the territory, and build new roadways from scratch whenever we are faced with a new challenge. Histories of our field are needed if we are to understand the context in which our present acts have meaning and if we are to learn from the knowledge others have gained.[5] For example, any teacher who wants to develop an "integrated" or "related arts" program could find in our professional literature a number of excellent models for selective adaptation.[6] Historical inquiry is basic research, and it can be of very practical use to teachers. But it is not a well-cultivated form of research in art education and not as well represented in the training of art teachers as it should be.

The contributions of philosophical and conceptual research to teaching practice are usually underestimated. Philosophical and conceptual research is so gradually assimilated into our thought that we are not even aware of the original sources of it. For example, the concept of creativity is taken for granted today as something we value. We have learned to define creativity in terms of fluency, flexibility, and originality. We forget that these ideas rest on basic research into the nature of intelligence—philosophical, conceptual, and empirical—spanning at least three decades.[7] Or consider the so-called elements and principles of design that many teachers try to introduce to youngsters. This way of thinking about design reflects a philosophy of art and concepts first articulated many years ago (1899) by Arthur Wesley Dow.[8] Dow, in fact, also served, early in this century, as professor of "aesthetic education" at Teachers College, Columbia University, while John Dewey was on the faculty. The concept of aesthetic education, like many others that have become familiar, has been forged over a period of time.

Basic research—philosophical, conceptual, and empirical—does produce knowledge of use to art educators and often in more direct and lasting ways than we may assume. Furthermore, this kind of basic research is the source of concepts and theories which are needed for the development of coherent observational or empirical research. Observational research describes events we can see and interprets what these events mean in relation to some theory or system of values.

In comparison to other areas of education, observational research in art education[9] is not abundant. Much of it has been aimed at description, more than explanation. Observational research may be based on a quantitative or a qualitative description of phenomena.[10] Both approaches to description share the common goal of explaining human experience and events. The content of most of our research, regardless of type, is the art activity of children.

The Content of Research

The extent of the interest in making art among art educators is apparent from the fact that the largest single body of theory and research in art education deals with the artistic process; that is, the psychology of making or creating art. Within this literature, the process of creating art is typically viewed as an individual effort marked by innovation, by freedom in expression of the "self," and by facility with a particular medium. These descriptions of artistic activity, as we have seen, are most applicable to the studio arts, especially those like drawing and painting which permit direct expression even by the very young.

In addition, drawing and painting are sometimes regarded as the most basic visual arts, and they are convenient sources of data for the researcher. It is physically more convenient to collect and study pictures than three-dimensional objects. For these and many other reasons, art educators have generated more theory and research about drawing and painting than other art forms. Our numerous studies of pictorial work, especially that of children, are not matched by a comparable body of theory and research on the dimensional arts of sculpture or the crafts,[11] or the development of artistic activity in adolescents and those who choose art as a career.

This body of research on child art has been influenced, of course, by the particular philosophical and theoretical orientation of the researcher. Because most of this research draws upon the discipline of psychology for theory, different schools of thought within psychology have left their mark on studies of child art. For example, art educators who favor psychodynamic theories as a basis for their research tend to look at the emotional content and symbolic meanings in the subjects children draw or paint.[12] When a cognitive or Gestalt theory is selected, researchers are more likely to study the design of children's drawings, whole-part relationships, and how complete the compositional arrangement appears to be.[13] Researchers who prefer behaviorist theories are more likely to attend to the cultural content of child art, the child's use of immediate perceptual cues, and the impact of art instruction on children's work.[14]

As we have seen, the general public, as well as some professionals, has reservations about whether children, especially young children, really need to have instruction in art from adults. It is not surprising, then, that our research literature is dominated by a "developmental," rather than "instructional" view of art education. Studies that demonstrate the effect of art instruction on artistic growth are less numerous than reports on typical stages of artistic development. In most developmental studies, the actual or potential effect of instruction is not well explained because the researcher is more interested in patterns of maturation—patterns of understanding, enjoyment, or skill in art—that are not the result of formal instruction.[15]

In all of our research and teaching literature, the public arts—architecture, environmental design, graphic and product design, photography, television, and film—are infrequently treated as examples of the artistic process. These art forms call for conscious choice and collaborative effort, and have built-in constraints which do not fit the concept of art that has dominated the field of art education. Although we express an interest in making art relevant to everyday life, we have little if any research that examines the concepts of art that children acquire at home or how the child may select and arrange ready-made, mass-produced forms.

Research on perception, response, and critical judgment is not plentiful. Much of the research we do have is firmly rooted in a formalistic aesthetic theory which, until recently, has dominated critical discussions of art in our century.[16] In keeping with this formalistic view, a child's response to the design or composition of a work is of particular interest. In some studies, a child's response to qualities of line, color, shape, form, and movement are considered more appropriate and "sophisticated" than the child's references to mood, feeling, imagery, technique, subject matter, or contextual observations about the work or artist. And while many researchers rely on slides and reproductions of art to study children's patterns of response, the researcher usually wants to make inferences that would apply to original works of art, if not all works of art. Here, too, the typical referents for "art" are the fine arts, especially two-dimensional forms. Because we so readily conceive of works of art as isolated, flat objects with qualities presented on a surface level, we know little about the impact of original works of art on children or how their responses are influenced by the physical, psychological, or social context in which they encounter visual forms.

Although we have many studies that report on children's preferences among works of art,[17] we still know very little about the way
preferences are shaped by the family, peer groups, or even by direct
instruction in school. We have not investigated whether children see
any connection between their own work, the art in museums and
galleries, and the many images they see in their daily lives. We know
little about the reasons why children and adults acquire, modify,
maintain, destroy, or ignore particular images and forms in their daily
lives. There is no shortage of research topics in art education.

The Scope of Research

In the same way that the content of research in art education has been
shaped by our values, so too have certain aspects of the educational
context been studied to a greater degree than others. Research has
been child-centered, focused on students—especially young children—far more than it has been directed toward the study of teachers,
or the curriculum, or the setting in which art education occurs. Why
have these other dimensions not been given as much attention?

The scarcity of research on teachers and the teaching of art may be
due, in part, to the active and visible role we give to the child, as
creator, and the supportive background role we seem to prefer for the
art teacher. Our research offers little insight into the way the art
teacher's beliefs and preferences may influence what students study,
or the character of interactions in the classroom, or what students
learn. Research on the teacher's own artistic and educational philosophy is of special importance in the visual arts precisely because the art
teacher is relatively free to invent the art curriculum—to determine the
objectives, content, and activities made available to children.

Accurate descriptions of art programs are rare. The curriculum
offered in schools has not been well researched. Surely the quality and
the character of art education hinges, in part, on the pacing of art
activities through a year or span of years, the variety and kind of
experiences made available to students, the options for student choice
presented, the degree and kind of emphasis on particular concepts,
skills, and values.[18] If we want to know the long-term effect of these
and related factors, sustained research on stable groups—longitudinal
research—is essential.

The study of educational settings and the conditions under which
the art teacher works are neglected in research. In addition to a need
for basic "census" data on art teachers—our national distribution, our

experience, and so on—we need more comprehensive information on factors such as community and administrative perceptions of art in schools, scheduling practices, class loads, and available resources. Census information should be complemented by studies that describe, compare, and contrast programs in ways that fully reflect the experiences of teachers and youngsters in different settings.[19]

Studies such as these are essential if we wish to understand relationships between children's access to art instruction, the quality of art education available, and its educational significance. In offering this brief analysis, I have not, of course, encompassed all research in our field, but I have tried to demonstrate that research, practice, and even the analysis of research are influenced by the value orientations and concepts we bring to our work.[20]

Obviously, the forces that shape our theory, research, and practice are not limited to those internal to the profession. The space race in the sixties, for example, produced great interest in art as both a means of nurturing scientific creativity and as an intellectual discipline. These developments, in turn, renewed the art educator's interest in cognitive psychology and in studies based on the work of Jean Piaget, the developmental psychologist who has traced the development of logical thought in children. Cultural pluralism and educational equity are acknowledged concerns today, and are both direct outgrowths of the civil rights movement. The issues raised by the civil rights movement, in turn, have given impetus in art education to ethnographic research (the study of cultural groups) and to policy studies (the study of decision making) as means of understanding educational processes at microscopic and macroscopic levels.[21]

And in the last decade, a back-to-basics, utilitarian concept of education has assumed a position of prominence. It is no mere coincidence, I think, that in this period of economic stress and general disenchantment with the performance of schools, research of "immediate and practical utility" is being called for. Let us examine this question, for there is a great deal of misunderstanding about what research can and cannot help us to do.

Does Research Matter?

All of us know that teachers bring a wisdom to their day-to-day work that is quite different from the kind of knowledge published in dissertations and scholarly journals. This difference is often cited to condemn the "gap" between research and practice. Some people think research should be more relevant to the "real" problems of teachers, thereby bringing about educational reform where it counts—in the classroom.

Concern about the so-called gap between research and practice is not new, but in the last decade it has been voiced with an urgency and tone of irritation that seems to call for sweeping reforms in the character of educational research. Consumers of educational research, like taxpayers in revolt, want their money's worth from research; they want the research "product" to have utility.[22] This demand for useful research can be seen as part of that same mind-set which supports the back-to-basics movement, and questions the value of any educational activity that does not produce an immediate payoff in the achievement of youngsters or improvement of schools.

What this attitude seems to require from those who conduct educational research is not merely a practical justification of their efforts, but a fundamental realignment of the form, content, and intent of scholarly inquiry to make it of immediate use to particular educational clients—teachers, administrators, parents, policymakers, and, most important, children and young people in public schools. Research is thus seen as a service operation valuable only when it 1) addresses those questions that clients want answered, and 2) offers answers that clients will find useful.

Since the early 1970s, most demands for applied research have been based on a comparison of education with business, where research may improve the efficiency of an organization and thus increase its output and profitability. By analogy, techniques for improving the efficiency of teaching and of learning are wanted. It is assumed that what is to be learned, and why it might be worthwhile, is not an issue; only the how of teaching is to be addressed.[23] Educational research is thus seen as a tool for streamlining methods of instruction, thereby producing more learning at less cost and effort. This general focus in research is highly valued today because it holds the promise of demonstrating to a skeptical public that schools are doing their job effectively, efficiently (in terms of time, cost, and so forth), and conscientiously (through research).

This emerging conception of the role of research as a service to educational practice is naive in several ways: It assumes that research tells us what we ought to do; it assumes that applied research can be conducted independently of basic research; and it assumes that persons employed in education are merely technicians who are hired to produce, in high volume, at low cost, a commodity called learning.

First, research does not, in any simple sense, tell us what we ought to do. The theories and the facts that we may produce through research do not speak for themselves. As I have tried to show in this chapter—indeed throughout this book—facts are sought out and interpreted within a theoretical or philosophical context, some framework of interest and value. Facts are useful in making decisions only as they are interpreted and judged within some system of values. Thus, facts become useful only when the decision-makers are committed to a system of values and to the reasoned use of facts as major ingredients in the decision-making process. There is abundant evidence that policy decisions about education can be, and are, made "in spite of the facts."

Second, utility is not a simple concept, and the risk in taking a narrow view of useful research is the wholesale neglect of basic research. Basic research is essential for nontrivial applied research. Basic research also has a more direct bearing on educational practice than we think.

Basic research is often characterized as the pursuit of knowledge for its own sake, without regard to its immediate application to specific problems or situations. Basic research is easily dismissed as useless by those who assume that research should give to teachers a product or procedure guaranteed to overcome a particular educational problem. For example, how to teach reading, or mathematics, or art, or how to improve discipline). But should we think of the teacher as little more than a technician who is employed to use specific products or procedures?

If art education is merely a technical field, it can be entered by anyone who is capable of being trained in teaching techniques to handle specific tasks. A technician does not need to understand why the particular product or course of action works, or why the results are worthwhile, only that the technical procedure has been proven effective if it is properly employed. But if art education is also an intellectual and a professional field, far more is required of its participants than the ability to use specific teaching techniques that have been proven useful in obtaining results. Instead, a broad understanding of art and art education is required.

Just as the study of science and medical practice is vital to the physician, the study of art and art education is essential to the teacher of art. Research in art education should have a direct bearing on teaching practice, in the same way that research in medicine guides the practice of medicine. For example, medical practice has been refined through basic research into the structure of cells and other aspects of human physiology, while applied research has produced reliable knowledge about the success of different treatments.

Physicians are more confident in administering a particular medical treatment, and justifying it, if there is evidence to support its use. So, too, should teachers of art be able to justify and offer supporting evidence to show that their actions are not merely personal whims or preferences, but are based on a substantial body of facts, theory, and analysis. Spontaneity in teaching is not automatically ruled out by this view of teaching, especially if we have evidence that a teacher's spontaneity has a positive effect on student learning.

Those who express dismay at the apparent gap between research and educational practice seem to want a more rapid demonstration of results than is typically found even in the physical sciences and technology. This expectation for immediate solutions is reinforced by our cultural experience in this century. In our own lifetimes, we have seen dramatic scientific breakthroughs, such as the invention of polio vaccine and of open-heart surgery. We have witnessed spectacular demonstrations of our technological prowess—the program of space exploration and the development of satellite communication. It is easy for us to think that research in the social sciences and education can produce equally dramatic results.

What we fail to appreciate is that the application of knowledge to practical problems or goals rarely occurs in a straightforward manner or instantly, even in the realm of the physical and biological sciences. For example, more than fifty years elapsed between early studies of fluorescence, totally separate research on patterns of electrical discharge in tubes, and the use of this knowledge to make fluorescent lighting.[24] Behind many of the dramatic changes in our lifetime is a body of theory and research that has been built up over years—about seventy years, in the case of space exploration. Yet most of the observational research in art education has been developed since 1950. It is not yet well organized in relation to philosophical and theoretical premises. Observational studies in art education are seldom replicated to help establish the reliability or validity of the findings.[25]

Perhaps our cultural fascination with dramatic events and instant success (along with instant coffee, instant replays, and instant news analysis) makes it difficult for us to value those human activities which, like research and education, are slow and evolutionary in character, centered on form and substance, yielding undramatic, inconstant, but discernable increments of change over time. When we have acquired an appreciation of these characteristics of both the research process and the educational process, we are less likely to expect overnight miracles from them.

In summary, scholarly activity in art education parallels the major value orientations that are implicit in the education and teaching practice of art teachers. Theory and research influence teaching in more subtle and long-lasting ways than is commonly supposed, but it is also true that many broad areas of concern within art education have been neglected by the community of scholars. Research should be construed as a process of vital importance to the profession as a whole and to individual teachers who seek trustworthy knowledge as the basis for their work.

Knowledge from research can be used in many ways—to justify budget requests, to add prestige and legitimacy to the claims one makes, and to bury unfavorable information while claiming that an impartial study has been made. But to conceive of inquiry in narrow utilitarian terms, to conduct it with the intention of proving a point, and to interpret the results so that they are self-serving—all under the cover of truth-seeking—is to corrupt the research process.[26] Research is a process of being honest with ourselves and others. That is what makes it so challenging, demanding, and necessary, both to the conduct of our work and to the perception that others have of the work we do.

Valid, reliable, and organized knowledge about teaching and learning in art is certainly needed, but it does not come with a built-in guarantee that it will be used to inform practice. Nor will it always be useful in solving every professional problem that we face, for many decisions about education are conditioned by social codes, by shifting priorities, and, increasingly, by political and economic considerations far removed from the immediate interests of researchers and teachers. In the next two chapters, we will examine some of the directions for art education which have been mapped by this kind of process—a process that is known as the politicizing of art education.[27]

9 | *Arts Education as a Political Issue: The Federal Legacy*

IN THE PRECEDING CHAPTERS, we have examined some of the attitudes and practices which have contributed to the neglect of arts education. In this chapter and the next, we will examine some of the recommendations for arts education which have their origin in federal programs in the arts.

When Congress established the National Endowment for the Arts in 1965, there was no nationally organized arts constituency. This is no longer the case. Indeed, what has emerged from more than fifteen years of federal activity in the arts is a new arts bureaucracy, consisting of state and local arts councils, and various groups established for the purpose of influencing public policies bearing on the arts. What kind of arts education has been endorsed and promoted by the new arts establishment? In federal policies and programs, in the recommendations for arts education issued by blue-ribbon panels, and in the promotional activities of various arts advocates we find elements of a national policy aimed at "de-schooling" arts education.

The Emergent National Policy for Arts Education

Recommendations for the de-schooling of arts education have emerged in piecemeal fashion over a period of time. This policy position, articulated in full form during the late 1970s, reflects how the new arts establishment—those who have political and economic power in the art world—envision arts education for American youth. Equally, the recommendations bear the imprint of decisions made within federal agencies having some responsibility for arts education, particularly (but not exclusively) the National Endowment for the Arts.

Before tracing the origin and the implications of this viewpoint, let me outline the major themes which define it. The main ingredients of the policy position are as follows:

□ Arts education means education in all the arts, not only music and the visual arts, but also dance, theater, and creative writing.

□ Education in the arts means making art—performing as a musician, dancer, actor, sculptor, and so on. Arts education also means being exposed to the making of art—seeing actors, painters, musicians and so on do their work firsthand. Of far less importance is studying art from an historical or cultural perspective, acquiring an understanding of artistic traditions, or gaining an intellectual understanding of art.

□ Arts education, thus conceived, should be de-schooled to a substantial degree. In other words it should be delegated to artists and to arts or social service agencies within the community. In addition, schools should be free to employ artists and other non-certified personnel to deliver arts services to children and youth within the schools.

□ Citizens should approach the problem of improving arts education as they would approach any other civic effort that involves 1) fund raising for special projects or 2) fund raising to provide community services for a special population. In effect, arts education is a special social service which citizens need not expect their schools to provide. Programs might be planned and implemented through arts councils or independent committees. The school is merely one of many agencies through which arts education might be delivered.

□ Just as arts services might be delivered through agencies other than the school, and persons other than certified teachers, so too might the instructional program within the school be financed by sources other than the regular school budget. Funds for arts education might come from corporate and private foundations, labor unions, fund-raising campaigns, as well as creative use of federal or state funds earmarked for special programs (arts for the handicapped, arts for the talented).

□ Given that much instruction could occur outside of school, the residual program of in-school arts instruction should be redesigned so that the arts are interrelated (as the sciences and social studies are said to be). In addition, the arts should be used as tools for learning other subjects, especially reading and mathematics, and integrated into the regular curriculum. Another important function of the in-school program is to make the school more interesting to children, thus reducing truancy and vandalism, and improving the general conduct of children.

□ Present and future arts teachers should be trained as "arts generalists" and have administrative skills. The arts generalist would be employed to 1) manage the arts services offered by individual artists and community agencies, and 2) monitor or teach the residual in-school program.

While the arts establishment might well have used its growing influence to urge the reform of in-school programs, it has, I believe, put a stamp of approval on the very ideas which have served to weaken arts education. And in emphasizing the cost of employing artists and "delivering" arts education to youth, the arts establishment has fostered an attitude that may persuade citizens and school administrators to judge that instruction in the arts is an expensive frill, beyond the expections we should have for school.

How have these recommendations surfaced as the key features of a national policy? In order to answer this question, we must understand something about the channels through which the recommendations have been forged and promoted, and some of the reasoning behind them. Most of them are the legacy of an arts-in-education movement spanning about fifteen years and encompassing a variety of interconnected programs, many of them federally supported. The concepts behind this movement have been widely disseminated and have been incorporated into the operations of advocacy groups and agencies whose work in arts education is not dependent upon federal funds.

Grand Visions of Curriculum Reform

The U.S. Office of Education Seminars

The stage for the arts-in-education movement was set in the mid-1960s through a series of seminars, as well as a short-term research program, conducted under the auspices of the Arts and Humanities Branch of the U.S. Office of Education and directed by Kathryn Bloom from 1963 to 1968.[1]

These Office of Education conferences stimulated discussions which set three major precedents. The first was the opportunity for art and music educators to think about the reform of school curricula on a fairly grand scale. Major centers for research and curriculum development were just being established with federal funds, and there was hope that one or more of these centers might address art and music. A second precedent was the direction of thinking taken by many professionals in education at that time. Following the example of the new mathematics and science curriculum projects, arts educators called upon artists and scholars in the arts to identify the "key concepts" and "methods of inquiry" they employed in their work. Their insights were to be used as source material for designing arts curricula that would be up to date and authoritative.

The Office of Education seminars also renewed interest in the idea that artists, in particular, might be brought directly into classrooms to demonstrate their methods of inquiry, strengthening the performance-based, studio curriculum in most schools, and protecting the arts from becoming a "packaged" curriculum.[2] Although it was clearly impractical to employ artists to reach over thirty million school-aged young people, these discussions foreshadowed and gave credibility to a later program known as Artists-in-Schools, sponsored by the National Endowment for the Arts, and initially supported by the U.S. Office of Education as well.

A third precedent was established through these exploratory seminars. Arts and music educators were informed that any major curriculum projects undertaken with federal funds must include all of the arts, in order to avoid the potential problem of favoring one art form over another. A report from one of the first seminars, held at the Pennsylvania State University in 1965, foreshadowed the requirements that would soon be placed on almost all federal programs for education in the arts.

Harlan Hoffa, then on the Arts and Humanities staff of the U.S. Office of Education, articulated the problem for visual arts educators:

> It is unlikely that an R & D [research and development] center would be established for [visual] art education alone. However, I think it is perfectly conceivable that a center could be structured around the concept of arts education . . . including the visual, performing, and literary arts, or around perceptual education, or around *aesthetic education* or any other related construct. . . . It could encompass . . . *interdisciplinary* activity between all of the various arts [italics mine].[3]

In response to these conditions, music educators and visual arts educators who were interested in fairly ambitious research and curriculum projects had the choice of bringing along "all of the arts" or receiving no federal funds. This early federal position left an imprint on later programs and helps to explain, in part, why arts educators were urged to reexamine various methods of relating the arts, integrating and correlating the arts to other subjects, and setting up interdisciplinary programs. This "all the arts" requirement also seemed to provide a means of strengthening instruction in dance and theater, which few schools offered.

The CEMREL Aesthetic Education Program

Beginning in 1967, the federal interest in arts education was channeled almost exclusively into a single curriculum development effort, the Aesthetic Education Program, located at one of the new regional educational laboratories established by the U.S. Office of Education, CEMREL, the Central Midwestern Regional Educational Laboratory in St. Louis. As coauthor of the planning proposal for the Aesthetic Education Program in 1967, I can attest to the fact that some of us objected to the scholarly and somewhat, alien title for the program, yet all who were initially involved in this venture thought it wise to take advantage of the opportunity for a major curriculum development effort, comparable to earlier mathematics and science projects.[4] Not until the early 1970s did it become apparent that the "new" mathematics and science curricula were far from perfect, and that the cost of an arts version of those curricula would be dear—not just in dollars for the production of instructional materials in the arts, but in the effect of those allocations on other federal activity in arts education.

The CEMREL Aesthetic Education Program was intended to address both the creative and appreciative dimensions of music, dance, theater, literature, and the visual arts. The curriculum, designed for use in grades one through six, would be presented through sets of instructional materials which had been thoroughly tried out in schools, then published and marketed. A teacher education program was also planned.

The Aesthetic Education Program was bound to be either a spectacular success or a gigantic failure. The federal gamble was that one well-supported program could deliver the goods. Although some federal support was given to two other centers for arts curriculum development, the CEMREL program was by far the most ambitious.

Questions about the effectiveness of the Aesthetic Education Program can best be answered by examining its status since it was officially terminated in 1978, ten years, and about twelve million dollars, after it began. Of the forty-four sets of instructional materials developed to the stage of publication, only twelve had been published by 1982.[5] Publishers had little interest in the project, primarily because the entire curriculum was costly and difficult to market to administrators whose primary concerns seemed to be the three R's and for whom the phrase "aesthetic education" had no meaning or an elitist connotation. In the absence of a complete and marketable set of curriculum materials, the supporting teacher education program was also severely handicapped.

One can hardly judge that the initial aims of the Aesthetic Education Program were achieved, but through related activities the CEMREL program had an indirect influence on arts education well beyond its major mission. In addition to a host of scholarly documents produced for the project,[6] the CEMREL materials developed for classrooms (though limited in number) became an ingredient in a number of pilot programs which were sponsored by other agencies. CEMREL also conducted the first tryout and evaluation of the program later known as Artists-in-Schools.[7]

A Mixed Bag of Other Federal Programs

During the years that the CEMREL Aesthetic Education Program was in full swing, its financial requirements preempted almost all other federal support directed exclusively to arts education. Other projects in arts education were financed, but through federal programs within the U.S. Office of Education that were not officially designated for the arts. Thus, the arts were tied to programs to forward school desegregation, to enhance reading performance, or to reach specific groups such as the talented, the handicapped, or ethnic groups.[8] The opportunity for the arts and humanities staff in the U.S. Office of Education to actively shape a more coherent program of research, teacher education, and curriculum development was also greatly reduced by several staff cutbacks and various reorganizations of the Office.

The mixed bag of projects supported by the Office of Education helps to explain, in part, why discussions of arts education have been shaped in a way that emphasizes the arts as means to promote better racial and ethnic understanding, as means to reduce truancy and dropping out of school, and as means to improve the reading or cognitive skills of children. Arts education was featured in a number of pilot programs having these missions, and became instrumental to achieving them. What children were learning about the arts was not the point of these programs and was not evaluated as systematically as other outcomes.[9]

So fragmented were federal programs bearing on arts education that in 1976 an effort was made to identify the scope of all arts education activity supported with federal funds and to develop a coherent federal policy for the future.[10] If it had not been obvious before, it became clear at that time that the interests of the National Endowment for the Arts had begun to dominate discussions of arts education, and would continue to do so. Since the Office of Education was handicapped in addressing critical needs—for improved in-service education for teachers, systematic evaluation of school programs, and other approaches to curriculum development and research—the Arts Endowment offered its own solutions to at least some of these problems, all of them keyed to the Artists-in-Schools Program.

Grand Visions of Artists in Schools

Although the National Endowment for the Arts (NEA)* might seem to be the logical agency to strengthen arts education in schools, the primary missions of the NEA were to expand employment opportunities for artists and to make the arts more accessible to all regions and sections of the American population.

Early in the history of the Arts Endowment, a policy was established that the NEA would not support projects that "actively and purposefully teach."[11] This policy seemed to be based on two major considerations. First, the original legislation which established the Endowment for the Arts and the Endowment for the Humanities made a distinction between the *practice* of the arts and the *study* of the humanities. Thus, the Arts Endowment was slated to emphasize the making or performing of art, not the study of art. The study of art, especially art history, was to be supported by the Humanities Endowment. To complicate matters, the Office of Education was responsible for programs addressed to elementary and secondary schools and teacher education. Nobody was clearly in charge of a school program that might include the study of art through studio practice as well as art

---

*I have used the terms Arts Endowment, National Endowment for the Arts, and NEA interchangeably.

history. By virtue of its title, the Arts Endowment seemed to have responsibility for all proposals dealing with the arts, including arts education in schools.

The Artists-in-Schools Program

These territorial problems among federal agencies contributed to the formation of a national direction for arts education in which the interests of the Arts Endowment and its constituency were well represented. Within the Office of Education, and in the Humanities Endowment, arts education was only one of many topics to be addressed. Increasingly pressed to answer questions on arts education, the Arts Endowment responded to most questions by placing an emphasis on amateur or professional training in the practice of art, as well as exposure to the arts through concerts, exhibitions, and so on. There was much less emphasis on formal programs to build an appreciation of the arts through the study of art history.

Through a pilot Artists-in-Schools program in 1969, the NEA discovered that artists could be employed in schools if several conditions were met.[12] The artists could not be identified as teachers, since that would cause problems with teacher certification standards. The school placement had to be attractive to artists—allow them time to work at their art, offer them a studio with decent equipment, and provide a better salary than they might receive with other part-time work. But this was a costly arrangement, and the program could not be advertised as "educational." In effect, schools were to become patrons of the arts. The Artists-in-Schools Program (renamed, in 1980, the "Artists in Education Program") became the showcase through which the Arts Endowment and arts councils could demonstrate an interest in arts education, employ artists, and win political points by demonstrating that children were being exposed to the arts.

The growth in state appropriations for arts councils has provided a channel for each state to fund variations on the Artists-in-Schools Program. Even if federal funding were withdrawn, state and local arts councils are likely to pursue the employment of artists in schools, and perhaps more vigorously, for the services offered to children are useful in generating public support for all of the operations of an arts council. Moreover, because school funds can be diverted to arts councils for the services they deliver to youth, schools can assist arts councils in financing the employment of artists. For example, a study of financial support for the Charlotte Symphony Orchestra (North Carolina) suggests that school programs accounted for "most of the increase in the orchestra's total budget from $101,000 in 1970–71 to $428,000 in 1974–75," primarily from local government support and funds from the county school board.[13]

Although the NEA did not officially call the Artists-in-Schools Program "educational," it sought to demonstrate that the program had educational value. Under pressure from arts educators who questioned the program, the Arts Endowment commissioned a study of it. However, the agency selected to do the study was heavily dependent on funding from the Arts Endowment for other aspects of its operation, and the report that it produced buried all negative results. Indeed, the final report was issued as a *publicity* package for the Artists-in-Schools Program (complete with a poster). The failure of the NEA to secure an impartial evaluation of this program was regrettable, to say the least.[14]

In spite of a number of criticisms of the program—including charges of a lack of solid documentation of the duration and amount of time artists spent with students, or of the cost of such contacts in each of the arts, or of the measured educational benefits—the Artists-in-Schools budget grew from $145,000 in 1969 to a projected $5.9 million for 1982, making it the largest federal arts program for school-aged youth.[15] In the meantime, regular school arts program and supervisory staff in the arts were being eliminated in many of the nation's schools. About this trend the NEA had little constructive to say. The general concept of employing artists in schools was to become a central theme in other reforms promoted by the Arts Endowment and to a lesser extent by the U.S. Office of Education.

Through the Arts Endowment and its various lobbies, the idea of placing artists in schools was elaborated into recommendations that artists not only be employed in schools, but also be engaged in curriculum design, teacher education, and other dimensions of policymaking for schools. In the movement to de-school arts education, one also finds suggestions that the arts education offered to youth might be planned and implemented by arts councils or other "independent" agencies. By the mid-1970s, almost all of these ideas had been charted through pilot programs and promoted through a number of channels.

The JDR 3rd Fund Arts in Education Program

One of the most important of these channels, particularly in regard to pilot or demonstration projects, was the Arts in Education Program of the JDR 3rd Fund, directed by Kathryn Bloom from 1968 to 1979.

Among the guiding premises of this private foundation program were 1) that all of the arts would be considered in the projects it would undertake; 2) that artists and community agencies would be considered as "major resources for teaching and learning about the arts"; and 3) that the arts should contribute to the general education of children—be infused into the total curriculum of schools.[16]

During the eleven-year history of the Arts in Education Program of the JDR 3rd Fund, approximately five hundred thousand dollars per year was invested in pilot projects, (about three million dollars in all). Because the program emphasized the use of artists and community agencies as "resources" for teaching, many of the Arts in Education projects served as the testing ground for the artists-in-schools concept, as well as the involvement of community arts councils in arts education planning. In the initial years of the Arts in Education Program, the focus was on pilot projects at the scale of a single school or small school district, and, in many cases, involved the use of the CEMREL curriculum materials. The resources of the JDR 3rd Fund were a stimulus for the school district to enhance its arts program and become better prepared to carry arts education forward after these special funds were withdrawn (usually after two to three years).

This early work of the Fund provided "case" material about the procedures for designing programs based on a school-community "partnership"—the hallmark of the JDR 3rd Fund projects. Following the pilot work in schools, grants were made to stimulate change in large school districts, as well as state departments of education and arts councils. Among the final activities of the Arts in Education Program were the development of two national networks to initiate change, and a strategy to place arts education on the agenda for discussion as a national policy issue.[17]

The first advocacy network directed its efforts toward state departments of education. The campaign strategy reflected its political intent and the experience of the Fund's work with the Pennsylvania State Department of Education.[18] Representatives from arts councils, professional associations of arts educators, and other civic and business groups were called together in each state to form an informal lobby and develop a plan for arts education within the state, based on an analysis of needs and resources. This process was carried out under the auspices of the Alliance for Arts Education (AAE), a program jointly sponsored by the U.S. Department of Education and the John F. Kennedy Center for the Performing Arts.

The general strategy, developed in consultation with the JDR 3rd

Fund staff,[19] called for each state AAE committee to develop a "comprehensive statewide plan for arts education." The AAE committee was to urge the state department of education to 1) identify the arts as eligible for support within programs earmarked for minorities, the talented, handicapped, and others, and 2) encourage schools to use community resources for arts education. States that participated in this comprehensive planning process became eligible to compete for grants to support demonstration programs in schools. The criteria for the pilot projects were similar to those for the statewide planning process. Representatives from local arts agencies, parents, and civic and business leaders were to be involved in designing the arts education program and implementing it. The model for change, in short, was essentially the same as that which had been employed in the JDR 3rd Fund Projects: a school-community partnership.[20]

A second network established by the JDR 3rd Fund's staff was the League of Cities for the Arts in Education. The main advocacy channels for this program were the American Council of the Arts and the Association of Junior Leagues. The mission of this network was to urge civic groups or arts councils to initiate a comprehensive plan for arts education within their communities.

The suggested model for change called for the arts council or civic group, in consultation with school officials, to establish a comprehensive plan, identify resources for schools, and set up a coordinating "hub"—administrative center—for the delivery of arts services to school-aged youth. In addition to coordinating the use of arts resources in schools, the hub was intended to serve as a fund-raising agency for special projects. In the initial years of its operation, the hub might be supported by a mixture of funds from civic and business groups, the arts council, foundations, and special grants from participating school districts. However, since the community agencies were to provide services in response to requests from schools, responsibility for most or all of the budget eventually would be assumed by schools.

Within this scheme, the initiative for planning arts education programs rests with the community, and so does the administration of the budget. Schools are urged to plan programs around available services—performances by members of the local symphony or opera company, dance groups, or exhibitions and demonstrations by local artists, poetry or storytelling sessions, puppet shows, and the like. Ultimately, these services are intended to become an integral part of the arts curriculum, so "infused" into the school program that the district would be expected to pay for those services.[21]

The Blue-Ribbon Treatment for Arts Education

Overlapping these two networking activities, and bringing the philosophy behind them into a position of national prominence, are the reports of several blue-ribbon panels. In the tradition of influencing national policy through the establishment of blue-ribbon panels to study issues and make recommendations to Congress or federal agencies, several panels were established to address arts education during the 1970s.

Without question, the most influential of these panels was the Arts, Education and Americans Panel, chaired by David Rockefeller, Jr., and including such distinguished citizens as author James Michener; Nobel physicist Glenn Seaborg; former CBS president Frank Stanton; and Francis Keppel, former U.S. Commissioner of Education, among others. The two-year effort of the panel was supported by a consortium of private foundations, as well as by the National Endowment for the Arts and the U.S. Office of Education. The project was initiated in 1974 at the suggestion of Nancy Hanks, then chairperson for the NEA, and Kathryn Bloom, among others.

The panel report, entitled *Coming to Our Senses: The Significance of the Arts for American Education,* offered ninety-eight recommendations for arts education, in a form and manner clearly intended to shape national policies.[22] The recommendations reflected the interests of the NEA, state and local arts councils, and, most important, the constituencies that these agencies represent—namely, artists and patrons of the arts.

The report calls for increased involvement of artists and arts councils in the education of children. Education is to be tied to "making art" and "exposure to art." Within the report, many of the case studies and reasons for teaching art which were promulgated during the first decade of the arts-in-education movement are reiterated. The arts are portrayed as tools for learning, and as a means of reducing truancy, improving reading, and pursuing similar goals. The report recommends that schools be free to employ noncertified personnel— artists—to work in schools. Although the report might seem to represent the views of arts educators, especially in its emphasis on making art, it was issued and presented to members of Congress without benefit of prior review by representatives from the four professional associations representing educators in music, the visual arts, dance, and theater, which have about two hundred thousand members in all.[23]

In order to sustain the momentum created by all of these activities and to implement the recommendations in *Coming to Our Senses,* a follow-up advocacy group called The Arts, Education, and Americans, Inc. was formed by David Rockefeller, Jr. In October 1979, this group established The National Advocacy Program for Arts-in-Education. Still in operation today, the program sponsors conferences, offers a speakers bureau, has initiated a national publicity campaign through the print and broadcast media, provides consultation service, and operates a publications program. In 1980 and 1981, a series of monographs addressed to "support groups" for arts education was issued. Four of the first ten monographs are addressed to planning and financing arts education for schools through techniques commonly used in fund raising for united appeal campaigns or other civic projects.[24] The monographs describe a planning and a budgeting process for arts education that would permit schools, if they wished, to do little more than serve as advisors to the program, publicly endorse it, and assist in fund raising, but otherwise leave the administration of arts education to an independent agency. That agency, most likely an arts council, would have the power to hire (and fire) persons who worked in or through the schools to deliver arts services to youth.[25]

A variation on the theme of de-schooling arts education was offered by a blue-ribbon panel of school administrators appointed by the U.S. Commissioner of Education in 1972 to study and develop recommendations on high school and adolescent education. The final report of this panel, published in 1976, recommends that education in the arts be provided to adolescents through new "Participatory Education" programs to be offered by "community arts centers closely associated with the high school." The panel suggests that such centers would be governed by "a community council for the arts [and] would provide facilities and support for all the arts and crafts for which sustaining interest was forthcoming." Opportunities would be provided for "joint participation of adolescents and other interested and qualified adults in the community . . . to learn by doing." The panel envisions such centers as operating day and night with amateurs, volunteers, paid staff, and professionals competing for program space, and of course, for clients.[26]

The panel on adolescent education apparently had no reservations about the quality of education that might be received in a community arts recreation center where the popularity of a class would be criterion for offering it, nor did this panel envision art as much more than a hobby. If these recommendations were taken seriously, art instruction in secondary schools might well be disbanded altogether, and school-aged youths would be free to determine what art activities they might wish to pursue. All of this adds up to another expression of the belief held within the educational establishment that making art is a re-creational activity, and little more.

Similar themes are found in the report of a task force appointed by the National Endowment for the Arts to make recommendations on the "Education, Training, and Development of Professional Artists and Arts Educators." Throughout the task force report issued in December 1978, one is struck again by the emphasis placed on the training of talented students outside of schools or through special schools; the use of artists as teachers of children and of educators; and the retraining of arts specialists as arts generalists who can help to administer the services delivered by artists and community agencies, teach related arts or interdisciplinary programs, and demonstrate the use of art to enhance learning in other subjects. This task force claims not to have addressed the issue of an appropriate curriculum for elementary and secondary schools, but assumes that whatever the curriculum is, the artist will, by definition, assure a program of high quality.[27]

What is significant about these reports is the willingness of highly influential groups—outside of the profession of arts education—to assume that the school is not, in some fundamental sense, responsible for transmitting knowledge about art to young people, and the most logical agency for doing so. It is as if the professional arts community, with the consent of the educational establishment, has determined that arts education is analogous to athletics. Like the professional sports community, everyone seems to be satisfied with scouting future talent and building fans for the arts by employing living artists as "coaches" and "stars" for children to see and emulate. Just as physical education has been reduced in many schools to competitive sports activities and athletics, art education too is portrayed as if it were a form of spectacle—an arena for the display of talent, a spectator sport in which the scheduling and financing of arts events is a major problem.

I believe that the emphasis being placed on the living artist as the star performer—agent of reform in education and highest example of "knowing about art"—reflects, in part, our general fascination with stardom, action, and spectacle in American culture. But it also reflects the dominance of the performing arts in the formation of national policies on the arts and arts education.[28] Unlike most of the visual and literary arts, the performing arts usually occur through a collaborative effort. The performance and performer are inseparable. The artistry in a concert, dance, or play is fashioned at the moment of encounter, and if the encounter is "live", so much the better. In addition to this tradition of collaboration, many performing artists (about four hundred thousand) are represented by trade unions whose officers are both skilled and authorized to speak on behalf of their interests in the councils where decisions about policy are made.[29]

The visual and literary arts are usually created and appreciated under more solitary, private circumstances and are identified with the creation and sale of art products. Most people who are trained in the visual and literary arts pursue their art as individuals. In the development of careers in the visual arts, being unique, creative, and innovative has taken precedence over efforts based on shared concerns. There are no powerful trade unions or well-organized support groups for the artist who works alone.[30] These and other differences in the structure of political and economic power within the art world have helped to produce recommendations for school programs that favor the employment of artists as performers, whose art is to be created in the presence of a young audience. Apart from the exposure of children to living artists, one finds little concern for the kind or amount of arts education regularly offered in the school curriculum.

Public Policy for Arts Education: Some Basic Issues

Federal programs, the thrust of statements being issued by arts advocates, and many of the policy recommendations offered by various blue-ribbon panels reflect a profound distrust of the school as an agency for art education, a skepticism about formal education in art (except for the talented), a lack of esteem for programs that transmit knowledge about art except through firsthand encounters with living artists or making art, and a willingness to use the arts as a means to ends other than learning about art. A number of issues are presented by these and other recommendations from the arts establishment.

The first issue is justice. At present, access to instruction in schools is so restricted that most young people have little more than a brief exposure to art. Because the majority of them are denied sound and continuous instruction in schools, intellectual access to art is restricted to youngsters whose parents already value art and can afford to provide their children with special opportunities for the study and enjoyment of art. The balance of influence in the adult world of art is kept in place through this privilege of birth and the special advantage of one's parents' education.

The second issue is trustworthy knowledge and its transmission. We are quick to bemoan the lack of public understanding of art, but in our schools we treat art as if it had no content worthy of study in its own right, as if art had no history, no context of meaning beyond that which one can discover oneself through making art or through exposure to individuals whose knowledge of art is presumed to be trustworthy because they are called artists. The ethical question is whether we believe that the self-proclaimed truths of artists are an adequate basis for education. This issue is particularly important in the visual arts, where, in their desire to be regarded as innovative and creative, artists not only may endeavor to insulate themselves from historical and other "outside" influences, but advocate that students of art do the same.

In almost every subject, we express concern about the accuracy and scope of knowledge being transmitted, the purpose and efficiency of the education children are receiving. In the arts, however, either we allow classroom teachers who have little or no grasp of art to teach it or we act as if the personal enthusiasms of artists solved all problems of the quality of instruction—its appropriateness to children and their general education, its efficiency, and so on. If useful and reliable knowledge about art is thought to consist solely in the individual opinions, preferences, and personal discoveries of the teacher (or the artist), then we must be prepared to define art as something so idiosyncratic, so free of social, cultural, and historical influence that teaching it really is pointless. Reasonable people know otherwise.

A third and related issue is power. The idea that knowledge is power is taken for granted in teaching reading, writing, arithmetic, and the so-called basic subjects. In our schools, art is treated almost exclusively as a manipulative activity. The ethical question is whether, in fact, we are setting low expectations for children in our schools—letting children of the working class use their hands, but not really expecting them to be capable of much more. The current insistence that school programs focus on "hands-on" manipulative activities is an effective way to restrict opportunities for children to discover that art can be perceptually and intellectually challenging even if one has little interest or skill in creating art. It is an effective way to restrict the growth of childrens' appreciations—especially of art forms that do require study and a background of knowledge beyond that which children may acquire by making art. Thus, while seeming to provide an equal opportunity for all to "participate" in art, our schools expect little more than engagement with art as a manual task, a skill, or a craft. Equal opportunity is not provided for young people to be engaged with art in a manner that broadens their horizons.

The fourth issue is freedom of choice. One of the arguments for de-schooling arts education is that the schools should not have a monopoly on arts education. The premise is false. If anything, it is the absence of school programs that contributes to the virtual monopoly on the arts now exercised by a particular social class. The majority of our citizens depend on our schools to transmit knowledge that would not normally be provided in the home or community. And citizens rightly expect that knowledge acquired in school will open doors for youth, extending their sense of human potential and accomplishment and giving them an opportunity to make informed choices.

As we consider the increased use of public funds to support the arts, the issue of freedom of choice in the arts is no longer just a matter of interest in the personal development of children. It becomes a matter of public interest to ask who will benefit from such funds and who will have a voice in how they are used. Clearly, those who are educated in the arts are best poised to speak on such matters and to benefit most from the arts which are supported. If, as a matter of national policy, we intend to support the production of art with public funds but, in effect, to restrict the circulation of knowledge about art to the college-educated, to the affluent and their children, let us at least be candid about what we are doing.

The fifth issue is priorities. Informed decisions about the future of art education must be made. To the credit of the arts establishment and the arts-in-education movement, some discussion has been stimulated beyond the professional field of art education. But this discussion has not been guided by a sensitivity to the larger social issues, to differences among the arts, or to the role of formal education in the appreciation and production of art.

Many educators and citizens who influence school policies are not well informed about the arts and easily conclude that art is being "taken care of" if there is the slightest bit of any of the arts in a school. Too rarely are questions asked about what is taught, to whom, how often, and toward what ends. Many parents likewise believe that art is being taught if there is evidence that children are permitted, now and then, to use art materials.

Art educators, too, have contributed to the problems in our schools, chiefly through a failure of vision and intellectual leadership within professional associations and at the university level. But as a professional group, we in art education have a disposition to be grateful for crumbs and leftovers; we have an affinity for the casual, improvised, teaching situation; and we are, I believe, more tolerant of shabby teaching than we ought to be.

Within most of our schools, we find that something called art is allowed to happen, but on such a haphazard basis that we are not doing much service to children or to art. As a nation we have reached a point where a choice must consciously be made to offer in our schools sound programs of basic instruction in art, or perhaps to exclude art education altogether.

Because current instruction in our schools is so meager, and so concentrated on making art, we already know a good deal about the consequences of the very programs and policies that are now being advocated at the national level—and advertised as if they were brand new. We have not, on a national scale, tried the other alternative— namely, offering in our schools sound, balanced, and continuous instruction in art and requiring the study of art as part of the basic education of all our children.

10 | *Problems and Opportunities: A Closer Look*

As WE HAVE SEEN, a pattern of activity on behalf of arts education has emerged at the national level in the last decade or so. It is noteworthy in its expressed concern for making "all of the arts available for all of the children."[1] This vision is admirable as a national goal, but the policies being recommended as means to achieve this goal have not been fully examined. Neither have the philosophical and practical implications of the new national viewpoint been exposed to the full discussion they deserve.

Several matters which have been touched upon now merit a closer look. These are: the models of teacher preparation and educational change being advocated for art education, as well as some of the reasons behind the emphasis on integrating the arts into the general curriculum, and interdisciplinary or related arts programs.

The Arts Curriculum and Teacher Education

The model for teacher education which has been proposed by the arts bureaucracy is based on the idea that arts educators and school children are "special populations" which arts councils must serve. Other special populations are the elderly, the handicapped, those in prisons and hospitals, and ethnic groups. If you look at arts education from this vantage point, children *and* educators are clients for the arts. They can be served by putting artists into schools, employing artists as teachers, and involving artists in the related activities undertaken by educators—curriculum planning, teacher preparation, in-service education.

I have pointed out that within the arts bureaucracy, experts such as art historians, art critics, other scholars, and university arts educators have not often been mentioned as contributors to the improvement of school programs, primarily because the interests of the National Endowment for the Arts, especially in the employment of artists, have dominated public discussions of arts education. We thus find that the recommendations reported by the NEA-appointed Task Force on the Education, Training and Development of Professional Artists and Arts Educators[2] are almost identical to those put forward by the Arts, Education and Americans Panel in *Coming to Our Senses*,[3] and both echo the school-community "partnership" philosophy of the JDR 3rd Fund's Arts in Education Program.

The NEA Task Force report on the training of arts educators offers a guiding image of the kind of curriculum schools should adopt, and hence also of how arts teachers should be prepared.

The task force envisions present and future teachers of the individual arts having a role similar to that now held by supervisors of art and music in fairly large school districts, but expanded across all of the arts.

On the education of art specialists, the report says:

In-service training for [arts] teachers should include all the arts.[4]

In-service workshops should be provided for arts specialists . . . to educate [them] in organizing and administering arts programs that encompass several arts, reach all students, use community resources and relate [the arts] to the general curriculum.

Teams of classroom teachers, artists, administrators and parents, led by arts specialists, should be developed . . . to provide in-service arts education, [and] to plan and initiate model arts curricula . . .

Funds should be made available . . . for training [arts teachers] in [the] use of community resources, teaching arts to special constituencies, team teaching, and interdisciplinary approaches.[5]

The classroom teacher is to be trained in the studio tradition, by artists, and with an interdisciplinary approach.

On the education of elementary school classroom teachers, the report says:

> Project funds should be available to colleges, universities, and arts institutions to provide . . . classroom teachers with interdisciplinary courses encompassing several arts disciplines, arts studio experience to broaden and deepen [their] understandings [of] the arts process in basic education, and innovative techniques.
>
> Resources should be created . . . enabling in-service programs in . . . schools to incorporate arts components, assisted by arts student interns, artists-in-schools, college faculty arts teams.[6]

The task force recommendations emphasize the importance of training teachers through studio experiences and across all of the arts. Each teacher must in some degree learn to perform as an actor, dancer, musician, vocalist, painter, potter, printmaker, and so on. This training, to be offered by artists, is also to have an interdisciplinary focus and equip teachers to interrelate the arts and integrate them into the regular curriculum of schools. The arts curriculum in schools is likewise envisioned as interdisciplinary and based on studio experience.

There are several explanations for all of these themes. First, the arts constituency is interested in "marketing" the arts and the services of artists. If a "package deal" can be designed to bring all the arts into a school, without placing the school in the position of hiring full-time teachers in each of the arts, it might be easier to market the arts to parents and school administrators. Second, if the retrained arts "generalist" or arts "administrator" can deal with more than one art form, or get more of the arts into existing classes through interdisciplinary, related arts programs or integrated arts programs, then the school district will seem to have less need for arts teachers, leaving money and curriculum time to employ artists and obtain other arts services from the community. Third, through this kind of approach, dance and theater—which rarely are taught in schools—would have a better chance of becoming established as part of the arts education program.

In advocating related arts and interdisciplinary arts programs for schools and teacher education, the models held up for arts educators to emulate are the sciences and the social studies, where it is claimed that the special concerns of each of the disciplines have been organized into school programs that can be taught by a generalist.[7] In principle, the science generalist can teach biology, physics, astronomy, and other sciences, while the social studies generalist, in theory, can teach history, geography, anthropology, and related disciplines. Several things are forgotten in this comparison.

First, teachers of science and social studies are not trained and socialized into their profession with the expectation that they should have the technical skills to function as professional geographers, historians, anthropologists, physicists, or astronomers. Instead, teachers in these subjects are asked to see themselves as lifelong students of the disciplines they teach. They are urged to cultivate an appreciation for the sciences and social studies; to grasp the issues and concepts associated with particular branches of study. Similarly, instruction in schools is not conceived with the idea that most students will become highly creative biologists, or skilled economists, or what have you. Talent is recognized and encouraged, but knowledge of general use to all students is the basis of the curriculum.

In contrast to this orientation, the arts educator is urged to identify with the role of the artist. Principals and teachers, children and parents have been socialized to think of art as a recreational activity, analogous to athletics, which can be enjoyed by all but is of primary value to the talented. This deeply engrained orientation cannot be changed if teachers are admonished, on the one hand, to train themselves as artists and place even more emphasis on making art, and, on the other hand, are urged to operate more like teachers of the sciences and social studies.[8] A parallel between the arts generalist and other generalists can be made only when imparting knowledge about the arts—knowledge of use to all citizens—is emphasized to a greater degree than teaching specialized crafts and skills for a recreational or vocational role in making art.

Second, it is misleading to compare arts education with the "interdisciplinary" or "holistic" character of science and social studies. Instruction in social studies, for example, is usually organized around the concept of an expanding frame of reference from grade to grade—beginning with the family and school, neighborhood and local community, state or region, national and international relationships. At each grade level, teachers may introduce only four or five major topics for the year. Moreover, the topics are usually selected to draw upon concepts in several (not all) of the disciplines encompassed by the social studies—history, geography, political science, economics, anthropology, sociology, psychology, and philosophy. When children study the "nation," for example, insights from history and political science are dominant, but those from psychology and sociology are not. In the elementary grades, anthropology and geography are likely to be called upon in studying say, Mexican culture—not political science or sociology.

In social studies, as in science, the special disciplines (which are analogous to the various arts) are brought into play in a highly selective manner. Comparable selectivity is vital for curriculum design in the arts, but the principles of selection are not likely to be examined through a teacher education program unless the program emphasizes the conceptual study of art and the uses of knowledge about art in various contexts. Indeed, curriculum design is not a job that anyone should undertake without considerable understanding of the subject matter and of children.

Third, curriculum resources are abundant in subjects other than art, and teachers are routinely trained and retrained to use new instructional materials. The National Science Foundation and the National Endowment for the Humanities have offered a wide range of services to schools, as well as summer programs and fellowships for school and university teachers, special conferences, and regional minicourses. The NEA has offered no comparable services. Because children are required to study the sciences and social studies, or required to take "options" within these areas, it has been profitable for educators and publishers to develop a wide range of instructional materials and services for teachers. The arts are not required subjects, and typically are introduced with the teacher's own art background serving as the major resource. As a consequence of these differences, equally valuable programs and services have not been developed for the improvement of arts education.

Fourth, if schools are expected to emphasize making art or performing arts activities, then specialist arts teachers must be employed. Why? Because the moment children enter into the role of artist, the teacher's guidance must concentrate on the child's actions in a particular medium. In making art, there are technical skills to be taught; ideational and aesthetic considerations also must come into play. The depth of learning one can achieve through the studio experience depends upon sustained engagement with an artistic medium. The kind of tutoring children need requires more expertise than most classroom teachers can be expected to supply. It also requires more pedagogical wisdom, patience, and sheer endurance than most artists have or willingly would offer. Specialist teachers will be needed if we care about the quality of learning as children engage in studio activities.

Fifth, it seems to be expected that if arts educators develop interdisciplinary, related arts, correlated, or integrated programs more arts instruction will be available to children, and childrens' learning will be more coherent. Since some of the arts instruction would be "infused" into other subjects, children would seem to have more art in their curriculum, without having additional time earmarked for art.

But as we look at some of the typical practices that flourish under related arts or interdisciplinary efforts, it is apparent that these approaches are not always carried out with a genuine concern for what children are learning about art. Let me illustrate some of the most common problems.

PROBLEM 1. CONTINUITY IN ART LEARNING: One typical method of integrating art into the curriculum is to add some art to mathematics, science, and social studies instruction. For example, if children are studying geometric shapes in mathematics, the art teacher might show children (and the classroom teacher) how geometric shapes have been used by artists. Children might also do an art project with geometric shapes. So far, so good. This kind of connection might be called "integrated," "correlated," or "interdisciplinary" teaching.

But suppose now that the art teacher says that the next logical step is to introduce these same children to other shapes and forms—naturalistic, fanciful, expressionistic. In this way, the children's study of shape would build toward an understanding of different types of shape as elements in different styles of art. Can the art teacher now count on the classroom teachers to adjust the scheduled science lessons to enrich the arts unit dealing with naturalistic shapes? The answer is, probably not. Why? Because it rarely occurs to anyone to ask whether other parts of the curriculum might be adjusted to improve learning in art—without sacrificing learning in other subjects. All too often, "integration" is merely a fancy word for patching a bit of art into a curriculum already planned, and planned without regard to art education.

PROBLEM 2. INTEGRATION OF ART CONTENT AND BASIC SKILLS: At least part of the impetus for integrated and related arts programs comes from the idea that creative activity in the arts will motivate children toward improved skills in reading, writing, and speaking.[9] However, the motivation to improve one's skill in any area may come from any number of sources, not just the arts. In fact, a recent review of studies on the teaching of reading shows that any experimental treatment will produce short-term gains, that gains under the phonics sound-blending system are the most dramatic in magnitude, and that visual-perceptual strategies and other combined methods of teaching are no more effective than any "new" approach one selects.[10] If children see art, read, speak, and write about art, and listen to discussions about art, they are practicing what is useful to them in art and in learning to command language. And that is the best, most direct way to integrate art and reading.

It is instructive, also, for arts educators to put the shoe on the other foot with regard to the so-called tool subjects. Are the tools for learning—reading, writing, mathematics, and other so-called basic skills—introduced so that they enhance children's learning about the arts? For example, are children taught a vocabulary appropriate to describe the qualities of action, mood, and meaning in various art forms? Do materials devoted to "critical-thinking skills" include examples that develop critical thinking about the arts? Do standardized tests for reading and vocabulary include basic concepts from other subjects, but exclude the arts from comparable assessment? Are reading and other textbooks examined not only for race and sex stereotyping, but also for arts stereotyping, by the omission of arts content or by the kind of treatment given to the arts content? If integration is to be a two-way street, then arts educators must begin to ask questions such as these.

PROBLEM 3. ADEQUACY OF ART CONTENT: Let me point out a few of the most typical problems in planning programs around broad concepts which are said to be common to many subjects besides the arts—sound, movement, energy, pattern, line, shape, color, mass, and so forth.[11] These concepts are part of "formalist aesthetic theories"—those which place great value on the form or design within a work of art. But in no other area do we find so much naive and misleading instruction in schools as when teachers try to deal with these so-called elements of art. No one reasonably knowledgeable in music and in art would ever equate "tone color" in music with color mixing in painting, or with color optics in physics, but this kind of comparison is easily made by a naive teacher.

Teachers attracted to the elements and principles of art must realize that this strategy for teaching emphasizes highly abstract connections among the arts. For example, everything in the universe may be portrayed to children as fitting a single concept such as "energy." But children must recognize and appreciate that in the arts, particular manifestations of energy differ in form and can be used intentionally. The forms of energy one can create in dance, for example, differ from the implied energy one can convey through painting.

Teachers may also become so enthralled with connecting a single concept like energy across disciplines that children may not grasp interactions within the discipline. Indeed, there is something quite misleading about isolating single concepts such as energy in dance—as if dance movement could be understood apart from the character of its flow, direction, effort, extension into and definition of space. These are precisely the interactions which must be grasped in the arts, and why instruction is needed in each of the arts.

While teachers appear to be fascinated with these "design" connections, the whole arts curriculum may become distorted when design concepts are taught without reference to other aspects of art. For example, the design vocabulary does not offer information about the role of myths, legends, and allegory in art, or the relationship of the arts to religious and political developments in a culture, nor does it provide all of the sensibilities required to study a single work in depth, especially if the work is expressive of more than its form or design.

PROBLEM 4. EFFICIENCY AND COMPLETENESS OF ART LEARNING: Another tendency is to invest a lot of time in teaching superficial connections among the arts through "flash and dazzle" activities, at the expense of teaching more subtle, but powerful, aspects of the arts. Here is an example. A lesson in color is planned. Children make their own slides using cellophane, vasoline, and various dyes, combine these with other visual-sound technologies popular in the youth culture, and, finally, stage a light show (with music and dance as well). This is a highly entertaining and time-consuming activity, but the fact that it is enjoyable does not, in itself, justify its inclusion in a program. Equally enjoyable and more efficient ways to introduce color concepts can be devised.

Another related problem is oversimplification. Perhaps the clearest example is when a teacher claims to be introducing "all of the arts" by having children produce a play, do a puppet show, make a film, or contribute to an arts festival. Learning in all of the arts is not the natural result of such activities. Children can obtain great satisfaction from undertakings such as these, but in the process of delegating tasks and managing such complex productions, individual children may spend much of their time on uninspiring activities. For example, using a sponge to make a brick pattern for the stage set, or mechanically producing posters, does not really promote much learning about the arts of stage design or poster design (or theater or graphic design).

For elementary school programs in which the classroom teacher has major responsibility for instruction, there are many alternatives to these often shallow or misleading ways of relating the arts and "integrating" the arts into the curriculum. To suggest only one of many options, consider the idea of units of instruction, similar to those that classroom teachers may set up for social studies.

Typically, a unit is set up so that children develop skills in reading, writing, speaking, and listening; in doing research; in working cooperatively on parts of a larger task; and in summarizing and sharing the results of the inquiry. Now let children study art under the same general scheme. One fourth grade teacher, for example, engaged children in a six-week unit of study that led them to investigate such problems as defining art, occupations in and the economics of artistic production, and issues in judging art. The children created art, read about it, wrote about it, did research, conducted interviews, and experienced field trips. Reading, mathematics, writing, science, and social studies were, in this case, tools for learning about art.

Classroom teachers who are trained in this general method of teaching have little difficulty in planning units or topics around the arts. They are attracted to it because their role is not to provide ready-made answers or to demonstrate their skills as artists, but to lead the inquiry of students. Moreover, the inquiry process can be designed to show that one can learn about the world of art in many ways—by reading, by interviewing people, by watching films or television, by studying the work of artists, or by creating art. Classroom teachers are masters of gathering resources that "carry" the content. They are rarely able to generate, from memory alone, the content that children will need or want to study from week to week.

Finally, even if they are well conceived and well taught, units or courses that focus on interrelations are not a substitute for basic education in each of the arts. Instruction in each of the arts is necessary, not only because the arts themselves have become highly specialized, but also because the experience of art is built from an appreciation of particulars. The proposed multiarts, integrated, and related arts strategies will not (in the near future) reduce the need for full-time teachers of the arts, or lessen the need for designated time and resources for instruction in each of the arts.

How To Prevent Educational Change

The improvement of art education through greater use of artists and community resources has been a central theme in the arts-in-education movement, but this approach to change has several drawbacks.

The general model for change is based on the expectation that artists, parents, school administrators, and other members of the community are willing and expert enough in arts education to plan model curricula, to conduct in-service education programs for teachers, and to develop courses in the humanities, aesthetics, and the arts. The arts specialists currently employed by schools are to serve as administrators of such activities and programs. In effect, the school district would add music and art teachers to the administrative payroll and pay for arts education by subcontracting for the services of artists, or community agencies.

In spite of frequent references to partnerships between schools and arts agencies, school administrators, parents and arts educators should understand that the proposed use of artists and other community resources in the arts is not expected to be free to schools. Fund raising for arts education becomes a major theme in the advocacy literature precisely because professional artists and nonprofit art agencies that provide services to schools are to be reimbursed for services rendered and the school budget is to be tapped for this purpose.[12] In *Coming to Our Senses,* it is recommended that state and district school personnel "have budgetary discretion to use non-school arts facilities and to hire non-certified personnel, that is, artists."[13]

This services-for-hire concept has several predictable consequences. Quite naturally schools will want to shop for the least expensive arts services within the community. One can expect that entrepreneurs in the arts will find it profitable to cultivate the school as a client. There are a number of disadvantages in this relationship, not the least of which is the opportunity for children to be exploited. Owners of music and crafts stores, tap and ballet schools, and private music teachers would welcome the opportunity to teach in schools and advertise their goods and services to students. If funds to employ artists are made available by or through schools, professionals in the arts—especially the performing arts—must either be paid their prevailing union wage or compromise their professional status by accepting less than the prevailing wage. Who benefits from this arrangement? Who indeed shall be counted as an artist, and who will decide?

Furthermore, schools may or may not be able to draw upon the best local resources. Financial incentives might help, but experienced artists and arts organizations do not normally plan their work and performance schedules around the needs of schools. It would be unrealistic for educators to count on regular and sustained services from such individuals and groups, or the scheduling of those services so that they make the maximum contribution to the arts education of children. Surely, available funds from within or without the school system would better be spent to employ full-time arts teachers, to obtain resources that can be used more than once in classrooms, and to employ arts supervisors and outside consultants for curriculum development and in-service education.

When we look at the suggested "partnership" models for planning arts education programs, other problems are evident. The models would not be taken seriously as serving children if they were applied to other subjects. The suggested approaches to planning not only call for a financial strategy which resembles a united-fund or comparable campaign drive, but also call for members of a community to assume responsibility for arts education, irrespective of their qualifications to do so.[14]

Suppose, for a moment, that we were to ask that physical education programs in schools be upgraded by the same planning process. Parents interested in sports, booster clubs and sports fans, professional athletics, representatives of athletic teams, and others with a vested interest in professional sports would be involved in roles comparable to those identified for the arts. Suppose we were to ask such persons to become involved in fund raising, planning and implementing programs in schools, and, in some cases, serving as teachers. If citizens and fans are to serve in these roles on more than a token basis, then there really is not much for the professional educator to do except to endorse the program, help to raise funds, and provide access to students through the school. Even if citizens and organizations are prepared to undertake this kind of work on a continuing basis, it seems likely that the resulting arts programs, like athletic programs, would stress the early identification of talent at the expense (literally) of general education in the arts.

What impression might parents and educators get about arts education from the reports of the various panels, task forces, and advocacy groups that I have mentioned? I believe they might conclude that providing arts education in a school is exceedingly difficult and expensive, not a normal responsibility of the school. The model of change being developed for arts education leaves one with the distinct understanding that the major problems in arts education are the financing, marketing, and management of a program. But surely this *becomes* the problem because the kind of arts education recommended for schools resembles a circus or sideshow. Arts education, as it is portrayed, seems impossible to put into schools unless an extraordinarily complex set of relationships is established in the community, calling for exceptional administrative expertise, special funds to hire artists and other part-time or temporary staff, and the cultivation of all sorts of networks that necessarily involve meetings, negotiations, and paperwork.[15]

Faced with this kind of model for change, the practical school administrator is likely to say, "No thanks."

What is built into this model for change, and to a degree that overshadows everything else, is an administrative system designed to serve performing artists, providing them with an audience and income based on their work as artists. While it is vital for children to encounter original works of art and live performances of music, dance, and theater, the programming of such encounters is educationally wasteful in the absence of a well-established in-school program which can prepare students for the experience and provide a follow-up to it. In the absence of such planning, the experience degenerates into an expensive form of entertainment, or, worse, can reinforce stereotypes about the arts.[16] The scheduling of arts events or appearances of guest artists for schools is no more or less exotic than scheduling a field trip or having other guests visit the school. Affordability and educational value are equally important criteria.

There is an alternative way to pursue educational change and to secure for arts education a more stable position in schools. The first step is to set accreditation standards for schools that will make studies of the arts a requirement in the curriculum, on a par with the social studies (humanities) and the sciences. A second step is to develop teacher preparation systems that provide for dual certification in the arts, allowing teachers who have an affinity for more than one art form to obtain certification in a second art form (not all the arts), but also encouraging teachers in one of the arts to become certified in an academic field. The number of experienced and entering teachers who might be trained under such programs would enlarge the general pool of arts-qualified teachers (including those in dance and theater), give local schools much more flexibility in making teaching assignments, and give teachers more flexibility in locating jobs.

The anticipated decrease in the number of school-aged children and increasingly tight job market argues for this approach. A well-placed program of fellowships for experienced teachers of the arts, allowing them to become certified in a second field, would be appropriate. Also, a system of financial incentives might be devised for schools or school districts that do include the arts as a requirement in the general education of children. The fund-raising and political expertise of support groups in the arts might be directed toward such projects.

Getting to the Heart of the Problem

The vision of bringing all of the arts to all of the children has, I believe, been transformed into complicated administrative proposals which are unnecessary and in many ways reinforce the impression that art is an extra, a frill in the curriculum. A proper legacy from the arts-in-education movement is a fundamental realignment of attitudes about arts education—within the arts bureaucracy, at every level of education, and within the professions of arts educators.

There is a clear need for greater public awareness that people who devote their lives to the study, creation, performance, and teaching of the arts are not merely engaging in a peculiar form of self-indulgence, but are contributing in quite fundamental ways to the definition of American culture. Moreover, almost everyone who is seriously involved in the arts wants to be acknowledged as a person who is doing a kind of work that is no more eccentric (and often less eccentric) than other activities which have broad public support. Nevertheless, almost everyone who works in the arts encounters some form of occupational discrimination simply because he or she has elected this kind of occupation.

The forms of discrimination felt by individuals who work in the arts carry over into educational activity in the arts, but with added force for arts educators who work in schools. Not only does the arts educator face an educational establishment that seems to regard the arts as luxuries, but he or she is also confronted by an arts community all too eager to judge that schools and arts educators have failed to do the job, and all too willing to delegate responsibility to other agencies and individuals. Educators in the visual arts often find, as well, that discussions of "all the arts" result in proposals more appropriate to the performing arts than to the visual arts.

Arts educators have, I believe, contributed to this pattern of discrimination, in part by insisting that children be engaged in the performance and production of art as if that were the be-all and end-all of their work. Most of the benefits claimed for this kind of activity are not apparent to the public or to arts professionals except through the exceptional work of talented students. The credibility of arts educators becomes open to question, in part, because they are not really able to develop studio skills in their students with the limited time and resources usually provided to them. Yet they insist on this emphasis in their teaching, at the expense of other aims for arts education, which, if pursued, would help to demonstrate that the arts are more than a hobby, or vocation for the talented. Thus, whether intending to or not, I believe arts educators have taught the larger educational community to equate arts education with having a marching band, doing macrame or papier-mâché, staging a pageant or play, or having disco-dancing on a rainy day.

Arts educators are also inclined to operate in a manner that is remarkably similar to that of many minority groups seeking full participation in the larger culture. Arts educators, collectively, are so eager to gain entrance into schools that we seem quite willing to compromise the identity of the arts for any token representation in the educational programs of children. This pattern of response from within the professional field of arts education allows the arts to enter schools, but under conditions that are fundamentally demeaning to the arts. We thus perpetuate the idea that the arts must be proven worthy of being allowed in schools, even though no comparable demands are made that the sciences and social studies prove their worth.

Having attempted to do the impossible for years (and with little organized support from the arts community), arts educators now find that their efforts to position the arts in schools are not perceived as constructive by the newly organized arts community. Instead, schools and young people are now seen by the arts community as clients to whom the arts can be delivered and from whom additional employment for artists can be obtained. In effect, the school is being asked to offer patronage to artists, and on terms that are more suitable to artists than appropriate to the education of children. The politicizing of arts education and the portrayal of the arts in education as an expensive social service have drawn attention away from the more pressing issues of concern to professionals in arts education. Within some segments of the arts community (and education establishment) a school district is judged to be doing very well if one school has a program designed for the talented and if here and there, now and again, all other students encounter a live performance or meet an artist in person.[17]

The arts establishment must recognize that the education of young citizens in the arts is a basic mission of schools, and one that cannot be met simply through introducing artists into schools, thereby exposing children to the arts occasionally. Not all artists are equipped or eager to undertake in-school education. To the extent that artists are willing to do so on a full-time basis, they are entering into a different career and should be thoroughly trained as art educators.

If many arts educators appear to be less than enthusiastic about current proposals for de-schooling arts education, or delegating it to artists, or establishing integrated arts programs, it is because this general pattern of operation has been characteristic of the past. Training artists to be teachers has been thoroughly tried as a model for visual arts teachers and music educators. Making art and performing in the arts are, as we have seen, if anything too much the focal point of instruction. So, too, have art and music teachers in elementary schools long worked with "integrated arts." Finally, the de-schooling of arts education can hardly be judged as an acceptable alternative to the present situation in the majority of schools where instruction from an arts specialist is limited to about 1 percent of a twelve-year curriculum.

Most important, in the long run, is a necessary and fundamental change in the way the educational establishment conceives of general or basic education. What must be changed is that habit of mind which leads educators, first, to exclude the arts from the working definition of general or basic education; second, to offer apologies for this exclusion and to acknowledge that the arts really should be included after all; third, to "allow" the arts back into the curriculum, as if that were a generous act; but fourth, to attach strings to this permission. What strings? Arts educators must prove that the arts are useful in serving other subjects, and arts educators must not expect the arts to receive equitable treatment in the curriculum.

A host of policies and practices within our schools actually demean the arts and the study of them. There is no legitimate social or educational reason why the arts should be slipped into schools through the back door, disguised as a means of teaching reading or as tools to "enrich" the teaching of other subjects. The arts are not illegal aliens in the history of human achievement, nor subservient in merit to other endeavors. If the idea of an integrated curriculum is sound, then the arts need not be the only subject to be examined in this way. Let the curriculum in other subjects be examined, and if necessary modified, so that learning in the arts is reinforced and enriched. It is time to release the arts from a bondage which has made them into all-purpose servants in the house of education.

I think that many would also agree that it is time for arts educators to challenge our colleagues on the question of basic education limited to the three R's. If students cannot in twelve years be taught to read, write, and compute well enough to manage personal finances and job applications, surely it is because producing this kind of minimum competency has become the aim of schools. The solution is not to pour more money into so-called basic programs that aim low, are not productive, and are so programmed toward minimum skills that they bore the daylights out of most students. Nor is the solution to be found in promises that putting children in touch with artists will work magic.

There are no simple solutions, but certain fundamental changes in attitude are essential. What is needed is a fundamental redefinition of general education, so that the arts are not automatically excluded, but routinely included. What is needed is a basic change in all those habits of mind that disparage the worth of instruction and study in art, making the arts seem to be so intuitive, mysterious, or mindless that education seems pointless. What will transform arts education is not better packaging, advertising, and marketing of the arts, nor more of the same kind of casual or instant-art instruction so typical in classrooms, and now to be resold and installed in schools by complex and costly managerial systems.

There is no reason why the arts should be expected to sit in the back of the bus of public education, especially when knowledge about the arts is so clearly reserved for an elite in our culture—the college-educated and their children. Discrimination against serious study of the arts in public schools reinforces the elitism found within the larger culture. What will improve arts education is a national commitment to policies and programs that reasonably assure that the arts are given full and fair treatment in the education of all our children. Why, indeed, should the nation spend millions to support the arts, if the actual and potential benefits are restricted to a few?

11

Recommendations

A NUMBER OF SPECIFIC steps can be taken to improve arts education in schools and to make effective use of community resources in the arts for the education of young people. The recommendations that follow are intended to serve as guidelines for parents, concerned citizens, members of the artistic and educational communities—all who wish to see the arts placed in a more central position within the curriculum of schools, on a par with the sciences and social studies.

A Change in Attitude

In order to extend and improve arts education in schools, we must put aside the popular belief that one does not really have to study art in order to enjoy, understand, or create it. Not only does this attitude demean the hard work and intelligence of individuals who devote their lives to the arts; it seriously underestimates the degree to which formal education can enhance one's response to the arts. Fortunately, many young people enjoy the arts, but art is more than fun; it is also a highly demanding field of endeavor which, like other fields, cannot be grasped without some fundamental or basic education.

147

The Role of Schools

Most citizens recognize that our system of public schools has been created to reasonably assure that young people are not deprived, by lack of education, of the opportunity to learn about subjects that will enhance their general understanding of the world and prepare them for the future. While we routinely ask our schools to teach children about science and the humanities (social studies), we routinely deny them the opportunity to study the arts in a comparable way. Until arts education becomes a required subject, like science and social studies, the opportunity to learn about the arts will remain a special privilege for a few. Indeed, insofar as the arts are neglected in school programs, the school directly and falsely reinforces the impression that the arts are for a particular social class, a luxury for the wealthy. Schools exist to assure equality of opportunity, but we have not yet applied this principle to education in the arts.

Reforming the Curriculum

Many of the problems faced in public education have been addressed in a patchwork fashion. One consequence is that the general curriculum has been fragmented, devoted to specific skills, leaving little time and few resources for instruction in the arts, sciences, and humanities. The result is a decline in the quality of education children receive. In upgrading the total curriculum, the arts should be given parity with the sciences and humanities, not introduced as a bonus, an enticement to learning other subjects, or a decorative addition to the curriculum.

□ Every school should provide a program of basic studies in the subject of art as part of the regular required curriculum—from kindergarten to at least the tenth grade—preferably, to the twelfth grade.

□ As a condition for school accreditation, state departments of education should make it obligatory for schools to provide sound and continuous instruction from certified teachers in the visual, performing, and literary arts. These programs should reach all students in elementary and secondary schools, not just the talented.

□ Community support groups should address their efforts toward advocating the arts as a core subject in the school curriculum, as

well as the employment of certified teachers of the arts to offer
instruction in schools.

☐ School districts should require at least one full year of study in the
arts as a condition for high school graduation. Adequate support
should be given for the development of arts courses that might
meet this requirement and be well suited to students not currently
served in arts courses.

☐ In every school district, a program of studies in the visual, literary, and performing arts should be developed and reviewed
annually to identify staff and resources for the future. Plans for
improving the program should be projected ahead for a three- to
five-year period and be placed on the agenda for discussion in all
major budget hearings for the school district.

Improving the Arts Curriculum

If young people are to receive a basic education in the arts, they must
be engaged in the process of studying the subject of art, and well
beyond the typical fare in many schools—making art projects, singing,
dancing, and the like. Programs of study should offer such activities,
but not at the expense of teaching young people to critically examine
the arts and develop skills which allow them to make informed decisions about the arts in everyday life.

Beyond the Making of Art

The arts curriculum should be coordinated so that studies are clustered
within three program areas: the visual arts, the literary arts, and the
performing arts. Within each of these areas, teachers of the respective
arts, in collaboration with experts in curriculum design, should develop a coherent program serving the majority of youth, who, as
citizens, will deal with the arts neither as professional artists nor as
amateur creators or performers in the arts.

☐ The arts curriculum should affirm the importance of creative,
imaginative thinking in art and also the importance of critical,
reflective thinking about art. Both modes of thinking are relevant
to creating art and responding to art.

☐ Teachers of the arts should recognize that their role is to guide
students so that their knowledge about the arts extends beyond
their personal ability to create art.

□ The arts curriculum should be framed to draw upon the skills, knowledge, and experience that young people acquire outside of school. It should expand upon that experience, illustrating its connection to human history and to facets of life beyond the immediate experience of children.

□ The curriculum should provide for the study of art forms which intersect with our daily life—the popular arts, mass-produced and mass-distributed art forms—and engage students with comparative studies of art forms associated with the fine arts tradition in Western culture. Equally important are studies of the arts of cultural groups outside of the Western European tradition.

□ Correlated, integrated, interdisciplinary, or related arts programs should not be conceived as alternatives to instruction in each of the arts. The practice of using the arts to enhance learning in other subjects without any consideration of appropriate and efficient learning in the arts should be stopped.

Vocational Guidance

Occupational roles in the arts are not limited to those which lead to performing as an artist, creating studio art, or doing crafts. In the visual arts, careers may be found in television, design, and architecture. Careers in art history, criticism, and journalism, as well as in the teaching and administration of the arts, are open to young people. *One can make a career of being an enlightened citizen-supporter of arts.* Early identification of talent is not easy, and particularly in the visual arts, premature technical training may be more of a liability than an asset.

□ In order to make an assessment of talent in the arts one must 1) examine what prior opportunities the student has had for studying art; 2) base judgments on a cumulative record of "work products" (visual, verbal, audio, and written) over a span of time; and 3) seek evaluations of performance from persons who have extensive experience in looking at the kind of work that young people can produce, with and without instruction.

□ As a practical procedure and as a tool for research, it is recommended that teachers of art identify, semiannually, students who in their judgment exhibit exceptional aptitude in art and assemble for those students a file of work products, along with supplementary observations about the students' performance. Such files should be standardized within a school district and assembled for the purpose of monitoring performance over a period of years. The file should not be considered confidential. If the student transfers to another school or district, the file should be transferred.

☐ Parents of students who have been identified as having special aptitude in art should be informed of this aptitude and offered counsel on special programs and home activities that would be appropriate. Art teachers are urged especially to note students who show aptitudes for talking and writing about art, and students who might be interested in fields within the arts that require a knowledge of science and mathematics, such as architecture and industrial design, and the technological aspects of theater, music, dance, and film.

☐ With few exceptions, school-sponsored apprenticeships and work-study programs in the arts for the talented should be reserved for the last two years of high school and, in every case, closely supervised by school personnel.

Teachers

Qualified Full-Time Art Teachers Are Essential

All students have a right to study the arts with persons who are committed to teaching art as their first choice of occupation. Teachers of the arts must emphasize issues and options in the world of art and serve as skilled, knowledgeable interpreters of art. Currently, there is greater likelihood that a student will be misinformed about art in school than provided with sound instruction. This is particularly true in the elementary grades, where persons who are not required to have studied art themselves are given the responsibility for teaching it to the young.

☐ It is essential that schools employ, as full-time teachers of the visual, literary, and performing arts, persons who are broadly knowledgeable within those arts, skilled in teaching young people, and committed to the importance of the subject of art within the curriculum as a whole, and to the principle of developing programs that will serve all students, not just the talented.

☐ The teacher's ability to perform as an artist can be an asset, but effective teachers may also come from the ranks of persons who have an extensive background in the history of the arts, in art criticism, and within the visual arts, in the several design fields, including architecture. Teachers should be encouraged to regard public education in art as their central responsibility. Toward that end, their skills in articulating ideas, engaging students in creative and critical thought, and their acquisition of a broad understanding of art are vital occupational skills.

□ Teachers must understand that the majority of young people will have no formal education in art beyond that offered in elementary and secondary schools. The content and methods employed in art education must therefore be efficient, powerful, and representative of opportunities and issues in art.

□ State departments of education should require evidence of such skills and commitments in teachers as a condition for teacher certification and for the accreditation of school art programs.

□ Teacher certification in art should be required for employment of any person who will teach art on a full-time or half-time basis during a school year. The employment of artists should not be given higher priority than the employment of full-time certified teachers of art. Adequate resources for the regular in-school art program must be provided, and this too, has greater priority than the use of community services which may be beneficial, but not essential.

Support Systems

Many arts teachers work in physical and psychological isolation, not by choice, but because they teach in an environment in which their efforts as educators are rarely noted. Teachers of the visual arts are frequently seen as little more than the persons responsible for bulletin-board displays, exhibitions of student work, posters, or the source of a needed roll of masking tape or a drawing for a school newsletter. The teacher of the performing arts may be seen as little more than a person who provides entertainment through special assemblies, a marching band, and a core of skilled baton twirlers. Teachers of the arts may, through their eagerness to respond to such requests, create the impression that their programs have value only as service operations for the school administration and community. In order to improve the quality of thought arts teachers bring to their work, to revitalize their morale, and improve their working conditions, several steps must be taken.

□ Arts teachers need to become more active in their professional associations and to form local communication networks to share their interests and solutions to problems. (Only 11 percent of the visual arts teachers who responded to the *School Arts* survey identified themselves as highly active in professional associations.)

□ In-service education in the arts should be extended to include released time and travel reimbursement to permit arts supervisors, arts specialists, administrators, and classroom teachers to attend state and national conferences on arts education.

□ Principals and school administrators should seek information from their own teachers and from outside experts about the current aims and content of the arts program, the conditions which facilitate or impede effective instruction, as well as resource needs that may have been neglected. Experts in arts education should be consulted in planning improvements in programs.

□ In-service education in art should be offered under the auspices of universities—ideally, by teams comprising experienced or "master" art teachers (who work in schools), art content specialists, and university faculty in art education. All in-service personnel should be superb models for teachers. Academic or other credits for in-service work should be made available to participants.

□ Supervisors of education in the visual, performing, and literary arts should be employed by school districts. They should be given resource and development funds, as well as staff assistance, to assure that curriculum materials and necessary community services are provided to arts teachers in a timely and efficient manner.

□ Parents and other support groups in the community likewise have a role to play in assisting arts teachers, not only by finding out what children are being taught, and why, but by influencing school policies. At a practical level, parents may assist arts teachers through securing resources or by offering various forms of expertise the parents may have.

Monitoring the Quality of Instruction

Members of school boards today routinely monitor the status of instruction and achievement in many subjects, and in almost all programs that have received special funds. Too rarely do administrators and school boards assess the status of instruction in the arts, often only when they are considering a cutback in the program. Periodic evaluations of art programs are appropriate, and needed.

□ Toward this end, local school districts should periodically conduct a year-long colloquium on basic education in the arts involving members of the school board, administrative staff, parents, art supervisors and teachers, educational personnel in arts institutions, and outside experts in art education. Bimonthly seminars for all participants and separate study groups for the visual, literary, and performing arts should be established to evaluate strengths in the existing programs, to conduct research if needed, to identify program strengths and weaknesses, and to formulate recommendations for action by the school board. Colloquia of this kind should be scheduled at least once every five to seven years.

□ State departments of education should schedule, within regions of each state, extended colloquia (similar to those recommended for local districts) to assist rural schools in solving problems they face.

□ Higher-education faculty should invite teachers in the several arts to suggest how the resources of the colleges and university might be brought into play to support their work. Few universities and colleges conduct follow-up studies of their graduates or secure from them suggestions for program improvements, courses, and other services that might be provided.

□ In too few communities do we find members of the artistic community and supporters of the visual, literary, and performing arts who are adequately informed about what teachers of these arts are doing or hope to accomplish in schools. Staff, volunteers, and administrators of local art institutions have an obligation to examine the conditions under which the art teacher works and to serve as advocates for strong in-school programs.

□ Each community should establish a highly publicized annual program of recognition for teachers, parents, administrators, volunteers, and members of the private sector who have made outstanding contributions to the arts programming available in schools.

Stimulating Change

Leaders, above all else, are able to discern the difference between the way things are and the way they ought to be. Leaders cannot bring about change without some power to stimulate action. Continuous and sound programs of basic education in art will require that persons who hold positions of influence develop new patterns of thought about the teaching of art in the school, the allocation of local resources and staff, and the most effective kinds of federal, state, and local support for school programs.

State Departments of Education Must Assume the Leadership Role

Of critical importance in the process of change are policies and standards that may be established by state departments of education in regard to school accreditation, as well as the certification of teachers, administrators, counsellors, and supervisors.

☐ Every state department of education should employ at least two full-time directors of arts education, one to serve the performing arts, a second to serve the visual arts. A third staff member should work in concert with these directors to strengthen instruction in the literary arts.

☐ Certification programs should be established by state departments of education to assure that all teachers of the arts, as well as supervisors or resource specialists in the arts, are well trained and recertified on a regular basis through appropriate continuing or in-service education programs.

☐ All administrators, teachers, and counselors who serve in schools should be required to present for certification, or renewal of certification, evidence of course work specifically designed to inform them of issues and opportunities bearing on arts education.

☐ Statewide curriculum guides should be reviewed, teacher and administrator workshops initiated, and public awareness programs planned to build a commitment to and action on behalf of programs offering basic education in the arts, sciences, and humanities.

Universities and Professional Associations Must Be Engaged

Equally important in the development of change and the exercise of leadership are universities and professional associations.

☐ Arts education departments in colleges and universities must engage in a process of self-renewal, taking assertive action to improve the quality of teacher education programs, as well as their standards for scholarship and in-service activities.

☐ New communication and activity networks within and between universities should be established to serve as vehicles for faculty de-velopment, to make better use of existing faculty talents, and to make more effective use of limited resources.

☐ University faculty, professional associations, and state and local education agencies should expand the scope of their educational activities to reach influential lay and legislative groups outside of the profession and to provide more direct support to art teachers in schools.

☐ Federal or state grants-in-aid should be made to local education agencies to work with university faculty on teacher reeducation, curriculum development, and resource development. Such grants-in-aid should be provided in order to strengthen basic education in the visual, literary, and performing arts, respec-tively.

Arts Agencies

Arts education frequently takes place outside of schools—in museums, in recreational and community centers, and as an adjunct to the activities of many other arts and social service agencies. Many worthy art-project programs and activities compete for the limited funds available through local and state arts commissions and related agencies. It is very important that arts agencies recognize the primary role of the schools in arts education, and do their utmost to assist school programs.

☐ Leaders in arts commissions and institutions must understand that it is educationally and economically wasteful to introduce community art resources into schools haphazardly, without a clear linkage to the ongoing program of studies in schools. Effec-tive in-school programming can occur when community agencies are given annual schedules and rosters, *prepared by teachers*, of essential in-school services. The school district should not be expected to pay for services not deemed essential to the curricu-lum, nor pay for outside services in lieu of employing full-time arts teachers.

☐ The scheduling of field trips, exhibitions, and visiting-artist and volunteer programs in schools all should be the responsibility of the supervisors of arts education employed in the school district.

☐ Community arts commissions and agencies are urged to develop rosters of professionals in arts education who are available for consultation or staff positions in local arts institutions, social service programs, and recreational programs, as well as in the arts commission itself. In every case, these specialists in arts education should be given fair compensation for their services.

□ In metropolitan centers where museum, recreational, and community-center programs exist, well-trained teachers of the arts should be employed to work with all programs reaching school-aged youths. A school liaison position, held by an arts educator, should be established among such institutions to facilitate linkages between in-school programs and community programs.

The Role of Federal and State Governments

Surely it is irresponsible to seek support for the arts at the highest levels of government while ignoring the need to cultivate in young people some understanding of the arts and their role in human history. Federal and state policies that bear on art education too often have been framed from political and administrative expedience, rather than from a genuine concern for the art education of the nation's youth.

The dependence on short-term pilot or demonstration projects in schools, in the hope that the projects will serve as models for other schools, is wasteful of limited resources. The underlying assumption is that the best features of the pilot program can be marketed (mass-distributed) or can be emulated by other schools. What is forgotten in this "manufacturing" concept of change is the fundamental instability and variability of school settings. Federal and state funds are more likely to yield long-term benefits when they are invested in upgrading standards for schools and improving the skills of educators.

Providing Incentives for Improving Arts Education

□ State departments of education should review and upgrade teacher certification and school accreditation standards so as to assure that all students receive a basic education in the visual, literary, and performing arts.

□ Following such reviews, state departments of education should establish a program of incentive grants, complemented by funds from state arts and humanities councils, for local school improvements. About one-fourth of the money earmarked for schools might be reserved for regional in-service programs within the state, the remainder allocated to school districts on a competitive basis.

☐ Grants for school improvement efforts should be made by arts and humanities councils, and these grants should not be restricted to programs that offer temporary employment for artists. For example, grants should be made available to develop seminars, workshops, and in-service programs for educational leaders, administrators, university faculty, arts teachers, parents, and citizen groups.

Supporting Improved Research

Both the quantity and quality of research in arts education must be improved.

☐ No less than five research consortiums in arts education should be established to develop programs of research that address the problems in teaching the arts to children and young people in school settings. Such centers could be organized by disciplines in the arts or be conceived as regional centers serving nine or ten states. At least one additional center should serve as a clearing house and stimulus for unrestricted basic or applied research in arts education.

☐ Regional centers could be funded by various agencies within the nine or ten participating states. For example, if each state department of education, state arts council, and state humanities commission contributed about ten thousand dollars per year to the regional consortium, nearly three hundred thousand dollars would be generated. Additional funds might be secured from universities and foundations.

☐ In addition to such consortiums, or as an alternative to them, centers might be established for research on educational problems in the visual, literary, and performing arts. Such centers might receive major support from an agency such as the National Institute of Education, or from major foundations. Such centers should sponsor seminars that put theoretical and methodological experts at the disposal of arts educators for short but intensive training, as well as offering financial assistance for arts educators who wish to design research programs on selected topics.

☐ Each such center should annually award from three to five research fellowships to encourage new researchers.

Increasing Public Awareness of the Arts and Education

America's arts and its system of public schools cannot thrive in the absence of support from an informed citizenry. Beyond the improvement of education within our schools, the adult population needs to be better informed about the arts and about schools. There can be little doubt that the press and broadcast media can play an important role in providing that information.

In virtually every community, news coverage on the arts—in or out of schools—typically features the arts as a form of entertainment or as social events. The performing arts, collectively, are covered more fully by the media than the visual and literary arts.

If space or time is devoted by the media to arts programs in schools, the events reported are likely to be a student play, art exhibit, or concert. Occasionally, reporters draw attention to talented students or show the ingenuity of arts teachers. Arts educators are remiss in failing to provide the news media with information about the curriculum and the full range of experiences they undergo on the job, not just the stunning successes and the annual art show.

So, too, are members of the artistic community unmindful of opportunities for informal public education about art events held in the community. In many communities with a population of one million or more, up to an hour and a half of locally produced television news is broadcast every evening. It is not unusual for eight to twelve minutes to be devoted respectively to the weather and to sports. Many stations employ special sports reporters, provide them with staff and camera crews, and feature on-camera announcers who are connoisseurs of sports and able commentators.

In larger communities there is, without question, sufficient newsworthy activity in all of the arts, daily—both in and out of schools—to merit at least the same amount of broadcast time, on-camera talent, and staff for news coverage that is presently devoted to the weather and to sports. Interviews, rehearsals, activities, workspaces of artists and craftsworkers, financial problems, new programs, issues in urban design, architectural developments, in-school arts education—all are potentially newsworthy and of interest to particular segments of the general population. Moreover, both the print and the electronic news media have found it profitable to offer special features and commentaries which initially are designed for particular segments of their audience but later become regular features by virtue of a broader interest than had been anticipated. This untapped resource for informal public education in art should be developed.

□ Art educators and arts advocates are urged to support more adequate coverage of the arts by the press and by the broadcast media in their communities. Particularly in television, coverage of the arts during prime-time hours should be sought. In developing formats for such coverage, particular attention should be given to the visual arts, which, in general, are less often featured than the performing arts (the latter are usually covered as "entertainment.") Press and broadcast media are urged to generate news files that might later be edited and arranged into programs for use in schools.

□ Locally produced news on the arts should be channelled to new regional and national news services specializing in the arts, thereby expanding citizen awareness of the scope of artistic activity in the nation. Through such news services, local and regional artistic activity can also be brought to the attention of a national audience. Through such programming the citizen can be reminded that the arts are an essential part of the nation's culture, and for that very reason are at least as newsworthy as the weather and competitive sports.

The preceding recommendations do not, of course, exhaust the possibilities for building better arts programs in schools and enhancing public awareness of the arts. But if efforts of this kind were made on behalf of arts education, surely the arts would be more generally understood, appreciated, and supported by the public.

The vitality of the arts is an important measure of the personal and civic aspirations of a society, and of the quality of life which it has attained. Taken together, the arts, sciences, and humanities encompass much of what we regard as civilization. Insofar as we regard these fields of endeavor as window-dressing in the education of children, we betray the superficial aspirations that we have for ourselves, each other, and future generations. If the arts are to function as civilizing forces in our society, we must come to regard them as something more than a cosmetic within the culture and within our schools.

As long as art is the beauty parlor of civilization neither art nor civilization is secure.
—John Dewey
Art As Experience

Appendix A
Teacher Viewpoint Survey: The Results

This appendix is an abridged version of my "Teacher Viewpoint Survey: The Results," *School Arts* 78 (1979):2–5, reprinted with permission.

A word about the analysis. First, this report only shows the percentage (rounded) of *art teachers* who checked each item. Time and resources did not allow me to find out some of the fancy things that can be discovered by computer analysis (e.g., Do answers differ according to amount of teaching experience?). Second, I do not know how representative our sample is of all art teachers. I am pleased that each level of instruction is fairly well represented, and that there is a good spread in teaching experience at each level. Third, teaching assignments are not uniform. Teachers were grouped into four levels of instruction, according to their major teaching responsibilities.

Table A.1. Art Teachers Who Replied

| | Teaching Experience | | | |
Grade Level	0–5 Years	6–10 Years	1 or More Years	ALL
Elementary	(80)43%	(54)29%	(53)28%	187
Middle school or junior high[a]	(56)33%	(62)37%	(50)30%	168
Senior high	(70)37%	(60)32%	(59)31%	189
K–12 or art supervisor[b]	(28)50%	(10)18%	(18)32%	56
Totals	(234)39%	(186)31%	(180)30%	600

Note: Not analyzed were 12 replies from classroom teachers, 18 from college students, 19 from college teachers, 10 from museum educators and art therapists, and 51 incomplete or damaged in mail.

[a]Majority of teaching responsibility in grades 5–9.

[b]Includes resource teachers, consultants, teachers assigned to more than 7 nonconsecutive grade levels.

Table A.2. Students Who Are Served

Grade Level	Art Teachers	Number of Students Served	Average Load per Teacher
Elementary	187	106,520	570
Middle school or junior high	168	44,410	264
Senior high	189	24,120	127
K–12 or art supervisor	56	72,250	1,290
Totals	600	247,300	412

Table A.3.   Teacher Viewpoints

	Elementary N=186	Middle School Jr.Hi. N=168	Senior High N=189	K–12 or Supervisor N=56	TOTAL N=600
1. *Which of these art forms will you teach this year?*					
Drawing	97%	96%	96%	89%	96%
Painting	94%	92%	93%	86%	93%
Basic design	89%	89%	94%	84%	89%
Printmaking	92%	82%	85%	86%	86%
Sculpture	80%	78%	79%	82%	80%
Ceramics	79%	76%	79%	77%	78%
Collage	87%	70%	70%	71%	76%
Weaving, stitchery	85%	65%	69%	79%	74%
Mixed media 2-D	82%	58%	68%	79%	71%
Lettering, com. art	55%	72%	74%	59%	66%
Batik	47%	51%	57%	55%	52%
Jewelry	18%	25%	42%	30%	29%
Architecture	32%	29%	22%	20%	27%
Enameling	14%	26%	38%	21%	26%
Photography (still)	14%	11%	15%	13%	14%
Interior design	09%	14%	12%	09%	12%
Moviemaking or T.V.	10%	12%	08%	11%	10%
Fashion design	06%	07%	15%	)7%	10%
Urban or environmental design	10%	10%	06%	16%	09%
Industrial design	05%	05%	04%	02%	05%
2. *Which will you have in your art program this year?*					
Major art exhibit or art festival	73%	73%	78%	80%	75%
Field trips to museums or galleries	45%	38%	60%	71%	50%
Local artists/visits or exhibits at school	35%	27%	43%	46%	37%
Team teaching, art with academic subjects	47%	28%	16%	46%	32%
Sponsor art club	17%	30%	46%	34%	31%
Obtain T.V. or news reports on art program	22%	17%	33%	30%	25%
Have open classroom with activity centers	22%	23%	19%	30%	22%

Table A.3.   Teacher Viewpoints (Continued)

	Elemen-tary N=186	Middle School Jr.Hi. N=168	Senior High N=189	K–12 or Super-visor N=56	TOTAL N=600
Team teaching, visual arts with other arts	26%	20%	10%	23%	19%
Workshops or classes for parents, adminis-trators or teachers	23%	13%	12%	39%	18%
Field trips to studios of local artists	11%	11%	24%	21%	16%
Fund-raising event for art program	05%	17%	23%	16%	15%
Have parents serve as art program volun-teers	23%	07%	05%	20%	12%

3. What two problems most concern you?

Inadequate space, equipment, storage	51%	49%	50%	59%	51%
Classes too large	32%	52%	32%	25%	37%
Inadequate budget, supplies, resources	25%	38%	44%	48%	37%
Class periods are too short	32%	18%	30%	25%	27%
Not enough planning, preparation time	32%	18%	22%	25%	24%
Too many classes to teach	28%	14%	13%	34%	20%

4. What two problems most concern you?

Not enough time for my own art work	52%	53%	51%	54%	52%
Unruly or apathetic students	35%	60%	44%	43%	46%
Lack of administrative interest, support	25%	25%	34%	38%	29%
Lack of parental, com-munity interest, sup-port	24%	27%	26%	21%	25%
Uncertainty about wanting to teach at all	11%	13%	15%	07%	13%
Not enough ideas for art activities	11%	08%	08%	04%	09%

Table A.3.   Teacher Viewpoints (Continued)

	Elementary N=186	Middle School Jr.Hi. N=168	Senior High N=189	K–12 or Supervisor N=56	TOTAL N=600
5. How important is it for the art teacher to be a practicing artist or craftsworker?					
Valuable, not essential	52%	60%	52%	39%	52%
Absolutely essential	36%	30%	36%	50%	36%
Depends on the level of teaching	05%	07%	09%	11%	07%
Not essential	07%	04%	02%	00%	04%
6. Have you exhibited your own craft work in the last three years?					
Have created, but not exhibited	46%	46%	43%	45%	45%
*Have received commissions and/or sold works	21%	22%	28%	36%	25%
*Exhibited, juried or invitational show	21%	19%	32%	27%	24%
None, do not work in crafts	22%	22%	13%	09%	18%
*Exhibited, one-person show	06%	04%	09%	11%	07%
Exceptionally active (checked 3 marked*)	02%	02%	04%	00%	03%
Very active (checked 2 marked*)	08%	09%	13%	06%	11%
7. Have you exhibited your own studio art work in the last three years?					
Have created, but not exhibited	41%	46%	38%	30%	41%
*Exhibited, juried or invitational show	41%	46%	38%	30%	41%
*Shown in sales gallery or sold works	19%	25%	27%	32%	25%
None, do not work in studio fields	14%	11%	09%	14%	12%
Exhibited, one-person show	08%	08%	12%	18%	10%

Table A.3.   Teacher Viewpoints (Continued)

	Elemen- tary N=186	Middle School Jr.Hi. N=168	Senior High N=189	K–12 or Super- visor N=56	TOTAL N=600
Exceptionally active (checked 3 marked*)	02%	03%	06%	07%	04%
Very active (checked 2 marked *)	09%	09%	12%	18%	11%
8. About how often do you personally visit museums or galleries during a year?					
1–5 times	46%	54%	48%	38%	48%
6–10 times	24%	19%	21%	21%	22%
11–15 times	10%	06%	11%	14%	10%
Rarely, none available where I live	08%	11%	08%	14%	10%
16–20 times	06%	02%	07%	07%	05%
21 times or more	08%	10%	05%	09%	08%
9. How active are you in art education profession-al associations?					
Rarely participate	56%	54%	54%	45%	54%
Moderately active	36%	36%	33%	34%	35%
Very active	08%	10%	13%	21%	11%
10. Will your students enter the Scholastic Art Exhibit this year?					
No	95%	67%	60%	77%	75%
Yes	05%	33%	40%	23%	25%
11. How often do you in-tegrate art into academic subjects?					
Occasionally, when the art doesn't get lost	35%	32%	30%	32%	32%
Frequently, to stimu-late creative thinking	28%	23%	15%	20%	22%
Regularly, part of my basic philosophy	24%	12%	13%	29%	18%
Rarely, not that valu-able or essential (us-ually)	04%	11%	10%	05%	08%
Rarely, not appropri-ate at my grade level	03%	08%	14%	02%	08%

Table A.3.   Teacher Viewpoints (Continued)

	Elementary N=186	Middle School Jr.Hi. N=168	Senior High N=189	K–12 or Supervisor N=56	TOTAL N=600
Rarely, not knowledgeable enough	04%	04%	08%	04%	05%
12. Which subject do you integrate most frequently with art?					
Social studies	45%	32%	20%	52%	34%
English/language arts	42%	25%	34%	14%	26%
Creative writing	11%	17%	13%	09%	13%
Science	15%	13%	08%	05%	11%
Mathematics	04%	05%	05%	02%	04%
Health/physical education	02%	01%	01%	02%	01%
13. Do you introduce your students to art history?					
Informally, in connection with creative art activities	61%	54%	52%	68%	57%
Regularly, as context for creative activity or during special class periods set aside for this	25%	32%	36%	25%	30%
Regularly, as a separate course	01%	04%	07%	05%	04%
Rarely teach it, not appropriate at my grade level	06%	05%	00%	00%	04%
Rarely teach it, not knowledgeable enough	04%	03%	04%	00%	03%
Rarely teach it, not that essential or valuable	01%	01%	01%	00%	01%
14. How do you most often teach art history?					
Historical designs and techniques related to creative art activity	33%	30%	39%	32%	34%
Visual arts of a selected culture or period, not chronological	24%	29%	18%	23%	23%

Table A.3.   Teacher Viewpoints (Continued)

	Elementary N=186	Middle School Jr.Hi. N=168	Senior High N=189	K-12 or Supervisor N=56	TOTAL N=600
Chronological, earliest times to present	05%	09%	20%	11%	11%
Comparisons and contrasts among very different cultures/ periods	12%	11%	07%	14%	11%
One broad theme as interpreted across many cultures (e.g. animals, war, seasons)	16%	07%	05%	07%	09%
Similarities in all of the arts of a culture/ period	03%	03%	06%	07%	04%
15. *How often do you teach relationships among the arts?*					
Occasionally, for perceptual awareness or art motivation/ learning	47%	40%	42%	43%	43%
Rarely, not knowledgeable enough	18%	27%	37%	27%	26%
Frequently, for perceptual awareness or art motivation/ learning	15%	08%	09%	09%	11%
Rarely, not that valuable or essential (usually)	05%	05%	08%	09%	07%
Regularly, as a special course or as part of my basic philosophy	06%	05%	05%	07%	06%
Rarely, not appropriate at my grade level	03%	08%	01%	04%	04%
16. *Check the two art forms you relate to the visual arts most frequently.*					
All of the senses—see, hear, touch, motion, etc.	67%	59%	56%	70%	61%

Table A.3.   Teacher Viewpoints (Continued)

	Elemen-tary N=186	Middle School Jr.Hi. N=168	Senior High N=189	K–12 or Super-visor N=56	TOTAL N=600
Music/sound	37%	40%	38%	32%	38%
Literature/poetry	18%	18%	21%	18%	19%
Creative writing	14%	14%	13%	18%	14%
Dance/movement	16%	11%	12%	13%	13%
Theater/acting	11%	12%	14%	04%	12%
17. How do you most often interrelate the arts?					
Emphasizing the elements and principles of design (line, color, etc.)	41%	49%	52%	52%	48%
Using other arts to enhance experience of the visual arts	19%	12%	08%	16%	13%
Emphasizing how each art might express the same broad idea (e.g. mystery)	14%	09%	11%	16%	12%
Emphasizing similarities in the creative process of the artist	09%	09%	11%	05%	09%
Using the visual arts to enhance experience of other arts	09%	05%	05%	00%	06%
Emphasizing similarities in all the arts of a culture/period	04%	05%	07%	07%	06%
18. Which statement best applies to your art program?					
Builds perceptual skills and ability to use media	38%	39%	35%	41%	38%
Develops openness to new ideas, originality, imagination	41%	32%	34%	29%	35%
Presents a good foundation in design elements and principles	16%	18%	19%	13%	17%
Nurtures awareness of the uses of art in everyday life	03%	13%	11%	16%	10%

Table A.3. Teacher Viewpoints (Continued)

	Elemen-tary N=186	Middle School Jr.Hi. N=168	Senior High N=189	K–12 or Super-visor N=56	TOTAL N=600
19. *Which statement best describes what you do?*					
Make sure students know I'm aware of their effort, prog-ress, achievements	34%	32%	38%	41%	35%
Get students involved cooperatively, solv-ing problems, shar-ing discoveries	28%	26%	25%	32%	27%
Make sure each stu-dent feels free to ex-periment, take risks	29%	20%	20%	25%	23%
Set high standards, let students know I ex-pect the best	08%	23%	17%	05%	15%
20. *Which statement best applies to you as a teacher?*					
Make art relevant to students' natural in-terests and ordinary experience	40%	26%	26%	45%	32%
Demonstrate that art is important, not a frill but a solid subject	24%	27%	26%	27%	26%
Make art exciting, spe-cial, different from anything else	22%	29%	16%	05%	21%
Show that art results from trial and error, patience and dedica-tion	15%	19%	26%	20%	20%

Appendix B
The Arts Audience: Income and Educational Background

The figures in this appendix illustrate some of the characteristics of the cultural elite in the United States—those who frequently attend arts and cultural events in their communities. Income, general educational background, and selected art experiences in the early education of the elite are noted.

Figure B.1. Art Museum Audience: Median Levels of Education. Percentage of Sample Audience

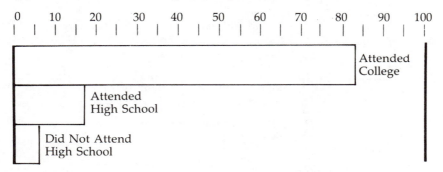

Note: Data from National Endowment for the Arts, *Audience Studies of the Performing Arts and Museums* (Washington, D.C.: National Endowment for the Arts, 1978), p. 20.

Figure B.2. Arts Audience: Median Income.

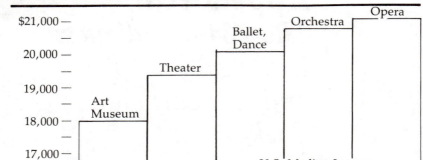

Note: Data from National Endowment for the Arts, *Audience Studies of the Performing Arts and Museums* (Washington, D.C.: National Endowment for the Arts, 1978), p. 30. The U. S. median income of $14,476 was figured in constant U.S. dollars.

Figure B.3. The Arts Audience (Frequent Attenders): Educational Background Compared with That of General Public.

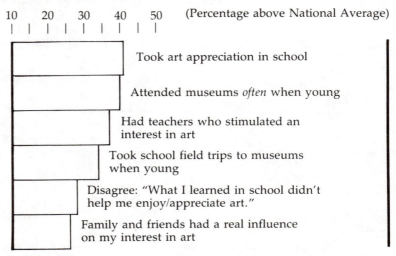

Note: Data cited by permission from *Americans and the Arts,* copyright 1976 by the American Council for the Arts, pp. 33, 68, 72–75.

Appendix C
The 1974–75 National Assessment of Educational Progress in Art:
Selected Results

Figures C.1 through C.4 present some questions asked, and some selected results from the 1974–75 National Art Assessment. Students were tested at ages nine, thirteen, and seventeen. All data in the figures can be found in National Assessment of Educational Progress, *Art Technical Report: Exercise Volume*, Report no. 06-A-20 (Denver: Education Commission of the States, 1978). Page references are noted at the bottom of each figure.

Figure C.1. Drawing Skills: Most Typical Drawings of a Table. Students were to pretend they were at one end of a room looking at the other end of the room where four people were sitting at a table. They were asked to draw the table and people "as you would see them from your end of the room." The exercise was scored on fourteen characteristics that indicated an ability to visualize three-dimensional space on a two-dimensional plane. An acceptable drawing included any seven of the fourteen characteristics. The perspective techniques most readily used by all students are overlap and the placement of major components higher or lower on the page. Foreshortening by the use of diagonals or by the placement and length of line *within* parts (table and chair legs) are skills which two-thirds of the seventeen-year-olds did *not* exhibit.

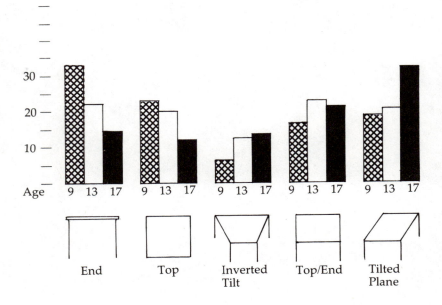

Note: Data from National Assessment, *Art Technical Report: Exercise Volume,* Report no. 06-A-20 (Denver: Education Commission of the States, 1978), pp. 148–56.

Figure C.2. Design Skills. Students were asked to draw a design or picture that would fit the shape of a bedroom wall interrupted by an off-center door. The exercise booklet contained a picture space with a predrawn blank wall and door. Drawings were judged on whether: 1) the design fit successfully within the shape of the wall (three points); 2) the elements were related to one another in an integrated, coherent, or consistent manner (two points); and 3) the door functioned as an integral part of the overall design (one point). Three points from any of these categories meant the exercise was completed acceptably. (Separate scores were obtained for unusual elements, but not included in the judgment of successful completion.) Achievement increases with age, and it is greater for the overall shape (whole) than for the part-to-part relationships.

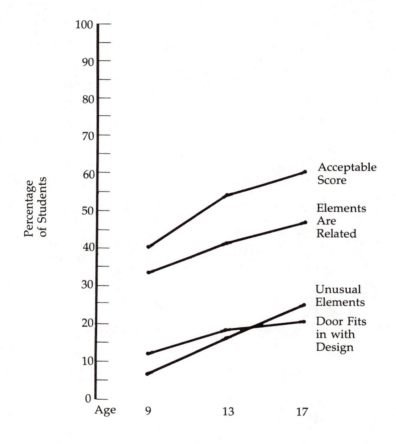

Note: Data from National Assessment of Educational Progress, *Art Technical Report: Exercise Volume,* Report no. 06-A-20 (Denver: Education Commission of the States, 1978), pp. 142–46.

Figure C.3. Attitudes Toward Art. Attitudes toward art were assessed by determining levels of student involvement in art outside of school and by direct and open-ended questions treating 1) the importance of art, 2) evaluations of works of art, as well as of 3) tolerance for experimentation and stylistic variety in art. Only a few of the values that students attach to art are noted in the chart. Of special interest is the fact that many of the seventeen-year-olds value art as a "means of communication and expression," but, at the same time, *disagreed* with the statement: "It's important for *me* to express my ideas and feelings through art."

In order to assess art preferences and "openness" to experimentation in art, students were presented with reproductions of works from a range of styles and asked to agree or disagree with statements such as "It's all right for works of art to look like this"; "The world would be better off without art like this"; or, following a description of how a work was made, "Do you think artists should experiment in this way?" In general, endorsements suggesting openness to styles of art increased dramatically from age nine to thirteen (from 30 to 60 percent as the modal response) with much less change from age thirteen to seventeen (from 60 to 70 percent as the mode).

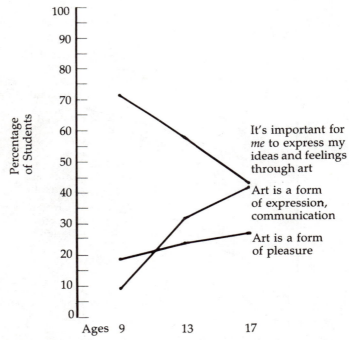

Note: Data from National Assessment of Educational Progress, *Art Technical Report: Exercise Volume,* Report no. 06-A-20 (Denver: Education Commission of the States, 1978), pp. 76–77.

Figure C.4. Response to a Work of Art. In one open-ended exercise, students were asked to state whether or not they enjoyed looking at a drawing (*Stammich*, by George Grosz) and to offer reasons for their answers in writing. Four points were awarded for a reason that touched on the sensory, formal (relational), or technical aspects of the work; three points were given for a "yes" to enjoyment. One point each was given for a reason that touched on the subject matter of the work, its overall quality, its meaning, or for a personal association or expression of preference. An acceptable response required six points. Few students at any age are able to move beyond general observations about the subject matter ("It's a picture of . . ." or "It looks like . . ."). The ability to mention qualities of line, shape, texture, composition, or technique was undeveloped in nearly 75 percent of these seventeen-year-olds. At each age, 20 percent of the students offered a preference statement of the form "I like it" or "I don't like it." The stability of this response serves as a reminder that simple expressions of personal preference are not a good measure of what students have learned.

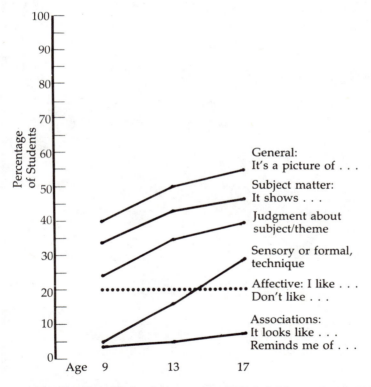

Note: Data from National Assessment, *Art Technical Report: Exercise Volume*, Report no. 06-A-20 (Denver: Education Commission of the States, 1978), pp. 58–60.

Notes

Introduction

1. National Assessment of Educational Progress, *Art Technical Report: Exercise Volume*, Report no. 06-A-20 (Denver: Education Commission of the States, 1978); also *Art and Young Americans, 1974–79: Selected Results from the Second National Art Assessment*, Report no. 10-A-01 (Denver: Education Commission of the States, 1981).

2. D. M. Rindskopf, A. Harnischfeger, and D. E. Wiley, "Arts Education in Public Secondary Schools: Opportunity and Participation," Technical Memorandum no. AH-21 (St. Louis: Central Midwestern Regional Educational Laboratory, 1978).

3. P. Dimaggio, M. Useem, and P. Brown, *Audience Studies of the Performing Arts and Museums: A Critical Review*, Research Report no. 9 (Washington, D.C.: National Endowment for the Arts, Research Division, 1978).

4. National Research Center of the Arts, *Americans and the Arts: A Survey of Public Opinion* (New York: Associated Councils of the Arts, 1975); also *Americans and the Arts* (New York: American Council for the Arts, 1981).

5. L. H. Chapman, "Teacher Viewpoint Survey: The Results," *School Arts* 78 (1979):2–5.

6. Commission on the Humanities, *The Humanities in American Life* (Berkeley: University of California Press, 1980), pp. 25–31.

Chapter 1:
Instant Art, Instant Culture: The Unspoken Policy for the Nation's Schools

1. The statistics in this paragraph will be documented at appropriate points in the text.

2. A. Toffler, *The Culture Consumers: A Study of Art and Affluence in America* (New York: Random House, Vintage Books, 1964).

3. P. Dimaggio, M. Useem, and P. Brown, *Audience Studies of the Performing Arts and Museums: A Critical Review*, Research Report no. 9 (Washington, D.C.: National Endowment for the Arts, Research Division, 1978).

4. National Research Center of the Arts, *Americans and the Arts: A Survey of Public Opinion* (New York: Associated Councils of the Arts, 1975), p. 76. Throughout this chapter, and in following chapters, the data are cited by permission from *Americans and the Arts*, copyright 1975 by the American Council for the Arts.

5. Ibid., p. 55.

6. Ibid.

7. National Research Center of the Arts, *Americans and the Arts* (New York: American Council for the Arts, 1981), pp. 25, 38. Throughout this chapter and in following chapters, the data are cited by permission from *Americans and the Arts*, copyright 1981 by the American Council for the Arts.

8. National Research Center, *Americans and the Arts* (1975), pp. 52–53.

9. National Research Center, *Americans and the Arts* (1981), p. 50

10. Ibid., p. 51.

11. National Research Center, *Americans and the Arts* (1975), p. 25.

12. Ibid., pp. 76, 110–12.

13. Dimaggio, Useem, and Brown, *Audience Studies*, p. 30.

14. National Research Center, *Americans and the Arts* (1975), pp. 33, 68–71.

15. A. L. Barresi, "Federal Commitment to the Arts: An Historical Tracing," *American Arts* 11 (1980):22–25.

16. See references for chaps. 9 and 10.

17. Exceptions can be found, of course. See H. S. Broudy, B. O. Smith, and J. R. Burnett, *Democracy and Excellence in American Secondary Education: A Study in Curriculum Theory* (Chicago: Rand McNally, 1964); E. W. Eisner, *The Educational Imagination* (New York: Macmillan, 1979).

18. See references for chap. 8.

19. See references for chap. 7.

20. See references for chaps. 5 and 6.

Chapter 2:
Reforming the Curriculum: A New Role for the Arts

1. See the following for each of these trends: D. A. Williams, J. Huck, C. Ma, and S. Monroe, "Why Public Schools Fail," *Newsweek*, 20 Apr. 1981, pp. 62–65; M. Kirst and R. Jung, "The Utility of a Longitudinal Approach in Assessing

Implementation: A Thirteen-Year View of Title I, ESEA," *Educational Evaluation and Policy Analysis* 2 (1980):17–34; D. L. Stufflebeam and W. J. Webster, "An Analysis of Alternative Approaches to Evaluation," *Educational Evaluation and Policy Analysis* 2 (1980):5–20; L. W. Anderson and J. C. Anderson, "Functional Literacy Tests: A Case of Anticipatory Validity?" *Educational Evaluation and Policy Analysis* 3 (1981): 51–56; J. G. Chambers, "An Analysis of School Size Under a Voucher System," *Educational Evaluation and Policy Analysis* 3 (1981): 29–40.

2. E. L. Boyer and A. Levine, *A Quest for Common Learning* (Washington, D.C.: Carnegie Foundation for the Advancement of Teaching, 1981).

3. A. Harnischfeger, "Curricular Control and Learning Time: District Strategy, Teacher Strategy, and Pupil Choice," *Educational Evaluation and Policy Analysis* 2 (1980):19–30.

4. C. M. Dorn, "The New Eclecticism, or Art Is Anything You Can Get Away With," *Art Education* 31 (1978):8.

5. L. H. Chapman, "Curriculum Planning in Art Education," *Ohio Art Education Newsletter* 8 (1970):6–20.

6. D. M. Rindskopf, A. Harnischfeger, and D. E. Wiley, "Arts Education in Public Secondary Schools: Opportunity and Participation," Technical Memorandum no. AH-21 (St. Louis: Central Midwestern Regional Educational Laboratory, 1978), pp. 17, 82–83.

7. A. Harnischfeger and D. Miller, "Resources for Art Education in the Nation's Elementary Schools: Opportunity, Time, and Instructional Staff Qualifications," Technical Report no. AH-78 (St. Louis: Central Midwestern Regional Educational Laboratory, 1979).

8. National School Boards Association, *The Arts in Education,* Research Report no. 1978–2 (Washington, D.C.: National School Boards Association, 1978), p. 89.

9. J. Goodlad, "Education in What Is Basic," in S. M. Dobbs, ed., *Arts Education and Back to Basics* (Reston, Va.: National Art Education Association, 1979), pp. 12–26.

10. Arts, Education and Americans Panel, *Coming to Our Senses: The Significance of the Arts for American Education* (New York: McGraw-Hill, 1977).

Chapter 3:
Back to Basics: Including Art

1. Many of the arguments presented in this chapter are presented more fully in my *Approaches to Art in Education* (New York: Harcourt Brace Jovanovich, 1978), especially chap. 6.

2. Ibid.; for an extended discussion, see chap. 5.

3. See Chapman, *Approaches,* especially chap. 6, and this volume, chaps. 3 and 4.

4. P. Dimaggio, M. Useem, and P. Brown, *Audience Studies of the Performing Arts and Museums: A Critical Review,* Research Report no. 9 (Washington, D.C.: National Endowment for the Arts, Research Division, 1978).

5. For a critical revieiw of these claims, see V. Lanier, "Schismogenesis in Contemporary Art Education," *Studies in Art Education* 5 (1963):10–19. For examples of such claims, see Art, Education and Americans Panel, *Coming to Our Senses: The Significance of the Arts for American Education* (New York: McGraw-Hill, 1977).
6. I first presented the model shown in an address presented to a meeting of the Ohio Art Education Association in November 1969. See also my "Curriculum Planning in Art Education," *Ohio Art Education Association Newsletter* 8 (1970):6–20. The present form is adapted from Table 6–1, *Approaches to Art in Education* by Laura H. Chapman, copyright © 1978 by Harcourt Brace Jovanovich, Inc. and used with their permission.
7. H. Gardner, *The Arts and Human Development: The Psychological Study of the Artistic Process* (New York: Wiley, 1973), pp. 242–98.
8. M. D. Day, "Effects of Instruction on High School Students' Art Preferences and Art Judgments," *Studies in Art Education* 18 (1976):25–39.
9. For a more detailed discussion, see Chapman, *Approaches*, chap. 19.

Chapter 4:
Basic Education in Art: Guidelines for Programs

1. Costs of reading program reported in *Cincinnati Enquirer*, 11 Nov. 1979. Junior high school allowance for art is based on my own budget while teaching in 1960–70. Even with adjustments for inflation, the contrast in allocations is striking.
2. For a commentary on these problems, see W. Raspberry, "Teaching Reading Remains a Problem," *Cincinnati Enquirer*, 7 Dec. 1981.
3. Listings can be found in most college texts for art-teacher education programs.
4. For an extended discussion, see my *Approaches to Art in Education* (New York: Harcourt Brace Jovanovich, 1978), chap. 18.
5. The discussion of Halloween art is adapted from my "Curriculum Planning in Art Education," *Ohio Art Education Newsletter* 8 (1970):6–20.
6. See J. C. Taylor, "The History of Art in Education," in E. L. Mattil, ed., *A Seminar in Art Education for Research and Curriculum Development* (University Park: Pennsylvania State University, 1966), pp. 42–59.
7. See J. E. Grigsby, Jr., *Art and Ethnics: Background for Teaching Youth in a Pluralistic Society* (Dubuque, Iowa: William C. Brown, 1977), pp. 125–27.
8. Chapman, *Approaches*, chap. 20.

Chapter 5:
The Most Crucial Years: Art in the Elementary School

1. A. Harnischfeger and D. Miller, "Resources for Art Education in the Nation's Elementary Schools: Opportunity, Time, and Instructional Staff

Qualifications," Technical Report no. AH-78 (St. Louis: Central Midwestern Regional Educational Laboratory, 1979), p. 10.

2. P. Greenberg, "Survey: Art and Music—State Requirements," *NAEA News* 21 (1979):8.

3. Harnischfeger and Miller, "Resources for Art Education," pp. 3–12.

4. E. W. Eisner, "Conservative Influences on Arts Education," in S. M. Dobbs, ed., *Arts Education and Back to Basics* (Reston, Va.: National Art Education Association, 1979), p. 73.

5. L. H. Chapman, "Teacher Viewpoint Survey: The Results," *School Arts* 78 (1979):2–5.

6. See, for example, V. Lowenfeld, *Creative and Mental Growth,* 1st ed. (New York: Macmillan, 1947), p. 1; also R. Kellogg, *Analyzing Children's Art* (Palo Alto, Calif.: Mayfield, 1969).

7. A. Efland, "The School Art Style: A Functional Analysis," *Studies in Art Education* 17 (1976): 37–44.

8. All of the data cited in the discussion of teaching practices in elementary schools comes from Chapman, "Teacher Viewpoint Survey," pp. 2–5. Presented in slightly abridged form, the survey has been included for reference; see appendix A of this book, pp. 163–170.

9. Chapman, "Teacher Viewpoint Survey," p. 4.

10. Ibid., p. 5.

11. Ibid.

12. Ibid.

13. Ibid.

14. Ibid., p. 4.

15. Ibid.

16. All citations of results from the first National Art Assessment are based on: National Assessment of Educational Progress, *Art Technical Report: Exercise Volume,* no. 06-A-20 (Denver: Education Commission of the States, 1978). All citations of results from the second National Art Assessment and on the changes in scores between the first and second assessments are based on: National Assessment of Educational Progress, *Art and Young Americans, 1974– 79: Results from the Second National Art Assessment,* Report no. 10-A-01 (Denver: Education Commission of the States, 1981).

17. National Assessment, *Art Technical Report: Exercise Volume,* pp. 147–55, 163–67.

18. Ibid.

19. Ibid., pp. 169–209.

20. Ibid., pp. 45–61, 101–41.

21. Ibid., pp. 61–67, 73–77, 84–88.

22. Ibid., pp. 61–75.

23. Harnischfeger and Miller, "Resources for Art Education," p. 10.

24. National Assessment, *Art and Young Americans,* p. 5.

25. Ibid., pp. 46, 55.

26. Ibid., pp. 65–70.

27. Ibid., pp. 20, 36.

28. Ibid., pp. 23, 27–34.
29. Ibid., pp. 13–16.
30. Ibid., pp. 35–42.

Chapter 6:
Rites of Passage: Art in the Secondary School

1. L. H. Chapman, "Teacher Viewpoint Survey: The Results," *School Arts* 78 (1979):2–5.
2. For an explanation of the analytical technique I employed, see my "Bearing of Artistic and Educational Commitments on the Teaching of Art," in G. L. Knieter and J. Stallings, eds., *The Teaching Process and the Arts and Aesthetics* (St. Louis: Central Midwestern Regional Educational Laboratory, 1979), pp. 193–216.
3. Chapman, "Teacher Viewpoint Survey," p. 4.
4. National Assessment of Educational Progress, *Art and Young Americans, 1974–79: Results from the Second National Art Assessment*, Report no. 10-A-01 (Denver: Education Commission of the States, 1981), p. 5.
5. Ibid., pp. 42, 50, 61, 77.
6. Ibid., pp. 13–14.
7. Ibid.
8. Requirements, course offerings, and enrollment data are from D. M. Rindskopf, A. Harnischfeger, and D. E. Wiley, "Arts Education in Public Secondary Schools: Opportunity and Participation," Technical Memorandum no. AH-21 (St. Louis: Central Midwestern Regional Educational Laboratory, 1978), pp. 17–83.
9. Chapman, "Teacher Viewpoint Survey," p. 4.
10. Percentages from Rindskopf et al., "Arts Education," for 1972 were similar to those in the *School Arts* survey in 1979, p. 4.
11. National Assessment, *Art and Young Americans*, p. 18–19.
12. For a picture of the earning power of artists, see Data Use and Access Laboratories, *Selected Characteristics of Artists: 1970*, Research Report no. 10 (Washington, D.C.: National Endowment for the Arts, Research Division, 1978).
13. Chapman, "Teacher Viewpoint Survey." All statistics cited in the discussion of teaching practices in high school are from this source. See also appendix A.
14. National Assessment, *Art and Young Americans*, pp. 18–19.
15. National Assessment of Educational Progress, *Art Technical Report: Exercise Volume*, no. 06-A-20 (Denver: Education Commission of the States, 1978), pp. 61–63.
16. National Assessment, *Art and Young Americans*, pp. 19–20.
17. Ibid., p. 21–22.
18. Ibid., p. 6.

19.   National Assessment, *Art Technical Report: Exercise Volume,* pp. 75–77; *Art and Young Americans,* p. 23.

20.   National Assessment, *Art and Young Americans,* p. 6.

21.   National Assessment, *Art Technical Report: Exercise Volume,* pp. 146, 155; also, National Assessment of Educational Progress, *Art Technical Report: Summary Volume,* no. 06-A-21 (Denver: Education Commission of the States, 1978), pp. 14, 22.

22.   Ibid.

23.   National Assessment, *Art Technical Report: Summery Volume,* pp. 14, 22; also National Assessment of Educational Progress, *Design and Drawing Skills: Selected Results from the First National Assessment of Art,* Art Report 06-A-01 (Denver: Education Commission of the States, 1977), pp. 88–89, 102.

24.   National Assessment, *Art and Young Americans,* pp. 13–16, 34, 42, 61, 77–78.

25.   National Assessment, *Art Technical Report: Exercise Volume,* p. 186.

26.   Ibid., p. 204.

Chapter 7:
The Most Important Ingredient: The Reform of Art Teacher Education

1.   Much of the discussion in this chapter is based on my address "Criteria for Effective Art Teachers," delivered at the Maryland Conference on Teacher Education, Frostburg State College, Frostburg, Md., 3 Apr. 1970, pp. 1–23.

2.   I developed these examples of metaphors in connection with the address noted above. They also appear in "Evaluating the Total School Art Program," multilith (New York: Arts in Education Program, JDR 3rd Fund, 1973), pp. 9–28.

3.   L. H. Chapman, "Teacher Viewpoint Survey: The Results," *School Arts* 78 (1979):2–5.

4.   For a discussion of these issues, see J. Loeb, ed., *Feminist Collage: Educating Women in the Visual Arts* (New York: Teachers College Press, 1979).

5.   National Research Center of the Arts, *Americans and the Arts: A Survey of Public Opinion* (New York: Associated Councils of the Arts, 1975), p. 33. Cited by permission from *Americans and the Arts,* copyright 1975 by the American Council for the Arts.

6.   See M. J. Sevigny, "Triangulated Inquiry: An Alternative Methodology for the Study of Classroom Life," *Review of Research in Visual Arts Education* 8 (1978):1–16.

7.   D. M. Rindskopf, A. Harnischfeger, and D. E. Wiley, "Arts Education in Public Secondary Schools: Opportunity and Participation," Technical Memorandum no. AH-21 (St. Louis: Central Midwestern Regional Educational Laboratory, 1978), p. 67.

8. For an extended discussion of the history of art education, see F. M. Logan, *Growth of Art in American Schools* (New York: Harper, 1955), or chap. 1 in my *Approaches to Art in Education.*

Chapter 8:
The Research We Have: The Research We Need

1. See, for example, the first sentence in V. Lowenfeld, *Creative and Mental Growth*, 1st ed. (New York: Macmillan, 1947), p. 1; also R. Kellogg, *Analyzing Children's Art* (Palo Alto, Calif.: Mayfield, 1969).

2. For a recent example of these themes, see C. M. Dorn, "The New Eclecticism, or Art Is Anything You Can Get Away With," *Art Education* 31 (1978):8.

3. For this definition, I am indebted to Dr. Elizabeth Steiner, Professor of Educational Theory and Philosophy, Indiana University, Bloomington.

4. For example, the single most comprehensive historical study, though out of print, is F. M. Logan, *Growth of Art in American Schools* (New York: Harper, 1955).

5. For example, see K. Rawlins, "Educational Metamorphosis of the American Museum," *Studies in Art Education* 20 (1978):4–17.

6. Some of these titles may be found in R. J. Saunders, "The Arts—Working Together to Make Education Work: An Idea Whose Time Has Come," *Studies in Art Education* 19 (1978):14–20.

7. H. Mearns, *Creative Power: The Education of Youth in the Creative Arts* (New York: Dover, 1929) might be taken as a benchmark for the acceptance of the idea. See also J. P. Guilford, *The Nature of Human Intelligence* (New York: McGraw-Hill, 1967).

8. See A. W. Dow, *Composition* (New York: Doubleday Page, 1899).

9. For a review of this literature, see D. J. Davis, "Research Trends in Art and Art Education: 1883–1972," in S. S. Madeja, ed., *Arts and Aesthetics: An Agenda for the Future* (St. Louis: Central Midwestern Regional Educational Laboratory, 1977), pp. 109–47.

10. See K. R. Beittle, *Alternatives for Art Education Research: Inquiry into the Making of Art* (Dubuque, Iowa: William C. Brown, 1973); E. W. Eisner, "On the Differences Between Scientific and Artistic Approaches to Research," *Educational Researcher* 10 (1981):5–9.

11. Exceptions can be noted. See, for example, R. Arnheim, *Art and Visual Perception* (Berkeley: University of California Press, 1966), pp. 202–12; and E. V. Brown, "Developmental Characteristics of Clay Figures Made by Children from Age Three Through Age Eleven," *Studies in Art Education* 16 (1975):45–53.

12. See E. Ulman, E. Kramer, and H. Y. Kwaitkowska, *Art Therapy in the United States* (Craftsbury, Conn.: Art Therapy Publications, 1979).

13. H. Schaefer-Simmern, *The Unfolding of Artistic Activity* (Berkeley: University of California Press, 1948); also Kellogg, *Analyzing Child Art*, and Arnheim, *Art and Perception.*

14. J. K. McFee, *Preparation for Art*, 2d ed. (Belmont, Calif.: Wadsworth, 1970).

15. H. Gardner, *The Arts and Human Development: A Psychological Study of the Artistic Process* (New York: Wiley, 1973).

16. See S. S. Madeja, ed., *The Arts, Cognition, and Basic Skills* (St. Louis: Central Midwestern Regional Educational Laboratory, 1978); H. J. Gans, *Popular Culture and High Culture* (New York: Basic Books, 1974).

17. G. W. Hardiman and T. Zernich, "Some Considerations for the Measurement of Preference in the Visual Arts," *Review of Research in Visual Arts Education* 4 (1975):1–14.

18. L. H. Chapman, "The Bearing of Artistic and Educational Commitments on the Teaching of Art," in G. L. Knieter and J. Stallings, eds., *The Teaching Process and the Arts and Aesthetics* (St. Louis: Central Midwestern Regional Educational Laboratory, 1979), pp. 193–217.

19. M. J. Sevigny, "Triangulated Inquiry: An Alternative Methodology for the Study of Classroom Life," *Review of Research in Visual Arts Education* 8 (1978):1–16.

20. V. Lanier, "The Five Faces of Art Education," *Studies in Art Education* 18 (1977):7–21.

21. For a review of some of these trends, and others, see F. M. Logan, "Up Date '75, Growth in American Art Education," *Studies in Art Education* 17 (1975):9–17. For a discussion of cultural anthropology and ethnography, see F. G. Chalmers, "Art Education as Ethnology," *Studies in Art Education* 22 (1981):6–14. For an example bearing on policy, see R. A. Smith, "Justifying Policy for Aesthetic Education," *Studies in Art Education* 20 (1978):37–42.

22. D. E. Mitchell, "Social Science Impact on Legislative Decision Making: Process and Substance," *Educational Researcher* 9 (1980):9–12, 17–19.

23. U.S. House of Representatives, National Institute of Education Appropriations Bill, Report 95, 1979.

24. Cited by W. Wolf in "A Trend that is Questionable," *Theory into Practice* 6 (1967):55.

25. D. W. White, "An Historical Review of Doctoral Program Growth and Dissertation Research in Art Education, 1893–1974," *Studies in Art Education* 19 (1977):6–20.

26. M. D. Day, "Point with Pride or View with Alarm? Notes on the NEA's Evaluation of the Artists-in-Schools Program," in Smith, ed., *Artists-in-Schools: Analysis and Criticism* (Champaign: University of Illinois Bureau of Educational Research, 1978).

27. For a variety of observations on this process, see R. A. Smith, ed., "Special Issue: The Government, Art, and Aesthetic Education," *Journal of Aesthetic Education* 14 (1980); also *Studies in Art Education* 19 (1978), entire issue.

Chapter 9:
Arts Education as a Political Issue: The Federal Legacy

1. C. Fowler, ed., *An Arts in Education Source Book: A View from the JDR 3rd Fund* (New York: JDR 3rd Fund, 1980), pp. ix, 203–5. For a review of the research programs, see J. Murphy and L. Jones, "Research in Arts Education:

A Federal Chapter," Report 76-02000, mimeographed (Washington, D.C.: Office of Education, 1978).

2.   H. Conant, ed., *Seminar on Elementary and Secondary School Education in the Visual Arts* (New York: New York University, 1965).

3.   E. L. Mattil, ed., *A Seminar in Art Education for Research and Curriculum Development* (University Park: Pennsylvania State University, 1966), p. 399.

4.   M. Barkan and L. H. Chapman, "Report on the Planning Phase: Aesthetic Education Program," mimeographed (Columbus: Ohio State University, Department of Art Education, 1967).

5.   *CEMREL Newsletter* (1980):7. Each unit contains materials for the teacher and six students. Through a telephone call to the Publications Department of CEMREL (in April 1982), I was informed that eleven units could be purchased for $704.00. One unit was no longer available.

6.   For a listing of these, see S. S. Madeja and S. Onuska, *Through the Arts to the Aesthetic: The CEMREL Aesthetic Education Curriculum* (St. Louis: Central Midwestern Regional Educational Laboratory, 1977), pp. 137–41.

7.   S. S. Madeja, ed. *The Artist in the School: A Report on the Artist-in-Residence Project* (St. Louis: Central Midwestern Regional Educational Laboratory, 1970).

8.   For examples, see L. Jones, "The Arts and the U.S. Department of Education: A List of Funded Projects and Activities," mimeographed (Washington, D.C.: U.S. Department of Education, 1979).

9.   M. Snow, "Arts in Education Evaluation, A Report to the Pennsylvania State Department of Education," mimeographed (Harrisburg: Pennsylvania State Department of Education, Bureau of Curriculum Services, 1979).

10.   J. Eddy, "Toward Coordinated Federal Policies for Support of Arts Education," mimeographed (Washington, D.C.: Alliance for Arts Education, John F. Kennedy Center for the Performing Arts, 1977).

11.   Quoted in J. Eddy, *Arts Education 1977—In Prose and Print: An Overview of Nine Significant Publications Affecting the Arts in American Education* (Washington, D.C.: U.S. Office of Education, Arts and Humanities Program, 1977. GPO Publication no. 260-934-2044), pp. 27–28.

12.   Madeja, ed., *Artist in the School*.

13.   D. Netzer, *The Subsidized Muse: Public Support for the Arts in the United States* (Cambridge, England: Cambridge University Press, 1978), pp. 114–17, 186.

14.   E. W. Eisner, "Is the Artist in the School Program Effective?" *Art Education* 27 (1974):19–24; Western States Arts Foundation, "A Study of the Poetry and Visual Arts Components of the Artists-in-Schools Program," Technical Report (Denver: Western States Arts Foundation, 1976); R. A. Smith, ed, "Artists-in-Schools: Analysis and Criticism," mimeographed (Champaign: University of Illinois, Bureau of Educational Research, 1978).

15.   Allocations of funds are cited from "Capital Comments," *Artspace* 4 (1981):2.

16.   Fowler, ed., *Source Book*, p. 7.

17.   Ibid., pp. 203–5.

18.   Ibid., pp. 153–79.

19.   Ibid., pp. 215–26.

20. G. C. Wenner, "Comprehensive State Planning for the Arts in Education," mimeographed (New York: JDR 3rd Fund, 1976); U.S. Office of Education, "Arts Education Program: Regulations," F. R. Doc. 76-11946 (Washington, D.C.: U.S. Office of Education, 1976).

21. Fowler, ed., *Source Book*, pp. 215–27; N. Shuker, ed., *Arts in Education
Partners: Schools and Their Communities* (New York: JDR 3rd Fund, 1977), p. 20.

22. Arts, Education and Americans Panel, *Coming to Our Senses: The Significance of the Arts for American Education* (New York: McGraw-Hill, 1977).

23. R. Klotman, "Statement on Behalf of the Music Educators National Conference, National Dance Association, and National Art Education Association," mimeographed (Washington, D.C.: Music Educators National Conference, 25 May 1977).

24. Arts, Education, and Americans, Inc., report no. 4, *Ideas and Money for
Expanding School Arts Programs;* report no. 5, *Method and the Muse: Planning a
School Arts Program;* report no. 6, *Developing Financial Resources for School Arts
Programs;* report no. 9, *Creative Collaborations: Artists, Teachers, and Students*
(New York: Arts, Education, and Americans, Inc., 1980–81).

25. Arts, Education, and Americans, Inc., *Method and Muse*, pp. 22–23.

26. U.S. Office of Education, *The Education of Adolescents: The Final Report and
Recommendations of the National Panel on High School and Adolescent Education*
(Washington D.C.: U.S. Department of Education, 1976), pp. 12–14. Available
from U.S. Government Printing Office, no. OE-76-00004 (1976).

27. National Endowment for the Arts, *Report of the Task Force on the Education,
Training and Development of Professional Artists and Arts Educators* (Washington,
D.C.: National Endowment for the Arts, 1978), pp. 27–35.

28. Netzer, *Subsidized Muse*, p. 187.

29. L. Kreisberg, ed., *Local Government and the Arts* (New York: American
Council for the Arts, 1979), p. 116.

30. For a comparison, see Rockefeller Panel, *The Performing Arts: Problems and
Prospects* (New York: McGraw-Hill, 1965).

Chapter 10:
Problems and Opportunities: A Closer Look

1. C. Fowler, ed., *An Arts in Education Source Book: A View from the JDR 3rd
Fund* (New York: JDR 3rd Fund, 1980), p. 25.

2. National Endowment for the Arts, *Report on the Task Force on the Education,
Training and Development of Professional Artists and Arts Educators* (Washington,
D.C.: National Endowment for the Arts, 1978).

3. Arts, Education and Americans Panel, *Coming to Our Senses: The Significance of the Arts for American Education* (New York: McGraw-Hill, 1977).

4. National Endowment for the Arts, *Task Force Report*, p. 28.

5. Ibid., p. 37.

6. Ibid., p. 38.

7. Arts, Education and Americans Panel, *Coming to Our Senses*, pp. 131,

140–47; S. S. Madeja, "Aesthetic Education: An Area of Study," *Art Education* 24 (1971):16–18.

8. Arts, Education and Americans Panel, *Coming to Our Senses*, pp. 138–39, 250–52.

9. Ibid., pp. 233–34.

10. S. W. Pflaum, H. J. Walberg, M. L. Karegianes, and S. P. Rasher, "Reading Instruction: A Quantitative Analysis," *Educational Researcher* 9 (1980):12–18.

11. Fowler, ed., *Source Book*, p. 234.

12. Arts, Education, and Americans, Inc. *Method and the Muse: Planning a School Arts Program*, report no. 5 (New York: Arts, Education, and Americans, Inc., 1981), pp. 20–22.

13. Arts, Education and Americans Panel, *Coming to Our Senses*, p. 262.

14. Arts, Education, and Americans, Inc., *Developing Financial Resources for School Arts Programs*, report no. 6 (New York: Arts, Education, and Americans, Inc., 1981), pp. 17–24.

15. For another example of the complexity of the recommended process, see U.S. Office of Education, "Arts Education Program, Advisory Bulletin for Prospective Applicants for Fiscal Year 1980," mimeographed (Washington, D.C.: U.S. Office of Education, 1980).

16. For some negative findings on the Artists-in-Schools Program, see M. Day, "Point with Pride or View with Alarm? Notes on the NEA's Evaluation of the Artists-in-Schools," in R. A. Smith, ed., "Artists-in-Schools: Analysis and Criticism," mimeographed (Champaign: University of Illinois Bureau of Educational Research, 1978), pp. 26–51.

17. See, for example, the brochure by Arts, Education, and Americans, Inc., entitled "Coming to Our Senses, Progress Report" (New York: Arts, Education, and Americans, Inc., 1980), and also N. Bush, ed., *Issues in Public Policy and the Arts: A Summary of Hearings on a White House Conference on the Arts* (New York: American Council for the Arts, 1978).

Bibliography

ALEXANDER, R. "The Ghost of Creativity in Art Education." *Art Education* 34 (1981):28–30.

American Educational Theater Association. *Humanities and the Theater.* Washington, D.C.: American Educational Theater Association, 1973.

ANDERSON, L. W., and ANDERSON, J. C. "Functional Literacy Tests: A Case of Anticipatory Validity?" *Educational Evaluation and Policy Analysis* 3 (1981):51–56.

ARNHEIM, R. *Art and Visual Perception.* Berkeley: University of California Press, 1966.

Arts, Education, and Americans, Inc. "Coming to Our Senses, Progress Report." Brochure. New York: Arts, Education, and Americans, Inc., 1980.

————. Report no. 1, *People and Places: Reaching Beyond the Schools;* report no. 2, *Your School District and the Arts: A Self-Assessment;* report no. 3, *Local School Boards and the Arts: A Call for Leadership;* report no. 4, *Ideas and Money for Expanding School Arts Programs;* report no. 5, *Method and the Muse: Planning a School Arts Program;* report no. 6, *Developing Financial Resources for School Arts Programs;* report no. 7, *The Case for the Arts in the Schools;* report no. 8, *Arts in the Curriculum;* report no. 9, *Creative Collaborations: Artists, Teachers, and Students;* report no. 10, *Arts in the Classroom: What One Elementary Teacher Can Do.* New York: Arts, Education, and Americans, Inc., 1980–81.

Arts, Education and Americans Panel. *Coming to Our Senses: The Significance of the Arts for American Education.* New York: McGraw-Hill, 1977.

Association of Junior Leagues. *Arts in Education Symposium: Revised Case Studies.* New York: Association of Junior Leagues, 1977.

BARKAN, M. and CHAPMAN, L. H. *Guidelines for Art Instruction Through Television for the Elementary Schools.* Bloomington, Ind.: National Center for School and College Television, 1967.

————. "Report on the Planning Phase: Aesthetic Education Program." Mimeographed. Columbus: Ohio State University, Department of Art Education, 1967.

BARKAN, M., CHAPMAN, L. H., and KERN, E. J. *Guidelines: Curriculum Development for Aesthetic Education.* St. Louis: Central Midwestern Regional Educational Laboratory, 1970.

BARRESI, A. L. "Federal Commitment to the Arts: An Historical Tracing." *American Arts* 11 (1980):22–25.

BAUMGARNER, A. A. D. *Conference on Curriculum and Instruction Development in Art Education: A Project Report.* Reston, Va.: National Art Education Association, 1966.

BEITTLE, K. R. *Alternatives for Art Education Research: Inquiry into the Making of Art.* Dubuque, Iowa: William C. Brown, 1973.

BERGER, J. *Ways of Seeing.* New York: Viking Press, 1972.

BOYER, E. L., and LEVINE, A. *A Quest for Common Learning.* Washington, D.C.: Carnegie Foundation for the Advancement of Teaching, 1981.

BROUDY, H. S., SMITH, B. O., and BURNETT, J. R. *Democracy and Excellence in American Secondary Education: A Study in Curriculum Theory.* Chicago: Rand McNally, 1964.

BROWN, E. V. "Developmental Characteristics of Clay Figures Made by Children from Age Three Through Age Eleven." *Studies in Art Education* 16 (1975):45–53.

BUSH, N., ed. *Issues in Public Policy and the Arts: A Summary of Hearings on a White House Conference on the Arts.* New York: American Council for the Arts, 1978.

CHALMERS, F. G. "Art Education as Ethnology." *Studies in Art Education* 22 (1981):6–14.

CHAMBERS, J. G. "An Analysis of School Size Under a Voucher System." *Educational Evaluation and Policy Analysis* 3 (1981):29–40.

CHAPMAN, L. H. *Approaches to Art in Education.* New York: Harcourt Brace Jovanovich, 1978.

————. "The Bearing of Artistic and Education Commitments on the Teaching of Art." In *The Teaching Process and the Arts and Aesthetics,* edited by G. L. Knieter and J. Stallings. St. Louis: Central Midwestern Regional Educational Laboratory, 1979.

————. "Criteria for Effective Art Teachers." Paper delivered at the Maryland

Conference on Teacher Education, Frostburg State College, Frostburg, Md., 3 Apr. 1970.

———. "Coming to Our Senses: Beyond the Rhetoric." *Art Education* 31 (1978):5–9.

———. "Curriculum Planning in Art Education." *Ohio Art Education Association Newsletter* 8 (1970):6–20.

———. "Evaluating the Total School Art Program." Multilith. New York: Arts in Education Program, JDR 3rd Fund, 1973.

———. "Teacher Viewpoint Survey: The Results." *School Arts* 78 (1979):2–5.

CHAPMAN, L. H., ed. "*Coming to Our Senses* and Related Matters." Special Issue. *Studies in Art Education* 19 (1978).

Commission on the Humanities. *The Humanities in American Life*. Berkeley: University of California Press, 1980.

CONANT, H., ed. *Seminar on Elementary and Secondary School Education in the Visual Arts*. New York: New York University, 1965.

Data Use and Access Laboratories. *Selected Characteristics of Artists: 1970*. Research Report no. 10. Washington, D.C.: National Endowment for the Arts, Research Division, 1978.

DAVIS, D. J. "Research Trends in Art and Art Education: 1883–1972." In *Arts and Aesthetics: An Agenda for the Future*, edited by S. S. Madeja. St. Louis: Central Midwestern Regional Educational Laboratory, 1977.

DAY, M. D. "Effects of Instruction on High School Students' Art Preferences and Art Judgments." *Studies in Art Education* 18 (1976):25–39.

———. "Point with Pride or View with Alarm? Notes on the NEA's Evaluation of the Artists-in-Schools Program." In "*Artists-in-Schools: Analysis and Criticism*," edited by R. A. Smith. Champaign: University of Illinois Bureau of Educational Research, 1978.

DEWEY, J. *Art As Experience*. New York: Minton, Balch, 1934.

DIMAGGIO, P., USEEM, M. and BROWN, P. *Audience Studies of the Performing Arts and Museums: A Critical Review*. Research Report no. 9. Washington, D.C.: National Endowment for the Arts, Research Division, 1978.

DIMONDSTEIN, G. *Exploring the Arts with Children*. New York: Macmillan, 1974.

DOBBS, S. M., ed. *Arts Education and Back to Basics*. Reston, Va.: National Art Education Association, 1979.

DORN, C. M. "The New Eclecticism, or Art Is Anything You Can Get Away With." *Art Education* 31 (1978):6–9.

DORN, C. M., ed. *Report of the Commission on Art Education*. Reston, Va.: National Art Education Association, 1977.

DOW, A. W. *Composition*. New York: Doubleday Page, 1899.

EDDY, J. *Arts Education 1977—In Prose and Print: An Overview of Nine Significant Publications Affecting the Arts in American Education*. Washington, D.C.: U.S. Office of Education, Arts and Humanities Program, 1977. GPO Publication no. 260–934–2044.

————. "Toward Coordinated Federal Policies for Support of Arts Education." Mimeographed. Washington, D.C.: Alliance for Arts Education, John F. Kennedy Center for the Performing Arts, 1977.

EFLAND, A. *Planning Art Education in the Middle/Secondary Schools of Ohio.* Columbus, Ohio: State of Ohio, Department of Education, 1977.

————. "The School Art Style: A Functional Analysis." *Studies in Art Education* 17 (1976):37–44.

EISNER, E. W. "Conservative Influences on Arts Education." In *Arts Education and Back to Basics,* edited by S. M. Dobbs. Reston, Va.: National Art Education Association, 1979.

————. *Educating Artistic Vision.* New York: Macmillan, 1972.

————. *The Educational Imagination.* New York: Macmillan, 1979.

————. "Is the Artist in the School Program Effective?" *Art Education* 27 (1974):19–24.

————. "On the Differences between Scientific and Artistic Approaches to Research." *Educational Researcher* 10 (1981):5–9.

EISNER, E. W., ed. *Reading, the Arts, and the Creation of Meaning.* Reston: Va.: National Art Education Association, 1978.

FELDMAN, E. *Becoming Human Through Art: Aesthetic Experience in the School.* Englewood Cliffs, N.J.: Prentice-Hall, 1970.

FOWLER, C. ed. *An Arts in Education Scource Book: A View from the JDR 3rd Fund.* New York: JDR 3rd Fund, 1980.

GAITSKELL, C. D., and HURWITZ, A. *Children and Their Art.* 3d ed. New York: Harcourt Brace Jovanovich, 1975.

GANS, H. J. *Popular Culture and High Culture.* New York: Basic Books, 1974.

GARDNER, H. *The Arts and Human Development: A Psychological Study of the Artistic Process.* New York: Wiley, 1973.

GARDNER, J. W. *Excellence: Can We Be Equal and Excellent Too?* New York: Harper & Row, 1961.

GOODLAD, J. "Education in What is Basic." In *Arts Education and Back to Basics,* edited by S. M. Dobbs. Reston, Va.: National Arts Education Association, 1979.

GREENBERG, P. "Survey: Art and Music—State Requirements." *NAEA News* 21 (1979):8.

GRIGSBY, J. E. JR. *Art and Ethnics: Background for Teaching Youth in a Pluralistic Society.* Dubuque, Iowa: William C. Brown, 1977.

GUILFORD, J. P. *The Nature of Human Intelligence.* New York: McGraw-Hill, 1967.

HARDIMAN, G., and ZERNICH, T. *Curricular Considerations for Visual Arts Education.* Champaign, Ill.: Stipes, 1974.

————. "Some Considerations for the Measurement of Preference in the Visual Arts." *Review of Research in Visual Arts Education* 4 (1975):1–14.

HARNISCHFEGER, A. "Curricular Control and Learning Time: District Strategy, Teacher Strategy, and Pupil Choice." *Educational Evaluation and Policy Analysis* 2 (1980):19–30.

HARNISCHFEGER, A. and MILLER, D. "Resources for Art Education in the Nation's Elementary Schools: Opportunity, Time, and Instructional Staff Qualifications." Technical Report no. AH-78. St. Louis: Central Midwestern Regional Educational Laboratory, 1979.

HAUSMAN, J. J., ed. *Arts and the Schools*. New York: McGraw-Hill, 1980.

HOUTS, P. L., ed. "Special Issue: The Uncertain World of Arts Education." *Principal* 60 (1980).

HURWITZ, A., and MADEJA, S. *The Joyous Vision: Art Appreciation in the Elementary Schools*. New York: Van Nostrand Reinhold, 1976.

JACKSON, P. W. *Life in Classrooms*. New York: Holt, Rinehart & Winston, 1968.

JDR 3RD FUND. *Comprehensive Arts Planning: Ad Hoc Coalition of States for the Arts in Education*. New York: JDR 3rd Fund, 1975.

JONES, L. "The Arts and the U.S. Department of Education: A List of Funded Projects and Activities." Mimeographed. Washington D.C.: U.S. Department of Education, 1979.

KELLOGG, R. *Analyzing Children's Art*. Palo Alto, Calif.: Mayfield, 1969.

KIRST, M., and JUNG, R. "The Utility of a Longitudinal Approach in Assessing Implementation: A Thirteen-Year View of Title I, ESEA." *Educational Evaluation and Policy Analysis* 2 (1980):17–34.

KLOTMAN, R. "Statement on Behalf of the Music Educators National Conference, National Dance Association, and National Art Education Association." Mimeographed. Music Educators National Conference, Washington, D.C., 25 May 1977.

KNIETER, G. L., and STALLINGS, J., eds. *The Teaching Process and the Arts and Aesthetics*. St. Louis: Central Midwestern Regional Educational Laboratory, 1979.

KREISBERG, L., ed. *Local Government and the Arts*. New York: American Council for the Arts, 1979.

LANIER, V. *Essays in Art Education: The Development of One Point of View*. 2d ed. New York: MSS Educational Publishing, 1976.

————. "The Five Faces of Art Education." *Studies in Art Education* 18 (1977):7–21.

————. "Schismogenesis in Contemporary Art Education." *Studies in Art Education* 5 (1963):10–19.

LANSING, K. *Art, Artists, and Art Education*. New York: McGraw-Hill, 1969.

LOEB, J., ed. *Feminist Collage: Educating Women in the Visual Arts*. New York: Teachers College Press, 1979.

LOGAN, F. M. *Growth of Art in American Schools*. New York: Harper, 1955.

————. "Up Date '75, Growth in American Art Education." *Studies in Art Education* 17 (1975): 9–17.

LOWENFELD, V. *Creative and Mental Growth*. 1st ed. New York: Macmillan, 1947.

McFEE, J. K., Preparation for Art, 2d ed. Belmont, Calif.: Wadsworth, 1971.

McFee, J. K., and Degge, R. M. *Art, Culture, and Environment: A Catalyst for Teaching.* Belmont, Calif.: Wadsworth, 1977.

McKim, R. H. *Experiences in Visual Thinking.* Monterey, Calif.: Brooks Cole, 1972.

Madeja, S. S. "Aesthetic Education: An Area of Study." *Art Education* 24 (1971): 16–18.

————. *All the Arts for Every Child.* New York: JDR 3rd Fund, 1973.

————. *The Artist in the School: A Report on the Artist-in-Residence Project.* St. Louis: Central Midwestern Regional Educational Laboratory, 1970.

————. *Arts and Aesthetics: An Agenda for the Future.* St. Louis: Central Midwestern Regional Educational Labortory, 1977.

————. *The Arts, Cognition, and Basic Skills.* St. Louis: Central Midwestern Regional Educational Laboratory, 1978.

Madeja, S. S., and Onuska, S. *Through the Arts to the Aesthetic: The CEMREL Aesthetic Education Curriculum.* St. Louis: Central Midwestern Regional Educational Laboratory, 1977.

Mattil, E. L., ed. *A Seminar in Art Education for Research and Curriculum Development.* University Park: Pennsylvania State University, 1966.

Mearns, H. *Creative Power: The Education of Youth in the Creative Arts.* New York: Dover, 1929.

Mills, E. A., and Thompson, D. R. "State of the Arts in the States." *Art Education* 34 (1981):40–44.

Mitchell, D. E. "Social Science Impact on Legislative Decision Making: Process and Substance." *Educational Researcher* 9 (1980): 9–12, 17–19.

Moore, T. G. *The Economics of the American Theater.* Durham, N.C.: Duke University Press, 1968.

Murphy, J., and Jones, L. "Research in Arts Education: A Federal Chapter," Report 76–02000. Mimeographed. Washington, D.C.: Office of Education, 1978.

Music Educators National Conference. *The School Music Program: Description and Standards.* Reston, Va.: Music Educators National Conference, 1974.

National Assessment of Educational Progress. *Art and Young Americans, 1974–79: Selected Results from the Second National Art Assessment.* Report no. 10-A-01. Denver: Education Commission of the States, 1981.

————. *Art Technical Report: Exercise Volume.* Report no. 06-A-20. Denver: Education Commission of the States, 1978.

————. *Art Technical Report: Summary Volume.* Report no. 06-A-21. Denver: Education Commission of the States, 1978.

————. *Design and Drawing Skills: Selected Results from the First National Assessment of Art.* Report no. 06-A-01. Denver: Education Commission of the States, 1977.

National Endowment for the Arts. *Audience Studies of the Performing Arts and Museums.* Washington, D.C.: National Endowment for the Arts, 1978.

————. *Report of the Task Force on the Education, Training, and Development of Professional Artists and Arts Educators.* Washington, D.C.: National Endowment for the Arts, 1978.

National Research Center of the Arts. *Americans and the Arts.* New York: American Council for the Arts, 1981.

————. *Americans and the Arts: A Survey of Public Opinion.* New York: Associated Councils of the Arts, 1975.

National School Boards Association. *The Arts in Education.* Research Report no. 1978–2. Washington, D.C.: National School Boards Association, 1978.

NETZER, D. *The Subsidized Muse: Public Support for the Arts in the United States.* Cambridge, England: Cambridge University Press, 1978.

NEWSOM, B. Y., and SILVER, A. Z. *The Art Museum as Educator: A Collection of Studies as Guides to Practice and Policy.* Berkeley: University of California Press, 1977.

PFLAUM, S. W., WALBERG, H. J., KAREGIANES, M. L., and RASHER, S. P. "Reading Instruction: A Quantitative Analysis." *Educational Researcher* 9 (1980):12–18.

PURVES, A. C. *Evaluation of Learning in Literature. Evaluation in Education: An International Review Series.* New York: Pergamon, 1979.

RASPBERRY, W. "Teaching Reading Remains a Problem." *Cincinnati Enquirer,* 7 Dec. 1981.

RAWLINS, K. "Educational Metamorphosis of the American Museum." *Studies in Art Education* 20 (1978):4–17.

REIMER, B. *A Philosophy of Music Education.* Englewood Cliffs, N.J.: Prentice-Hall, 1970.

REMER, J. *The League of Cities for the Arts in Education.* New York: JDR 3rd Fund, 1977.

RINDSKOPF, D. M., HARNISCHFEGER, A., and WILEY, D. E. "Arts Education in Public Secondary Schools: Opportunity and Participation." Technical Memorandum no. AH-21. St. Louis: Central Midwestern Educational Laboratory, 1978.

ROCKEFELLER PANEL. *The Performing Arts: Problems and Prospects.* New York: McGraw-Hill, 1965.

SAUNDERS, R. J. "The Arts—Working Together to Make Education Work: An Idea Whose Time Has Come." *Studies in Art Education* 19 (1978):14–20.

SEVIGNY, M. J. "Triangulated Inquiry: An Alternative Methodology for the Study of Classroom Life." *Review of Research in Visual Arts Education* 8 (1978):1–16.

SCHAEFER-SIMMERN, H. *The Unfolding of Artistic Activity.* Berkeley: University of California Press, 1948.

SHUKER, N., ed. *Arts in Education Partners: Schools and Their Communities.* New York: JDR 3rd Fund, 1977.

SILVERMAN, R. *Art Education and the World of Work: A Handbook for Career Education in Art.* Reston, Va.: National Art Education Association, 1980.

SMITH, R. A. "Justifying Policy for Aesthetic Education." *Studies in Art Education* 20 (1978): 37–42.

SMITH, R. A., ed. *Aesthetic Education Today: Problems and Prospects.* Columbus, Ohio: Ohio State University, 1973.

————. "Artists-in-Schools: Analysis and Criticism." Mimeographed. Champaign: University of Illinois, Bureau of Educational Research, 1978.

————. "Special Issue: The Government, Art, and Aesthetic Education." *Journal of Aesthetic Education* 14 (1980).

SNOW, M. "Arts in Education Evaluation, A Report to the Pennsylvania State Department of Education." Mimeographed. Harrisburg: Pennsylvania State Department of Education, Bureau of Curriculum Services, 1979.

STAKE, R. E. *Evaluating the Arts in Education: A Responsive Approach.* Columbus, Ohio: Charles E. Merrill, 1975.

STUFFLEBEAM, D. L., and WEBSTER, W. J. "An Analysis of Alternative Approaches to Evaluation." *Educational Evaluation and Policy Analysis* 2 (1980):5–20.

TAYLOR, J. C. "The History of Art in Education." In *A Seminar in Art Education for Research and Curriculum Development,* edited by E. L. Mattil. University Park: Pennsylvania State University, 1966.

TOFFLER, A. *The Culture Consumers: A Study of Art and Affluence in America.* New York: Random House, Vintage Books, 1964.

ULMAN, E., KRAMER, E., and KWIATKOWSKA, H. Y. *Art Therapy in the United States.* Craftsbury, Conn.: Art Therapy Publications, 1979.

U.S. House of Representatives. National Institute of Education Appropriations Bill, Report 95, 1979.

U.S. Office of Education. "Arts Education Program, Advisory Bulletin for Prospective Applicants for Fiscal Year 1980." Mimeographed. Washington, D.C.: U.S. Office of Education, 1980.

————. "Arts Education Program: Regulations." F. R. Doc. 76–11946. Washington, D.C.: U.S. Office of Education, 1976.

————. *The Education of Adolescents: The Final Report and Recommendations on the National Panel on High School and Adolescent Education.* Washington, D.C.: U.S. Office of Education, 1976. GPO no. OE–76–00004.

WENNER, G. C. "Comprehensive State Planning for the Arts in Education." Mimeographed. New York: JDR 3rd Fund, 1976.

————. *Dance in the Schools: A New Movement in Education.* New York: JDR 3rd Fund, 1974.

————. "Interdisciplinary Courses: Mythology and Methodology." *Art Education* 26 (1973):23–26.

Western States Arts Foundation. "A Study of the Poetry and Visual Arts Components of the Artists-in-Schools Program." Technical Report. Denver: Western States Arts Foundation, 1976.

WHITE, D. W. "An Historical Review of Doctoral Program Growth and Dissertation Research in Art Education, 1893–1974." *Studies in Art Education* 19 (1977):6–20.

WILLIAMS, D. A., HUCK, J., MA, C. and MONROE, S. "Why Public Schools Fail." *Newsweek*, 20 Apr. 1981, pp. 62–65.

Index